THE LORD OF THOUGHT

THE
LORD OF THOUGHT

A STUDY OF THE PROBLEMS WHICH
CONFRONTED JESUS CHRIST AND THE
SOLUTION HE OFFERED

BY

LILY DOUGALL
AUTHOR OF "PRO CHRISTO ET ECCLESIA," ETC., AND
JOINT AUTHOR OF "THE SPIRIT," ETC.

AND

CYRIL W. EMMET, M.A., B.D.
FELLOW OF UNIVERSITY COLLEGE, OXFORD, AND EXAMINING CHAPLAIN TO THE
BISHOP OF OXFORD
AUTHOR OF "THE ESCHATOLOGICAL QUESTION IN THE GOSPELS"
"CONSCIENCE, CREEDS AND CRITICS," ETC
JOINT AUTHOR OF "THE SPIRIT," ETC

WIPF & STOCK · Eugene, Oregon

Wipf and Stock Publishers
199 W 8th Ave, Suite 3
Eugene, OR 97401

The Lord of Thought
A Study of the Problems Which Confronted Jesus Christ
and the Solution He Offered
By Dougall, Lily and Emmett, Cyril W.
Softcover ISBN-13: 978-1-7252-9945-0
Hardcover ISBN-13: 978-1-7252-9947-4
eBook ISBN-13: 978-1-7252-9946-7
Publication date 2/2/2021
Previously published by Student Christian Movement, 1922

This edition is a scanned facsimile of the original edition published in 1922.

PREFACE

SINCE the publication of Schweitzer's *Quest of the Historical Jesus*, and of other books by writers who accept his interpretation, emphasis on the eschatological interest has characterized nearly everything that has been written about the teaching of Jesus Christ. It is now widely held that the whole thought of Jesus was governed by the belief that "the end of the world" was very near, or, at least, that this belief was a confusing element in his outlook. Our aim in the present study is to show that Jesus did not expect a speedy and supernatural destruction of the world, but that he did expect the termination of an order of society based on oppression—the result of his appeal to the Jews to fuse their fervid patriotism in a world-embracing zeal for the God he knew to be Father of all mankind.

In proof that this is no mere reading into the past of modern ideas we offer some account of the Jewish literature current at the beginning of the Christian era, with a critical examination of the eschatological passages in the first three Gospels, as together affording evidence of the strong contrast between

THE LORD OF THOUGHT

the teaching of Jesus and the religious thought common in his day. It is evident that this view, if established, materially affects our estimate of the originality and power of the mind of Jesus, and gives us a conception of his dominance in the sphere of thought commensurate with the historical results of his impact on the world of men.

L. D.
C. W. E.

Cutts End, Cumnor,
  September 1922.

CONTENTS

CHAPTER | PAGE
I. INTRODUCTORY 1

PART I

THE WORLD INTO WHICH JESUS CAME

II. JEWISH FANTASY 13
III. THE JEWISH IDEA OF GOD AS JUDGE . 24
IV. THE PROBLEM OF GOD'S LOVE AND CRUELTY 38
V. THE JEWISH IDEA OF MAN . . . 62
VI. THE PROBLEM OF INADEQUATE SALVATION 73
VII. JOHN THE BAPTIST 83
VIII. THE *DIES IRÆ* AND THE GOSPEL OF THE KINGDOM 93
IX. THE SON OF MAN AND THE OFFER OF ESCAPE 100

PART II

THE GENIUS OF JESUS

X. THE SYNOPTIC PORTRAIT . . . 113
XI. NEW IDEAS OF GOD AND MAN . . 126
XII. SALVATION INTERNATIONAL BECAUSE NATIONAL 136

THE LORD OF THOUGHT

CHAPTER		PAGE
XIII.	TEACHING CONCERNING CONSEQUENCE	154
XIV.	TEACHING CONCERNING PUNISHMENT	175
XV.	TEACHING ON FORGIVENESS	191
XVI.	TEACHING ON SIN AND SALVATION	200
XVII.	SUMMARY	210

PART III

Critical Verification

XVIII.	WHAT DO WE KNOW OF THE TEACHING OF CHRIST?	227
XIX.	ANGER AND PUNISHMENT	236
XX.	TEACHING ABOUT FORGIVENESS	250
XXI.	THE KINGDOM OF HEAVEN	256
XXII.	SALVATION NATIONAL AND INTERNATIONAL	266
XXIII.	THE SON OF MAN	275
XXIV.	THE FUNDAMENTAL IDEAS OF APOCALYPTIC: TRUTH AND ERROR	297
	GENERAL INDEX	313
	INDEX OF BIBLICAL, APOCRYPHAL AND APOCALYPTIC PASSAGES	319

THE LORD OF THOUGHT

CHAPTER I

INTRODUCTORY

Is the teaching of Jesus difficult to interpret, or is it so simple that all who wish may understand? The answer to both these questions is in the affirmative. The soul that in its devotional moments seeks spiritual help and wisdom in the recorded words of Jesus will find what it seeks. The devotional reading of the Gospels has always provided what satisfies and stimulates those who are hungry for the best that life can give. But the human soul has other legitimate moods than that of unquestioning devotion. The time in which we live is, like that of the Renaissance, a time when fresh knowledge from many sides is impinging rudely upon the religious life. In particular, new discoveries of the religious literature of the age of Jesus provide data of immense importance to all who are trying to understand what he was and stood for, but in so doing make it far less easy than of old to be sure that we have done so fairly.

Modern literary discoveries show how original was the thought of Jesus.

The genius of Jesus, his originality, his contribution to the world's wisdom, can only be understood if considered in relation to Jewish beliefs current in his day about the End of the World, the Last Judgment, final rewards and punishments, and the Reign of God or

THE LORD OF THOUGHT

the Heavenly Kingdom—beliefs summed up under the term Eschatology.[1] In addition it must be seen in relation to certain non-Jewish writings, now more carefully examined, which give us a clearer idea of the then prevailing Pagan notion of personal salvation. But the more all these are studied the more clearly, by contrast, does the teaching of Jesus stand out as distinctive.

In the light of the new and more accurate knowledge, some modern theologians have discovered in the teaching of Jesus what amounts to inconsistency of thought. These interpreters see that Jewish eschatology looked forward to the destruction of the world, not its regeneration, which implied a conception of God as a God not so much of love as of wrath, and they suppose that Jesus both taught a religion of love and also accepted the current Jewish eschatology that was really inconsistent with it.[2] Others, again, seek to give consistency to the teaching of Jesus by forcing upon all his sayings and parables an interpretation in harmony with the more fanatical Judaism of his time, thus depriving his message of any originality.[3]

Only a second-rate mind confidently holds inconsistent beliefs.

This book seeks to maintain that Jesus had a philosophy of life, in which all his ideas found a place. In other words, his ideas formed one consistent scheme of thought. Philosophy, as distinguished from the pursuit of philosophy or the historical knowledge of past philosophies, is the systematization of all that

---

[1] We have Jewish eschatology fully and picturesquely given to us in writings called "Apocalypses." The word means an "unveiling" or "disclosure." The books record visions supposed to disclose the events connected with the end of the world.

[2] Cf. e g Baron von Hugel, *Essays in the Philosophy of Religion*, pp. 124-6; Mr H. G Wood in *Peake's Commentary*, p 661A

[3] See Schweitzer, Tyrrell, and others. Cf also C. W. Emmet, Chaps. xxi., xxii , and xxiii.

INTRODUCTORY

is known or believed. Philosophy is to knowledge what, according to Plato, justice is to all the virtues—the organized unity of the whole. In this sense, like every great teacher who deals with the relation of what is to what ought to be, Jesus must have exercised the philosophic mind, must have achieved a philosophy of life.

In sympathy with the many who desire to make such research without orthodox presuppositions, it is as the words of a human thinker that we would examine the teaching of Jesus.[1] And this need not distress the most orthodox of readers for, while this method does not allow any question-begging assertion, it involves no contradiction of traditional doctrine. A Catholic thinker says, " A real Incarnation of God in man can only mean Incarnation in some particular human nature. Man in general is only an idea, it is not a fact, a reality. . . . The Incarnation could not be made other than the entering into, and possession of, a human mind and will endowed with special racial dispositions and particular racial categories of thought. . . . Otherwise the Revealer would begin His career by being simply unintelligible to His first hearers, and even, in the long run, to the large majority of mankind; and He would, in Himself, not be normally, characteristically, man." [2]

I start with the presumption that in Jesus human intellect attained high development. He must therefore have formed a judgment on the popular religious books of his time, as upon the law and prophets, and upon the reports of other religions which would

Genius an element in human perfection.

---

[1] In harmony with this treatment of our problem we discard the convention which puts capital letters to pronouns referring to Jesus.
[2] *Essays in the Philosophy of Religion*, Baron von Hugel, p. 125.

have entered Palestine; and that judgment must have been unified with all else that he believed. The power thus to unify ideas divides the philosophic from the unphilosophic mind, the higher grades of human intelligence from the lower. As, then, it is only the second-rate mind that is able to hold some beliefs shut off from the rest, or to be a confident teacher of obvious inconsistencies, we must be slow to attribute such weakness to Jesus.

<small>Genius the most important factor in human development.</small>
The phenomenon of human genius has played so large a part in the elevation of the race that it is strange that its importance has been so little noticed, so little lauded, by the Christian Church. Two causes have contributed to this. One is the tendency of mankind at large to insist upon the infallibility of religious oracles by seeking to minimize the part of the human intellect in any process of illumination. To this universal tendency of mankind was added the direction given to Christian piety in that long, chaotic period of low education and low civilization called " the dark ages." In such a period the light of truth came chiefly from the past. The ecclesiastical shepherds, with their uneducated flocks, naturally feared the originality and indocility which usually accompany exceptional intellectual power. Private judgment upon books or formulæ when the private person could not understand them would have been particularly futile and dangerous. When the Church emerged into a better age and general education revived, the habit was clearly fixed of belittling the moral value of intelligence as compared with that of literal obedience; and this, unfortunately, is still the orthodox tendency.

Yet new ideas come to us only through the medium

INTRODUCTORY

of intellect, and it is only by new ideas that the world changes from one phase of social or institutional life to another. It has been well said that discovery is the human side of what on God's side is revelation. Believing in God, we are obliged to believe that He imparts His truth through human minds, for the whole history of mankind exemplifies this. To accept this testimony of history is not, as some unthinking people are apt to cry, to reject revelation; it is simply to recognize that God's ways in revelation are harmonious with His other processes of creation. Nor is it to deny the action of divine super-wisdom and goodness; it is rather to affirm universally the great principle on which Christianity is founded, that the mind of God, which is partially manifest in nature, can only be perfectly manifested to man in human nature. Nor does the contention that Jesus was a great thinker involve any denial of his divinity: rather it insists that intellectual power is an element in even human perfection.

The dynamic of new ideas.

As the history of all human development, from totem tribes to modern societies, is the history of individual men great enough to lead their fellows, and as the force by which these leaders have been moved and have been able to move others has always been the new idea, let us ask what kind of idea has been most potent in the world. We find that what has always been most essential, most formative, to the character of any group or society, has been its idea of God. It is true to say that as men are, so they conceive God to be; but it is more true to say that as they conceive God, so they grow to be. For the idea of God, remaining for long periods little changed, is a steady force shaping the minds of generations, not by means of voluntary piety but through the social imagination. The character of an acknowledged and unseen power, whether conceived as fetish or warrior or judge or as vast mechanical force, is always in the background of the imagination of the community, and thus becomes the foundation of its philosophy of life. As the image of power, it shapes in man's subconscious mind both ideal and endeavour. Thus, a new idea of God involves a new idea of man. This is incontestable, and it follows that the leader from whom springs a new and truer idea of God has, in the long run, much more power than those leaders whose genius is occupied with what is less fundamental. For the new idea of God involves new laws, new political grouping and new art.

<small>The supreme importance of religious genius.</small>

As the idea of God, even when mainly some monstrous figment of man's fancy, has such power, it is plain that the greatest discovery in any place or epoch would be a better God. Further, if, as we believe, there is a Supreme Being whose influence environs all human life, the greatest of all discoveries would be knowledge of His true character. Such a discovery would involve a knowledge of man's true nature, and when accepted would be the remaking of man. I believe that such a discovery was made by the historic Jesus, and by him made for the first time, although many partial discoveries of God had been made earlier.

The peculiar genius which belongs to great moral or religious teachers is always coupled with a life lived in the power of the teaching. It could not be otherwise. Morality or religion can only be fully taught by being exemplified in life; and no teacher could be great who was not so possessed with his message as

INTRODUCTORY

to live in its power. If Socrates could have been suspected of dishonesty, or Plato have been seen distracted with the cares of life, or Paul have been melancholy or slothful, what a difference it would have made! The weakness would have crept into the teaching; the world would not have listened so well. Life is more than intellect; a great life is very much more than the great intellect which is one of its powers. But the two cannot be separated; and to acknowledge that Jesus lived and died so greatly as to fascinate the heart of the world is also to affirm that he must have thought greatly. We should expect, then, that he would make a discovery about God. It is the thesis of this book that he made an original discovery, the meaning and supreme importance of which have not even yet been fully recognized.

As a preliminary to any estimate of the Gospel teaching, we need to consider how we shall deal with any inconsistencies contained in the record. When we find, in the record of any great teacher, inconsistency and mistaken forecast, is it not the most reverent course to subject the record to the strictest criticism, on the assumption that confusion is more likely to belong to tradition or to the mind of the writer than to the master mind portrayed? In the history of any one of the canonized Christian saints, when sayings and acts are attributed to him or her which to us appear inconsistent and unworthy, our first proceeding is to suspect the accuracy of the narrator. If we discover independent reasons for thinking such things as we deprecate may have crept into the record as unwitting inaccuracies, we proceed, if we are scientific and honest, to sift that record care- *The Gospels written in the classic age of brief moral biographies.*

THE LORD OF THOUGHT

fully in the light of all relevant facts, on the hypothesis that the inspiration of the saint for goodness and wisdom was greater than the inspiration for accuracy enjoyed by his disciples. This is not true only of saints: it is true of all the great men of the past. The more we study the lives that have been written of them and the allusions to them in other histories, the more do their characters, shaped with fundamental consistency by certain strong, characteristic ideas, stand out clearly from a cloudy background of minor inaccuracies and mistaken interpretations.

But, it may be said, if the Gospels are inaccurate history, why believe their testimony? This question is not rational; it arises as a fretful reaction from the long tradition of verbal inspiration. The Gospels, as we have them, were written in the Golden Age of ancient biography. Plutarch's *Lives*, the *Agricola* of Tacitus, are contemporary instances of brief biographies written with a moral purpose. The application of the principle of criticism does not in any way discount the general truth of these records. Plutarch's stories are in general so true to fact, so entirely in harmony with the known results of each recorded life on the course of the world, so psychologically convincing, that his work is one of the great mines in which historians humbly and diligently dig. Yet every edition of his book is annotated to point out this and that detail as untrue or doubtful. Moreover, there are many statements to which no such critical note is appended which yet no one believes—tales of meticulously fulfilled prophecies, miraculous portents or mythical ancestors. Nor does the moral purpose of these records vitiate their truth. The facts they con-

<small>The substantial truth of the Synoptic narrative.</small>

INTRODUCTORY

tain still influence and shape men's characters—so moral they are, so true, and yet inaccurate.

Now the Gospels are by far the most beautiful and powerful specimens of the kind of biography characteristic of the age. We thus see that the life of Jesus comes to us through a natural channel which we may yet believe to be a channel of divine inspiration for us. God's way with life, from the amoeba to man, has never been to fulfil desire but to tempt to effort. From the dawn of history God's way with man has not been to instruct but to tempt to discovery. If, then, the most important of all truths is given us in the story of Jesus, we should not expect to find that truth spread out as an advertisement, but rather hidden as a treasure. If we think of God's spirit as ever creating us, we should expect to have to seek below the surface for what is most worth having.

The divine creative Mind does not instruct but tempts man to discovery.

If then, as appears, a fuller knowledge of the period in which Jesus lived has made it quite evident that there is inconsistency in the teaching attributed to him, we may well agree, considering the circumstances in which the Gospels were compiled, that it is more becoming for us, in the first instance, to suspect the records of inaccuracy than to assume that the inconsistency lay with Jesus. The course of investigation suggested in this book is based upon the belief that the great Subject of these biographies is more likely to have possessed a consistent philosophy of life than his historians to have possessed an infallible tradition of his words and works, that he was more likely to have made a new discovery of God than his recording disciples to have understood the full significance of that discovery.

THE LORD OF THOUGHT

Part I. World Problems.
The first part of this book is a brief review of the Jewish books which reflect the beliefs of the generation in which Jesus lived; for in order to know how far Jesus was original we must make what survey we can of the religious thought that he found to hand in his environment.

Part II. Their solution in thought.
In the second part I attempt a brief survey of the teaching as we have it in the Synoptic [1] Gospels, and suggest a critical hypothesis which, if it can be verified, would free the energies of Christian society from certain old and hampering traditions, and give new vividness to the stimulating vision of an international salvation.

Part III. Critical corroboration.
The third part of the book, contributed by Mr Emmet, shows how far sober critical examination of the Synoptic Gospels in relation to the Apocalyptic literature justifies our hypothesis, and how far the present results of such examination point to its complete justification.

[1] The first three Gospels are called Synoptic because the main facts of the narrative are common to all three. Our inquiry has been confined to these, although our position would have been greatly strengthened had we permitted ourselves further to substantiate it by reference to the Fourth Gospel.

PART I
THE WORLD INTO WHICH JESUS CAME

CHAPTER II

JEWISH FANTASY

THE prophecies of God's speedy judgment of the world, embedded in the Gospels, form an outstanding difficulty. Let us seek first their source, for, whether or not adopted by him, they are not original to Jesus.

The extinction of the old Jewish kingdom, the Exile, and the repatriation of only those Jews who were most intensely religious and patriotic, had resulted in a community which was more like our notion of a church than of a nation. Their statecraft was a religion. They bore to the older Jewish state that had passed away much the same relation as the Roman Catholic enthusiasts of the Counter-Reformation bore to the Roman Church as it existed before the Reformation. If we can imagine the Roman Catholic Church reduced to a few thousands of its most religious adherents, keeping alive a little "Holy Roman Empire" of their own in some border state, their land constantly trampled by the armies of neighbouring powers, convinced, not only of the right of their community to rule humanity, but that humanity could only be saved by submission to such rule, we can picture Judea after the Exile. Further, if we can imagine the members of this nucleus of a Holy Roman Empire at last completely convinced that they could never gain the audience

[sidenote: Judea after the Babylonian exile.]

THE LORD OF THOUGHT

<small>Persecution of Antiochus Epiphanes, 167 B.C</small>

of the nations by natural means and expecting a supernatural triumph, we may form for ourselves some picture of the community at Jerusalem during the period when Antiochus Epiphanes seized both the city and Temple, set up the worship of Zeus and burned the Books of the Law, and finally tortured and slew those who publicly upheld the sacred law. The average religious mind, under such circumstances, could only find refuge from insanity in fantasy.

<small>Origin of apocalyptic ideas, judgment, hell, etc</small>

Psychology recognizes that the human mind, when faced with distress too hard to bear, creates compensation for itself in day-dreams and fantasies picturing conditions exactly opposite to those of actual experience. This mental tendency is entirely consonant with sanity: it is the way in which nature roughly preserves sanity in the ordinary mind. This everyday fact may be illustrated, in a small way, from the experience of a well-known person in Victorian society who, morbidly self-conscious and shy, was able to overcome the distress of joining in public functions by fancying himself to be floating through interstellar spaces. The illustration, odd as it is, will recall to most of us similar devices of our own imaginations which psychologists now call " the compensations of fantasy." The mental law thus seen in trivial things works also in great. The form of much of the poetry of the world has this for explanation. Bunyan, immured in a cell, wrote of the inner life of a soul as a far journey in open country and full of adventure; Milton, in his later work, enthrones in heaven the Puritanism dethroned on earth; Dante glories in the fixed order and justice of the after-life while political chaos and injustice romp together over his beloved

JEWISH FANTASY

Italy. The popularity of any poetry or fiction is mainly due to the adoption by the many of compensating fantasies created for them by more gifted minds. Into the moulds of such written fantasy a poet or dramatist naturally pours such of his own favourite convictions as he desires should prevail. There may be great truth in his convictions and, if so, his imaginative work will have religious and moral value as well as its chief and proper value of relieving overcharged hearts by offering channels of agreeable relaxation.

Jewish fantasy, in the dire crisis of the national religious life when the first apocalypses were written, took the form of visions of supernatural and immortal triumph—a triumph which included cruel revenge upon their oppressors and apostate brethren. A glance at their history will make this appear natural.

During their exile in Babylon the Jews learned thoroughly the superiority of their own ethical and theological conceptions over those of the heathen. The superiority was real, but it was expressed in scripture which contained both superior and inferior matter. Their religion was enshrined in the final revision and canonization of a written law. Two things are noticeable about the idea of juridical law: *The legal outlook exalts innocence rather than goodness,*

(*a*) It has penalties, but no rewards. Though the idea of bestowing desert implies reward as well as punishment, legal systems are penal only. This makes the idea of virtue negative, for to do nothing worthy of punishment becomes virtue. Thus virtues tend to be regarded as unimportant as compared with iniquities, which are positive and cannot be overlooked. An unwholesome stress is laid upon wickedness.

(*b*) All legal systems have also a forward look, for the

THE LORD OF THOUGHT

ideal they contemplate is perfect obedience to them. They never are perfectly obeyed, but every infraction of the law has associated with it the idea that it ought not to be, while penalties are nearly always deterrent in aim as well as retributory. Thus every penal code points forward to its own negation, as theoretically it exists only in order to produce a condition in which it will not be needed—a time when the will of the law-giver shall be done universally. Thus from the deification of divine power as Law arose both an identification of innocence with virtue—producing an undue emphasis upon human iniquity, and the magnificent hope of the future Golden Age of God. These two ideas were implicit in the thought of the nation before it suffered the religious persecution that awoke an insatiable thirst for revenge.

<small>and implies a future paradise.</small>

Up to the time when the *Book of Daniel* was written, except for a few apocalyptic fragments, both the law and the prophets spoke to the Jews of that future good time in which the law would be obeyed as coming *in the natural process of human history*. God in the past had performed for them many and marvellous deliverances, but these had always been worked on earth, and through natural agents—kings, even the worst heathen kings, law-givers, generals, locusts and other plagues and pestilences of nature. The sun had stood still in Ajalon; the waters of Jordan had parted to let the tribes pass on; but these things had been but as adjuncts to common warfare. It was in the natural course of history (as history was then interpreted) that the prophets had taught them to expect the triumph of the Jewish religion and of God.

<small>The world-regenerating genius of the prophets</small>

When these high hopes born of the prophetic tradi-

JEWISH FANTASY

tion were turned to despair; when the confines of the known world had become greatly enlarged, and the power and wealth of Western nations recognized; when the more educated Jews at last perceived that the geographical position of Palestine made it impossible for them to be left in peaceful independence, and that their feebleness made it impossible for them to conquer their enemies by natural means, the devout among them naturally turned to the belief that the hope of a universal reign of God, implicit in the law, would be realized *by supernatural means*. But this national faith was not quite adequate to give to all of them serenity in adverse circumstances: the mere indefinite belief that God would some time vindicate His truth, in this world or another, was not sensational enough to give relief to their not only disappointed but naturally enraged hearts. Many of them—perhaps the greater number—could not rise to the height set forth in the *Book of Job*, that of repose in spiritual communion with God, leaving the problem of evil with Him. Far less could they find satisfaction in the thought of God's care for the heathen as well as for themselves as set forth in the *Book of Jonah*, or accept, with all its implications, the doctrine of vicarious national suffering taught by the Second Isaiah. Many who nobly endured the ruthless persecution of Antiochus Epiphanes still sought compensation for present suffering in visions of speedy supernatural triumph in which vengeance upon their enemies bore the largest part.

<small>The world-abandonment of lesser seers</small>

Both the law and the prophets, when written and re-edited and written again, contained passages of primitive origin in which the desired doctrine of God as a vindictive God found large corroboration. Thus the

THE LORD OF THOUGHT

apocalyptic seers took over and stereotyped from a cruder and coarser past a crude and cruel conception of God.

The sacred scripture taught God's love, but its history of the past was self-contradictory; the laws laid down in it were not consistent with each other; the prophets contained inconsistent statements. Within it there were the noblest visions of goodness and mercy, together with savage conceptions of deified cruelty. But no doubt was entertained of the veracity of every verbal statement. Whatever was believed had been revealed; whatever had got into the traditional revelation must be believed.[1]

With regard to this, Professor Burkitt, in *Jewish and Christian Apocalypses*, says (pp. 5, 14):

<small>When scripture is sacrosanct primitive errors are esteemed divine.</small>
"The returned exiles (of the age of Ezra) aspired to play no great political part. . . . But, insignificant as they might be in numbers and immediate influence, they were now a peculiar people. . . . They were the People : the rest of the world were Gentiles. They now possessed the Law of God in black and white, a law that had been given to them to keep at all costs. . . . The Word of God had been already given to them, and so the race of the Prophets came to an end and that of the Scribes took its place. . . . The Scribes had not in themselves the direct and masterful authority that belonged to the Prophets who went before them. They were not themselves commissioned to say ' Thus saith the Lord.' "

It is important to fix firmly in our minds how fundamental to the world of Jewish thought was this doctrine of an infallible revelation from the past.

---

[1] The extraordinary value—religious, historic and literary—to the world as well as to the nation of the ancient Jewish literature need not be dwelt on here. This value is recognized not only by all pious but by all educated men. What we are here concerned to note are the religious drawbacks attending their uncritical acceptance.

JEWISH FANTASY

In an article upon Jewish religion in the first century A.D., Mr Claude Montefiore says:

"Between God and the Jew there was a middle term. Bare man ... did not make his way to God alone and as best he could, serving and worshipping Him to the best of his ability ... with no dictation or demand from on high. What, then, was the mediation, or who were the mediators? Institutions or sacraments, demigods or angels? The link, the middle term, was the Law, or, more properly and accurately, the Torah. What is the Torah? ... Torah means instruction, teaching; thus it is a wider term than the Pentateuch or the Law. It could be used to include all the teachings contained in, or to be elicited from, all the Sacred Writings. ... The burden of the supposed possession of a perfect Scripture and of a perfect and authoritative Law had its drawbacks."[1]

These drawbacks seem to be: (1) As we have seen, passages that come from a lower civilization may be cited as giving authority to man's baser passions. (2) The paradox created by contradictory statements, to all of which equal value must be assigned, creates mental confusion. (3) The doctrine of infallible revelation belittles human intelligence.

It is not hard to see that this doctrine of an infallible revelation in human speech involves the belittling of human reason and values. If any intelligent man sits down and asks himself, How can this thing be? the natural answer would be that the perfectly inspired man must, in his hour of inspiration, be overshadowed and overcome by the power of the Highest, so that the erring or divided mind or self, of which all men are habitually conscious, would, for the hour, be dumb. All men know that "to err is human," and a man who received and gave forth an infallible "word of the Lord" must be, for the time, not himself, not at home

<small>Doctrine of verbal infallibility belittles human values.</small>

[1] Art in Dr Peake's *Commentary*, pp. 620, 623.

THE LORD OF THOUGHT

in his own brain and senses—in other words, beside himself. Hence human values could not be brought forward as tests of such revelation; human reason could have no power to criticize it. Thus, in a nation believing in such revelation, man's values and reasons were held to be on a level inferior to his religious visions, and the virtues of self-directed moral action inferior to those brought into play by painstaking docility of behaviour. With the Jews, copying and repeating the Law, and ordering the life to the end of its practical observance, were duties higher than the duty of thought, higher than any duty of obedience to that intense sense of value which we call personal insight or intuition.

Reason was set aside and truth sought for in dreams and visions. Another result of belittling human intelligence was that the Jews in national depression sought relief in dreams and emotional visions, believing that God's truth came to them by these channels; and because they believed that pure revelation came to them only from the past, each consoling vision, each helpful instruction, now put forth was credited to some religious hero of the past. Professor Burkitt says:

" So when the crisis (the persecution of Antiochus Epiphanes) came we find a new phenomenon. The Jew who feels himself to have a new message for his brethren shelters himself under a pseudonym. The original literature of the two centuries and a half that preceded the capture of Jerusalem (by the Romans in 70 A.D.) is either anonymous, or it professes to be the work of some worthy of old time. . . . It is well, I think, to remind ourselves at the outset that the authorship of the Book of Daniel is no isolated problem. Baruch, Ezra, Solomon, Moses, the Twelve Patriarchs, Noah, Enoch, Adam—all these had Apocalypses or Testaments fathered upon them. It is difficult to know in particular cases how far the pseudonymity was an understood literary artifice and how far it was really deceptive.

JEWISH FANTASY

What, I think, is clear is that both authors and readers believed that if any Revelation from God was true, it could not be new. It must have been given to the great Saints of antiquity."[1]

They had, as we have seen, the basis of a belief in a coming Golden Age. This was now expected to come by divine catastrophe. But the martyrs who were already dead, and such as must die before it came, must share its bliss. A life after death must be accepted. The form which this life took was also moulded, as we shall see, by the need of a compensating "projection." When the nation, out of its disappointment and cruel suffering, developed the immortal hope, the notion of spiritual life beyond the grave was in surrounding nations formless and shadowy in the extreme. One nation thought one thing about it, and another another. In the flux of life round the Mediterranean several doctrines floated; but as the only definite pictures that man can form are compounded of earthly material, the doctrine of re-incarnation alone among Gentile beliefs offered an *imaginable* future. Even on this view definite expectation for the future was only to be had, as it were, in patches; for in the discarnate intervals through which the soul must pass, everything that could be affirmed of it was vague because bodiless. The doctrine of successive re-incarnations, moreover, carried with it the notion of the endless wheel—the mere repetition of cycles of events which contradicted that notion of goal implicit in law. By deifying law the Jews committed themselves to faith in a definite purpose for the universe and a definite goal for human history which ruled out the idea of endless repetition. When, then, their de-

(margin note: Immortality and Resurrection.)

[1] *Jewish and Christian Apocalypses,* p 6

pressed hearts demanded an imaginative picture of compensating bliss that should come after the martyr's death, they were logically bound to postulate the resurrection of the body and the kingdom of God on earth.

In storm and stress this God-fearing nation divined some truths that bear the test of ages. It passed them on in transitory images. How far the authors of the apocalypses knew that they were writing poetic fiction, how far they may have been subject to trance visions and voices, cannot be known. It is, however, certain—and it is important to keep this in mind—that not all the Jews—not all the religious Jews—accepted the apocalypses as inspired, or even in thought dallied with their fantastic imagery. In this period we have Wisdom books which are not apocalyptic. After the conquest by Alexander many pious families of the returned exiles emigrated to other parts of the Hellenized world. These early " Jews of the Dispersion," while faithful to God and the law, absorbed Greek culture, and, most likely going backward and forward between Jerusalem and Greek cities, would be critical of the doctrine of the bodily resurrection and the hope of a speedy supernatural catastrophe. The resurrection of the body was a materialistic idea compared with the highest Greek conceptions of the immortality of the soul. The apocalyptic visions were materialistic and sensational compared with the spiritual teaching of Jeremiah and the Second Isaiah. One truly religious party in the state even rejected the then modern notion of personal immortality. This party — afterwards called Sadducees — jeered at the supposed authority of these apocalyptic books. The only one that, after long debate

JEWISH FANTASY

in the rabbinical schools, found access to the Jewish Canon was the *Book of Daniel*, which obviously had other points of interest. The great rabbis of the first century of our era finally rid the orthodox Jewish religion of all belief in a supernatural catastrophe and its attendant eschatological beliefs. The assumption made by some in recent times that all pious Jews accepted the apocalyptic panorama of the future and therefore Jesus must have accepted it, is not justified. The problems raised by it were still in debate in the time of Jesus. What appears certain is that no intelligent Jew could have been ignorant of these apocalyptic books [1]; no intelligent Jew could have failed to ponder the conceptions of divine justice and divine power which they so graphically set forth. If Jesus in his public teaching contradicted their fundamental doctrines of God and man, he could not have both contradicted those doctrines and held them.

It is important to realize that, while the notion of a supernatural catastrophe as God's way to right the wrong was not common to all religious Jews, those who held themselves aloof from it had the same underlying conception of God and man, of law and punishment; and also that neither the one party nor the other was satisfied with any current thought concerning the problems of divine justice and power which are the main themes of all the literature of the period.

But underlying conceptions of God and man were common to all.

We shall first see what conceptions of God and of man are put forward in this pseudonymous literature, and next hope to show how clearly the writers apprehended the unsolved problems to which these conceptions gave birth.

---
[1] The fact that these apocalypses were translated into the several languages spoken in the Jewish world is evidence of this.

CHAPTER III

THE JEWISH IDEA OF GOD AS JUDGE

IT was in the two centuries preceding the birth of Christ and in the first century A.D. that the books that we are to examine were written, collected, edited and re-edited, copied and translated into the many languages spoken in Syria and Egypt.[1] In these books we have the conception of God which Jesus found in his environment. It is with this conception that we must compare his own teaching about the Father if we would discover what is original and essential to that teaching.

<small>Temporary torture for the good;</small> In these apocalyptic writings the main idea associated with God is that of discipline and judgment. Nothing happens to men by chance, and the operation of natural law is scarcely recognized. In this world God sends many afflictions to the righteous. His reasons for this are stated differently by different authors, but all agree that He inflicts considerable torture on the righteous in this life. His mercy, however, is always <small>age-long torture or destruction for the wicked.</small> available for the righteous; and after their afflictions He provides for them the reward of eternal satisfactions. God's providential mercy to sinners simply takes the form of giving them a long chance. This degree of mercy is greatly extolled. Whenever that chance ends

---

[1] The more important of these books are now easily accessible in a series of translations published by S P C K.

THE JEWISH IDEA OF GOD AS JUDGE

His judgment is final; His vengeance upon them is terrible and implacable. During the long chance God provides for him in this life the human sinner may repent, that is, he may cease to be an unrighteous person and become a righteous one; but in the case of human beings after this life or of fallen angels, no grief for their sins, no recognition of God's righteousness, will be of any avail.

The Hebrew seers of this period thought of the divine power as personal, universal and moral. All history was regarded as moving, under divine control, to the entire elimination of evil and the realization of good. Their ethic was in many ways the purest the world then knew. Their God regarded nothing in man but his righteousness or unrighteousness; so pre-eminent was the importance of moral conduct that a man's strength or beauty or skill went for little or nothing in God's sight. The domestic and neighbourly virtues required of men were on a high level and were positive as well as negative; although any degree of positive virtue was valueless if combined with neglect of ritual law. The righteous man had continual access to the spiritual world, and his conception of his share in the joy of God when righteousness should be consummated gives rise to some of the noblest hopes and aspirations ever expressed in human language. The picture of friendship between righteous souls and a righteous God is a priceless gift which Judaism gave to the world. *High moral and religious value of the legal idea of God.*

But the main burden of these books is the scarcity of righteous souls and God's implacable vengeance on the unrighteous. This judgment is regarded as divine, whether conceived as executed by God in person or *But the emphasis is on divine vengeance.*

THE LORD OF THOUGHT

through an agent such as the "Son of Man" of the *Book of Enoch*. The spirit of cruelty breathes in their doctrine of divine justice. The very bliss of the righteous, even when otherwise nobly and spiritually conceived, is described as consisting partly in witnessing the torments God is inflicting on the unrighteous.

The Gentiles were not thought of as ruled by a different idea of God, but as merely "ungodly." Impious Jews were even worse than ungodly. Worst of all were the Gentiles who oppressed the Jews. God was not thought of as able to overcome sin and save the sinners; it was only by the destruction of all the ungodly and sinners that God and good could prevail. In the sight of God, as they conceived Him, the crime of *lèse-majesté* was the worst of crimes.

From the parables and visions ascribed to Enoch[1] I quote a few passages concerning the punishment of sinners.

In the description of the day of God's self-revelation we read:

The belief that God tortures men to establish His own honour.

> "And behold! He cometh with ten thousands of His
>   holy ones
> To execute judgment upon all,
> And to destroy the ungodly;
> To convict all flesh
> Of all the works of their ungodliness which they have
>   ungodly committed,
> And of all the hard things which ungodly sinners have
>   spoken against Him."—*Book of Enoch*, i. 9.

[1] In quoting the apocalypses I for convenience assume, for the most part, unity of authorship in each book, though, as a fact, many are of composite authorship. All that concerns us, however, is the way in which the books reflected and affected the beliefs of the religious mind of that day, for which consideration the manner of compilation is immaterial.

THE JEWISH IDEA OF GOD AS JUDGE

It is not enough that the Gentiles should suffer; unfaithful Jews are condemned:

> "But ye—ye have not been steadfast, nor done the commandments of the Lord. . . .
> Therefore shall ye execrate your days,
> And the years of your life shall perish,
> And the years of your destruction shall be multiplied in eternal execration,
> And ye shall find no mercy."—*Ibid.*, v. 4, 5.

Thus the angel Raphael describes the use of a hollow in the rocks of Sheol: *The first vision of hell.*

> "And this has been made for sinners when they die and are buried in the earth and judgment has not been executed upon them in their lifetime. Here their spirits shall be set apart in this great pain, till the great day of judgment, scourgings and torments of the accursed for ever, so that there may be retribution for their spirits."—*Ibid.*, xxii. 9.

Thus God upholds His own honour, making the hell of souls who have spoken ill of Him a spectacle for souls in heaven:

> "Then Uriel, one of the holy angels who was with me, answered and said: 'This accursed valley is for those who are accursed for ever: here shall all be gathered together who utter with their lips against the Lord unseemly words and of His glory speak hard things. Here shall they be gathered together, and here shall be their place of judgment. In the last days there shall be upon them the spectacle of righteous judgment in the presence of the righteous for ever.'"—*Ibid.*, xxvii. 2, 3.

Origin of the mediæval hell

This scene is still depicted over the west door of many mediæval churches:

> "And there I saw the mansions of the elect and the mansions of the holy, and mine eyes saw there all the sinners being driven

THE LORD OF THOUGHT

from thence which deny the name of the Lord of Spirits, and being dragged off: and they could not abide because of the punishment which proceeds from the Lord of Spirits."—*Ibid.*, xli. 2.

Here are the demons likewise familiar in Gothic art:

" There mine eyes saw a deep valley with open mouths.... I saw all the angels of punishment abiding there and preparing all the instruments of Satan. And I asked the angel of peace who went with me: ' For whom are they preparing these instruments ? ' And he said unto me: ' They prepare these for the kings and the mighty of this earth that they may thereby be destroyed.' "—*Ibid.*, liii. 1, 3-5.

In Enoch's hell we also find angels. This is explained —in part at least—by the fact that in many of the books of our period, both in the Apocalypses and in the Wisdom literature, this obvious problem confronted the thinking Jew: if God's law was the only means of salvation, why did the great majority of men neglect it ? They commonly took refuge in the traditional belief that some angels had fallen into sin and then beguiled men. This only moved the problem further back, and was not used to exonerate man, for it does not appear that they thought God less angry with men because they had been beguiled, or had inherited this angelic transgression. The fall of the angels is described as caused by love for the daughters of men. Having come to earth and taken each a wife, they taught men the arts and crafts of a corrupt civilization. They are represented as having human affections, through which God tortures them. Their transgression and fate, as described below, illustrate our point, which is, that God was conceived as dealing

The blame laid on wicked angels.

28

THE JEWISH IDEA OF GOD AS JUDGE

out implacable vengeance on all unrighteous and all oppressors of His people.

We get this traditional explanation of the cause of sin set forth vividly and with poetic power in the *Book of Enoch*. The fallen angels are called " Watchers " :

> " And again the Lord said to Raphael,
> ' Bind Azazel hand and foot, and cast him into the darkness ; and make an opening in the desert, which is in Dudael, and cast him therein. And place upon him rough and jagged rocks, and cover him with darkness, and let him abide there for ever, and cover his face that he may not see light. And on the day of the great judgment he shall be cast into the fire.' . . . And to Gabriel said the Lord : ' Proceed against the bastards and the reprobates, and against the children of fornication : and destroy the children of the Watchers from amongst men.' . . . And the Lord said unto Michael : ' Go, bind Semjaza and his associates, who have united themselves with women so as to have defiled themselves with them in all their uncleanness. . . . In those days they shall be led off to the abyss of fire : and to the torment and the prison in which they shall be confined for ever.' "

. . . .

> " And I, Enoch, was blessing the Lord of majesty and the King of the ages, and lo ! the Watchers called me—Enoch the scribe—and said to me : ' Enoch, thou scribe of righteousness, go, declare to the Watchers of the heaven who have left the high heaven, the holy eternal place, and have defiled themselves with women, and have done as the children of earth do, and have taken unto themselves wives : " We have wrought great destruction on the earth : and ye shall have no peace nor forgiveness of sin." . . . Over the destruction of their children shall they lament, and shall make supplication unto eternity, but mercy and peace shall ye not attain.'

<small>No forgiveness for the repentant in the spirit world.</small>

. . . .

And Enoch went and said: 'Azazel, thou shalt have no peace: a severe sentence has gone forth against thee to put thee in bonds: and thou shalt not have toleration nor request granted to thee, because of the unrighteousness which thou hast taught, and because of all the works of godlessness and unrighteousness and sin which thou hast shown to men.' Then I went and spoke to them all together, and they were all afraid, and fear and trembling seized them. And they besought me to draw up a petition for them that they might find forgiveness, and to read their petition in the presence of the Lord of heaven. For from thenceforward they could not speak with Him nor lift up their eyes to heaven for shame of their sins for which they had been condemned. Then I wrote out their petition, and the prayer in regard to their spirits and their deeds individually and in regard to their requests that they should have forgiveness and length of days."—*Ibid.*, x. 4-13 ; xii. 3-6 ; xiii. 1-6.

Enoch returns to them this answer, which well illustrates the Jewish idea of God's righteous judgment :

" I wrote out your petition, and in my vision it appeared thus, that your petition will not be granted unto you throughout all the days of eternity, and that judgment has been finally passed upon you : yea, your petition will not be granted unto you. And from henceforth you shall not ascend into heaven unto all eternity, and in bonds of the earth the decree has gone forth to bind you for all the days of the world. And that previously you shall have seen the destruction of your beloved sons and you shall have no pleasure in them, but they shall fall before you by the sword. And your petition on their behalf shall not be granted, nor yet on your own : even though you weep and pray and speak all the words contained in the writing which I have written."—*Ibid.*, xiv. 4-7.

Enoch then proceeds on his journeys, and thus again reports on the punishment of the angels :

" I saw a horrible thing : a great fire there which burnt and blazed, and the place was cleft as far as the abyss, being full of great descending columns of fire : neither its extent nor magnitude could I see, nor could I conjecture. Then I said, ' How fearful is the place, and how terrible to look upon ! ' Then Uriel answered me, one of the holy angels who was with me, and said unto me : ' Enoch, why hast thou such fear and

THE JEWISH IDEA OF GOD AS JUDGE

affright?' And I answered: 'Because of this fearful place, and because of the spectacle of the pain.' And he said unto me: 'This place is the prison of the angels, and here they will be imprisoned for ever.'"—*Ibid.*, xxi. 7-10.

The tortures which these fallen angels undergo, and also those heaped upon the potentates who oppressed Israel, are referred to so often that it would seem that the various authors of the *Book of Enoch* and its innumerable readers must have delighted in these descriptions of divine vengeance. Later on in the book Noah is represented as prophesying what seems to be a contrivance by which the bodies of the angels who beguiled mankind, and the kings of the earth who oppressed men, should be sustained to endure prolonged torture: *[margin: Vengeful delight in the spectacle of pain.]*

"And He will imprison those angels who have shown unrighteousness in that burning valley . . . in which there was a convulsion of the waters. . . . Through its valleys proceed streams of fire, where these angels are punished who had led astray those who dwell on the earth, for the healing of the body, but for the punishment of the spirit. . . . And in proportion as the burning of their bodies becomes severe, a corresponding change shall take place in their spirit for ever and ever; for before the Lord of Spirits none shall utter an idle word. For the judgment shall come upon them, because they believe in the lust of their body and deny the Spirit of the Lord. . . . Therefore they will not see and will not believe that those waters will change and become a fire which burns for ever."—*Ibid.*, lxvii. 4-13.

These vivid fragments would not of themselves be so important but for the fact that there is nothing in any part of the Hebrew literature of our period to contradict the idea of God's vengeance upon sinners as implacable and insatiable.

THE LORD OF THOUGHT

Pre-Christian teaching on forgiveness.
Of the pre-Christian books, the *Testaments of the Twelve Patriarchs* gives us the most gentle and noble idea of man's duty to man. This book comes nearest to Christian teaching concerning forbearance and forgiveness between brothers of one race; it seems, however, to be urged for the sake of creating a union of hearts in face of a non-Jewish world. There is little scope in this book for discussing the final judgments of God because all its injunctions are addressed by a father to his own children and grandchildren, a chosen race for whom final salvation is here assumed to be for the most part secure. Yet the same idea of God's vengeance on the wicked is in the background, and occasionally appears:

" Hear, therefore, regarding the heavens which have been shown to thee. The lowest is for this cause gloomy unto thee, in that it beholds all the unrighteous deeds of men. And it has fire, snow, and ice made ready for the day of judgment, in the righteous judgment of God; for in it are all the spirits of the retributions for vengeance on men. And in the second are the hosts of the armies which are ordained for the day of judgment, to work vengeance on the spirits of deceit and of Beliar. And above them are the holy ones. And in the highest of all dwelleth the Great Glory, far above all holiness."—*Testaments of the Twelve Patriarchs—Levi*. iii. 1-3.

There are other descriptions of the results of God's future judgment, but this is enough for our purpose. Here is a statement of God's providence for the unruly on earth:

" Therefore the temple, which the Lord shall choose, shall be laid waste through your uncleanness, and ye shall be captives throughout all nations. And ye shall be an abomination unto them, and ye shall receive reproach and everlasting shame from the righteous judgment of God. And all who hate you shall

THE JEWISH IDEA OF GOD AS JUDGE

rejoice at your destruction. And if you were not to receive mercy through Abraham, Isaac, and Jacob, our fathers, not one of our seed should be left upon the earth."—*Ibid.*—*Levi.* xv. 1-4.

The strongest and most beautiful exhortation to brotherly love and to forgiveness of the brother who has committed an injury ends upon the note of God's vengeance:

"If he be shameless and persisteth in his wrongdoing, even so forgive him from the heart, and leave to God the avenging."—*Ibid.*—*Gad.* vi. 7. Forgive because God will not forgive.

Nor is this conception of God confined to the highly visionary language of the apocalypses.

In the *Wisdom of Ben-Sira* (*Ecclesiasticus*) also there is a lofty teaching as to the duty of human forbearance, but behind it is the same belief in God's vengeance:

"Woe unto the faint heart; because it believeth not,
 Therefore it shall not be sheltered.
Woe unto you that have lost patience,
 And what will ye do when the Lord visiteth you?"
    Wisdom of Ben-Sira, ii. 13-14.

"Yea, and if there be one that is stiff-necked,
 A marvel would it be if he were not punished.
For mercy and wrath are with Him,
 He forgiveth and pardoneth, but upon the wicked doth He cause His wrath to alight."
    Ibid., xvi. 11. Divine vengeance in Wisdom books.

"Like tow wrapped together is the gathering of the ungodly,
 And their end is a flame of fire.
The way of sinners is made smooth, without stones,
 And at the end thereof is the pit of Hades."
    Ibid., xxi. 9-10.

"There are winds that are created for vengeance,
 And in their wrath lay on their scourges heavily;

THE LORD OF THOUGHT

> And in the time of the end they pour out their strength,
>   And appease the wrath of Him that created them.
> Fire and hail, famine and pestilence,
>   These also are created for judgment.
> Beasts of prey, scorpions and vipers,
>   And the avenging sword to slay the wicked,
> All these are created for their uses,
>   And are in His treasure-house, and in their time shall be requisitioned."—*Ibid.*, xxxix. 28-30.

In the *Wisdom of Solomon* we get these lines concerning the retribution that shall come upon the ungodly:

> " And them shall the Lord laugh to scorn.
> And after this they shall become a dishonoured carcase,
> And for a mockery among the dead for ever.
> For he shall dash them speechless to the ground.
> And shall shake them from their foundations;
> And they shall be utterly desolated,
> And shall be in torment,
> And their memory shall perish.
> And they shall come, at the reckoning up of their sins, in coward fear,
> And their lawless deeds shall convict them to their face."
>   *Wisdom of Solomon*, iv. 19-20.

In this connection we may read such passages as Ezekiel vii. 1-9 with its refrain: " Mine eye shall not spare, neither will I have pity," or Malachi iv. or the imprecatory Psalms.

It is needless to quote from the *Book of Daniel* and the *Book of Esther* to show that these books also breathe an undoubting belief in the divine vengeance. In Daniel viii. there is a vision in which a goat with a notable horn came upon a ram and " ran into him in the *fury* of his power. . . . There was no power in the ram to stand before him, but he cast him down to the ground and stamped upon him." In the next chapter this

[margin: God pitiless to the wicked]

THE JEWISH IDEA OF GOD AS JUDGE

same quality of fury is attributed to God. This same word translated " fury " is used in a prayer in which Daniel, while extolling God's mercy, entreats that His " fury " may at last be " turned away from Jerusalem," which is now suffering because of sin. In Daniel also we have an early record of belief in the resurrection of the wicked.[1] They shall " awake " from the long sleep of death; they shall awake and arise to life on this beautiful earth, but, by God's ordaining, only to " shame and everlasting contempt."

The *Book of Esther* is a story written in cruel times. It may not have been as cruel in its original form as in the form we know; but it could only have been written and enjoyed by a religious people who believed that vengeance was an attribute of God.

When we pass to the latter part of the first century A.D. after the ministry of Jesus, we certainly get, in the reflections of thoughtful Jews upon the fall of Jerusalem, a softened tone with regard to the suffering even of the wicked; but there is no suggestion of divine relenting towards them. We quote these books because, although written after Jesus had passed from earth, they represent the continuum of the traditional atmosphere that surrounded him. [Authors who were young when Jesus preached.]

In the *Apocalypse of Ezra* we find, among other references to God's punishments, these passages:

> " And the Most High shall be revealed upon the throne of judgment;
> and the end shall come,
> and compassion pass away,
> and pity be far off,
> and long-suffering be withdrawn."

[1] Dan XII. 2.

THE LORD OF THOUGHT

Pity may well be " far off," for the joy of the saved is to be heightened by contrast with the torments of the lost :

> " And the pit of torment shall appear,
> but over against this the place of rest ;
> the furnace of Gehenna shall be revealed,
> and over against it the Paradise of delights.
> And then shall the Most High say to those nations that have been raised :
> Gaze and see what ye have denied,
> or whom ye have not served,
> or whose commandments ye have despised !
> Look, therefore, over against you :
> behold here rest and enjoyments,
> and there fire and torment !
> Thus shall he speak to them in that Day of Judgment."[1]
> *Apocalypse of Ezra*, Vision III. vii. 33, 36-38.

When the seer himself compassionates the lot of the wicked he receives this final reply from God :

God indifferent to the perishing multitudes

> " Do not thou, therefore, again ask any more concerning the many who perish ; because they have received liberty and
> they have despised the Most High,
> his Law also have they scorned much,
> and have made his ways to cease :
> Yea, his saints they have trampled upon, and they have said in their heart that there is no God, while they verily know that they shall surely die.
> Therefore as these things aforesaid await you, so also thirst and torment are destined for them."—*Ibid.*, viii. 55-59.[2]

In the *Apocalypse of Baruch*, much of which has its origin in the same period as the *Apocalypse of Ezra*,

---

[1] This conception is in line with such passages of Christian literature as the rejoicing of the saints over the destruction of Babylon in Revelation xviii. 20 and xix. 1-3.

[2] Cf. *ibid.*, viii. 1-3 and ix. 15-16, showing the vast preponderance of those doomed to perish.

THE JEWISH IDEA OF GOD AS JUDGE

we again see a human compassion for the wicked not emphasized in earlier books; but again there is no echo or reflection of this pity in the divine vengeance. Baruch in his last prayer is represented as saying:

"For at the consummation of the world there shall be vengeance taken upon those who have done wickedness according to their wickedness; . . . And those who sin Thou blottest out from among thine own."—*Apocalypse of Baruch*, liv. 21, 22.

It is on this note that the book ends.

Thus in reading the Jewish literature of the period we see plainly, both in the Apocalyptic and Wisdom books, that Jesus Christ came into a world which could not conceive of a God who did not, in the long run, take terrible vengeance on all His enemies.

CHAPTER IV

THE PROBLEM OF GOD'S LOVE AND CRUELTY

Jewish seers and mediæval monks

THE Jews were a keen-minded people, but, as we have seen, they had to contrive to use their minds within the strict limit of a received revelation, beyond which limit reason and moral insight were held to be invalid. We have an analogous situation in Christendom in the monastic speculations of the Middle Ages. In both cases reason was confined within the bounds of a received revelation, and in both cases the religious insight and the moral values of good men were on a higher level than much of the supposed revelation, and tended to degenerate to match what were really the primitive premisses and dimmer insight of a less developed civilization.

The result was twofold. What was best, what was true, in the earlier religion was emphasized and carried forward by the religious experience and reflection of thoughtful and high-minded men; but, also, what was unworthy and degrading in the earlier religion was so rationalized and stereotyped that it acquired a permanent and unnatural importance, sucking the life-blood of religious thinking. Strange exaltations of savage fancies[1] were not the only bad result of a belief in a finished revelation. God in His relation to man was

[1] Cf. Chap. II. p. 19.

PROBLEM OF GOD'S LOVE AND CRUELTY

seen, not simply as the best and wisest being of whom man—at that stage of his development—could conceive, but as a mixture of good and evil, and therefore hostile, not to all those things to which man at his best was hostile, but to much that was best in man.[1] This contradiction between man's highest ideal and what he conceived God to be, felt even when not admitted to open-eyed consciousness, produced necessarily a complex system of doctrine at variance with the plain man's reason and values. Before the ideal of a God thus conceived man's reason inevitably faints and fails. Now, reason never quails before the realization that knowledge is inadequate, that there is more to know about the object of research than is, or apparently can be, known. It is only before contradiction that reason quails, and thus has always quailed and been unable to accept the God of an ancient and final revelation. Thus, as pointed out in the second chapter, irrational opposition of good and evil in the doctrinal God fostered the idea that religious truth was to be found, not by the use of all man's powers working upon the problems of life, but chiefly in states of ecstasy or divine obsession, causing men to reverence abnormal mental conditions and to undervalue their normal and natural powers. With the Jews of this period reason seems to have given up the religious problem as hopeless: they had no religious philosophy. Religious emotion and the imaginations it quickened tended to be more esteemed than sober religious thinking.

God thought of as hostile to human pity for wicked men.

Consolation only to be found in unreasoning adoration.

[1] "The wish that of the living whole
No life may fail beyond the grave,
Derives it not from what we have
The likest God within the soul?"
TENNYSON, *In Memoriam*, lv.

THE LORD OF THOUGHT

With such inconsistency in his God, if man is to be truly religious it must be by exercising his affections and imagination upon the only attributes of this complex and inconsistent God that do not contradict human values. That is precisely what the best of the Jews did, what the saints of every religion founded on an ancient and closed revelation must do, with the result that emotion is supposed to find God where reason can produce only scepticism.

The books of our period give us many examples of this outgoing of the heart of the Jew to all that he recognized as wholly good in the divine character. These books taught that God loved the Jew who obeyed Him ; His mercy was over all who feared Him ; His compassion surrounded all men, even the unrighteous, while as yet there was any hope of their repentance. These traits in God's character the good Jew could understand and adore ; and his understanding and adoration of God's love have been the chief tributary of the river of the water of life which has flowed through all human generations since man first became conscious of the unseen Presence whose name is Love.

God's friendship with the righteous is the great Jewish contribution to the world's thought.

Many of the Psalms are well-known instances of this conscious love and adoration. Psa. cxix. is typical of our period. In Job we find the inscrutable doctrine that all evils are due to the direct fiat of a good God, troubling a mind which only finds escape in unreasoning adoration of God's creative power. These and other instances in our Old Testament are too well known to quote. From the *Wisdom of Solomon* we cite one or two beautiful expressions of the love of God, to be found in the midst of much about law-breakers and their punishment :

PROBLEM OF GOD'S LOVE AND CRUELTY

> " But Thou, our God, art loving and true,
> Long-suffering and in mercy ordering all things.
> For even if we sin, we are Thine, knowing Thy strength;
> But we shall not sin, knowing that we are accounted Thine.
> For to know Thee is perfect righteousness,
> And to know Thy power is the root of immortality."
> *Wisdom of Solomon*, xv. 1-3.

This is an apostrophe to Wisdom :

> " For there is in her a spirit of understanding, holy,
> Sole-born, manifold, subtil,
> Mobile, lucid, unpolluted,
> Clear, inviolable, loving goodness, keen,
> Unhindered, beneficent, loving towards man,
> Steadfast, sure, free from care,
> All-powerful, all-surveying,
> And penetrating through all spirits
> That are quick of understanding, pure, and most subtil.
> For Wisdom is more mobile than any motion,
> Yea, she pervadeth and penetrateth all things by reason of her pureness.
> For she is a vapour of the power of God,
> And a clear effluence of the glory of the Almighty;
> Therefore nothing defiled findeth entrance into her.
> For she is a reflection from the everlasting light,
> And an unspotted mirror of the working of God,
> And the image of His goodness.
>
> . . . .
>
> And from generation to generation passing into holy souls,
> She maketh men friends of God and prophets."
> *Ibid.*, vii. 22*b*-27.

In the following beautiful passages in the *Wisdom of Ben-Sira* we have the complex emotions of worship grouped under the ambiguous word " fear " :

> " The fear of the Lord is glory and exultation,
> And gladness and a crown of joy.

THE LORD OF THOUGHT

> The fear of the Lord delighteth the heart,
>   And giveth gladness, and joy, and length of days.
> For him that feareth the Lord it shall be well at the last,
>   And in the day of his death he shall find grace."
>
> " Ye that fear the Lord, wait for His mercy ;
>   And turn not aside lest ye fall.
> Ye that fear the Lord, put your trust in Him,
>   And your reward shall not fail.
> Ye that fear the Lord, hope for good things,
>   And for eternal gladness and mercy.
> Regard the generations of old, and see :
>   Who ever trusted in the Lord, and was put to shame ?
> Or who did abide in His fear, and was forsaken ?
> Or who called on Him, and was overlooked ?
> For the Lord is compassionate and merciful,
>   And forgiveth sins, and saveth in time of trouble."
>   *Wisdom of Ben-Sıra,* i. 11-13 ; ii. 7-11.

In the *Apocalypse of Enoch*, after many and horrible visions of judgment, we get this beautiful imaginative picture :

A vision of heaven.

> " And he translated my spirit into the heaven of heavens,
> And I saw there as it were a structure built of crystals,
> And, between those crystals, tongues of living fire. . . .
> And I saw angels who could not be counted,
> A thousand thousands, and ten thousand times ten thousand,
> Encircling that house. . . .
> And they came forth from that house,
> And Michael and Gabriel, Raphael and Phanuel,
> And many holy angels without number.
> And with them the Head of Days,
> His head white and pure as wool,
> And His raiment indescribable.
> And I fell on my face,
> And my whole body became relaxed,
> And my spirit was transfigured ;

PROBLEM OF GOD'S LOVE AND CRUELTY

> And I cried with a loud voice,
> . . . with the spirit of power,
> And blessed and glorified and extolled."
> *Book of Enoch,* lxxi. 5, 8, 9-11.

In the *Apocalypse of Baruch*,[1] after the seer has been instructed concerning the destruction of all sinners, this passage comes as an escape for the dismayed heart:

> " And it shall come to pass, when He hath brought low everything that is in the world,
> And hath sat down in peace for the age on the throne of His kingdom,
> That joy shall then be revealed,
> And rest appear;
> And then healing shall descend in dew,
> And disease shall withdraw,
> And anxiety and anguish and lamentation shall pass from among men,
> And gladness shall proceed through the whole earth. . . .
> And it shall come to pass in those days that the reapers shall not grow weary,
> Nor those that build be toilworn;
> For the works shall of themselves speedily advance
> With those who do them in much tranquillity. . . .
> And I answered and said:
> ' Who can understand, O Lord, Thy goodness?
> For it is incomprehensible.
> Or who can search into Thy compassions,
> Which are infinite?
> Or who can comprehend Thy intelligence?
> Or who is able to recount the thought of Thy mind?
> Or who of those that are born can hope to come to those things,
> Unless he is one to whom Thou art merciful and gracious?'"
> *Apocalypse of Baruch,* lxxiii. 1, 2; lxxiv. 1; lxxv. 1-5.

But who can hope unless he knows himself elected to mercy?

[1] This apocalypse, although written after the ministry of Jesus, shows the continuity of ideas from 200 B.C. to 100 A.D.

THE LORD OF THOUGHT

But, after all, in all the books we have quoted there is little, comparatively very little indeed, concerning a pure delight in God.

The law, with its rich and reiterated promises of reward, was much nearer to men, and on that law all those who hoped for its rewards lavished their affectionate adoration.

But the great strength of Jewish religion was the intensity of the conviction that the power that ruled the world was personal. In personality, defined as a self-conscious centre of feeling, reason and will, the human soul instinctively discovers the greatest reality and power of which it can conceive. Thus, in attributing to God this supreme conception of reality, a righteous personality, Judaism made its great contribution. It is obvious, however, that their conception of a personal God must rise as their conception of human duty became more civilized. At the time when the books of the Old Testament came to be recognized as a final revelation, it had become difficult for the Jew to love whole-heartedly a character in whom cruel vengeance was so conspicuous.

Distinction between punishment and consequence. The problem was closely connected with the confusion between punishment and consequence.[1] Here we need only to mark the difference between them. Nature deals out consequences, never punishments. Justice as interpreted by persons deals out punishments. The universal system of causation has no visible moral focus. A fireman brought from a burning house, wrapped in his fireman's coat, a child unscathed; the rescuer suffered months of agony. Here we see

[1] The problem of the divine will in relation to the system of causation is dealt with in Chap xiii.

PROBLEM OF GOD'S LOVE AND CRUELTY

what we call natural consequence : we cannot call it punishment. If a schoolmaster whips a boy for not knowing his lesson we do not call it natural consequence, for the schoolmaster might have done something else ; we call it punishment. It was the arbitrary infliction of punitive torture by God upon His enemies, in a supernatural world, which the Jewish religion of our period teaches.

To-day we say, what would be the character of any person who treated disobedient children by burning them alive for ages in the way these writers represent God as treating disobedient Jews ? To-day we ask, what would be the character of a conqueror who, when no longer afraid of his victims, kept them in life-long torture chambers ? Such torture would have no utility, as the victims were not to be benefited by it, and the joy of the conquerors in seeing it inflicted could hardly be a moral benefit to them. Faith to-day insists upon the goodness of God in defiance of tradition ; but to the Jewish seer no such argument from human values was valid as against the revealed cruelty of God declared in their sacred writings, and so they were not satisfied. Some of the extracts that follow indicate that had they felt free to set up their own value-judgment as against these sacred writings they would have taught a new doctrine of God.

These are the more important because, as we have seen,[1] in recent years some eminent religious writers, impressed with the prevalence of apocalyptic thought at the beginning of the Christian era, have endeavoured to explain the teaching of Jesus on the hypothesis that he must have accepted these pious beliefs because

[1] See Introduction, p 2

THE LORD OF THOUGHT

no fundamental criticism of them was possible to a Jew of his time. So far from this being the case, we can show literary evidence that the problems raised by the deification of cruelty had long perplexed righteous Jews and even the apocalyptists themselves.

While in the Old Testament there are many passages in which whole nations that have oppressed Israel are doomed by God to final impenitence and destruction, we have the *Book of Jonah*, written some hundred years before our period, controverting this view. In an article published long ago in the *Interpreter*,[1] Dr Peake pointed out the magnificent testimony borne by this writer to the contrast between God's tender care for all His sentient creation and the fanatical cruelty of the Judaic doctrine. Jonah—the personification of Israel—desired nothing so much as the destruction of Nineveh, the capital of that Assyrian Empire which stood as the most unscrupulous and violent of ancient oppressors. He is angry at the repentance and salvation of the Ninevites, showing that he had none of the true missionary desire for the salvation of the world.

The love of God for wicked Nineveh.

In Dr Peake's interpretation of the parable of the gourd we read:

" For while Jonah had no part in the creation of the gourd, nay, had not even tended its growth, each inhabitant of Nineveh had been the direct creation of God's hand, had lived in His love, had grown under His fostering care. If the whole people meant nothing to Jonah, each single individual meant much to God. If they must be destroyed, it must be only when all means to save them had been tried, and in spite of the pang God felt in their death. And if it might be urged that the Ninevites had sinned beyond forgiveness, yet the judgment Jonah longed for was

[1] Reprinted in Dr Peake's *Commentary on the Bible.*

PROBLEM OF GOD'S LOVE AND CRUELTY

utterly indiscriminate. In that city there were more than six score thousand children, who had not come to years of moral discernment, and were therefore innocent of the crimes of Nineveh against humanity. 'And also much cattle,' the author adds in one of the most striking phrases of the book. It was possible even for Paul to ask, 'Is it for the oxen that God careth?' But this writer knows of a pity of God from which even the cattle of the Ninevites were not excluded."

This doctrine of God's universal love and care, of His universal offer of the gift of repentance, is, of course, not explicitly at variance with the destruction of the finally impenitent; but it is at variance with the spirit of God's vengeance as described in various visions of the Last Judgment, and with much apocalyptic denunciation of heathen as worthless and without any virtue. In the Second Isaiah we have the expression of the evangelical love for all humanity which may well have laid the foundation for the great parable of Jonah. The *mise en scène* of the lofty debates in Job is altogether in Edom the hated. In some passages in the Psalms we get the same sympathy with men as men. "Thou, Lord, art good ... plenteous in mercy unto all them that call upon thee. ... All nations whom thou hast made shall come and worship before thee."[1] In Psa. xcvi. also we seem to get a protest against the destruction of the world so often foretold. "Say among the heathen, the Lord reigneth. The world also shall be established, it shall not be moved. He shall judge the people righteously."[2]

Evangelical teaching in the great prophets.

In Psa. lxxxv. we have a clear suggestion that righteousness and peace ought somehow to unite. The problem which in that whole period divided Jerusalem into two

[1] Psa. lxxxvi. 5, 9.
[2] Psa. xcvi. 10.

THE LORD OF THOUGHT

parties was whether the righteous Jew could or could not give the kiss of peace to an ungodly world. The popular separatists, who denounced all but themselves as ungodly, but who thus succeeded in preserving for the world a higher conception of divine holiness and human duty than was known in other nations, were at enmity with the world. The liberal party, who, by their international outlook and sympathies, might have allowed what was characteristic in the Jewish inspiration to be lost in the in-wash of Hellenic speculation, proclaimed the virtues of charity and peace. All thoughtful men were asking, how was it possible to think of God's personal attitude to the ungodly and vicious as other than hostile without lowering the divine holiness, and, on the other hand, how could God be merciful and condemn the multitudes He had created? Neither party found an answer, for both accepted the same revelation; but neither was uncritical. The best men felt a haunting desire that mercy might unite with truth even in judging the impenitent majority; that righteousness might make peace with sinful multitudes. The apocalyptic belief that in the end God's only way to get rid of sin was by the extermination of unrepentant sinners from the earth, exactly as men might rid themselves of the trouble of vermin, was certainly not uncriticized.

Conflict between separatists and godly Hellenizers.

In the *Book of Enoch*, in which we get the earliest and most horrible pictures of the final punishments God visits upon fallen angels and deluded men, we have more than one indication that the author of such a picture realizes that the punishment would be unjust if inflicted by anyone but God. The author—slaking his own thirst for revenge—evidently delights to invent

PROBLEM OF GOD'S LOVE AND CRUELTY

punishments and put the responsibility on God; but the artist in him warns him that he cannot carry the sympathy of his readers unless he admits that they do not appeal to the sense of justice in any being lower than God. As we saw in Chapter II., when the torments of the fallen angels are announced, these queer beings are described as repenting and making supplication to God for mercy, and Enoch is moved to write out their petition and present it to the Most High. The petition is not granted : God is implacable. The artistic effect of God's implacability is greatly heightened by the fact that a mere man like Enoch was moved to mercy.[1]

Later on the angels who have not fallen see their fallen brethren in the burning valley. They, too, are touched with pity :

<small>Consciousness of the problem in pre-Christian books.</small>

" And on that day Michael answered Raphael and said : ' The power of the spirit transports and makes me tremble because of the severity of the judgment of the secrets, the judgment of the angels : who can endure the severe judgment which has been executed, and before which they melt away ? ' And Michael answered again, and said to Raphael, ' Who is he whose heart is not softened concerning it, and whose reins are not troubled by this word of judgment that has gone forth upon them because of those who have thus led them out ? ' And it came to pass when he stood before the Lord of Spirits, Michael said thus to Raphael : ' I will not take their part under the eye of the Lord ; for the Lord of Spirits has been angry with them.' "
—*Book of Enoch*, lxviii. 2-4.

Again, in later books where the horrors of God's punishments—either in this life or in the life after death—are described, there is an immediate overstatement of the iniquity and entire worthlessness of

[1] *Book of Enoch*, xiii. and xiv.

those punished. It is as though the writer were conscious that there was room for human protest. There are many examples of this.

In the *Wisdom of Solomon*, when the writer has been teaching that the ungodly, however they may enjoy themselves on earth, will be punished hereafter, he at once goes on :

> " Useless are their labours,
> Unprofitable their works.
> Their wives are foolish,
> And evil are their children;
> Accursed is their generation."
> *Wisdom of Solomon*, iii. 11-12.

Such sweeping statements about any class of heathen or irreligious people belong not to the region of fact but to that of moral theory; and here, clearly, the theory of the entire worthlessness of the ungodly is a buttress—felt to be needed—to the doctrine of their punishment after death. In later chapters, after depicting the torment and desolation of the wicked, the righteous and unrighteous are pictured as confronting one another in the Judgment; and the unrighteous are described as themselves confessing to the entire worthlessness of their former lives and characters, evidently in order to forestall natural criticism on the severity of their punishment.

The entire worthlessness of sinners justifies penal fires

In the second part of the same book, when the question of punishment was not to the fore, we get a loving appreciation of God :

> " Thou lovest all things that exist, and abhorrest nothing that
>   Thou didst make,
> For Thou wouldst have formed nothing if Thou didst hate it.

PROBLEM OF GOD'S LOVE AND CRUELTY

And how should aught have endured unless Thou didst so will?
Or how could that be preserved which was not called by Thee?
But Thou sparest all things for they are Thine, O sovereign Lord that lovest souls.
For Thine incorruptible spirit is in all things.
Wherefore them that err Thou dost convince little by little, . . .
That escaping from their wickedness they may believe on Thee, O Lord."—*Ibid.*, xi. 24-xii. 2.

"Thine incorruptible spirit is in all things," even in "them that err." That is a very different view of the world from what is implied in the worthlessness of the wicked and their wives and children from generation to generation. No sooner, however, has the editor inscribed this beautiful passage declaring God's universal immanence and love, than he sees its incongruity with the accepted doctrine of God's treatment of sinners. He bethinks himself at once of the classic instance of God's command to his forefathers to exterminate the Canaanites. He at once begins to justify this by a passage declaring them to have been guilty of extraordinary brutalities, describing their most horrid rites without admitting a redeeming feature. He enters into an elaborate statement of God's forbearance—how He sent them one by one horrid plagues, thus warning them and giving them time to repent, and adds that, although so long-suffering, God was not ignorant

". . . that their nature by birth was evil,
And their wickedness inborn,
And that their manner of thinking would in no wise ever be changed,
For it was a seed accursed from the beginning."
Ibid., xii. 10-11.

THE LORD OF THOUGHT

Quite clearly there is room here to challenge God's justice, and the writer of the passage is conscious that some of his readers will challenge it, for immediately he apostrophizes God, saying :

> "Who shall say, What hast Thou done ? Or who shall oppose Thy judgment ?
> Or who shall accuse Thee for the destroyed nations which Thou didst create ?
> Or who shall come before Thee as the avenger of unrighteous men ? "—*Ibid.*, xii. 2.

That last is a great question. It betrays an imaginative grasp of the situation as he has just described it. God omnipotent, the creator and sustainer of all men, who has of His own will set them " in the midst of so many and great dangers that they cannot always stand upright," who indeed permits them to be so " accursed from the beginning," so born in wickedness that they cannot turn from it, at the same time visits them with torments and destroys them from the face of the earth. Does not the blood and the misery of man " cry aloud for vengeance " upon God ? The poet seems, as it were, to sweep the universe with his inquiring glance. Who is able to challenge God ?

The Wisdom of Solomon acknowledges the riddle of a lost world

So the answer to the problem of God's cruelty is merely that might is right, that weakness may not challenge power. God is all-powerful, and therefore He must be just. Shall the clay complain of the potter ? This old, unsatisfactory answer, that the potter has the right to do what he will with the clay, is the only answer that Judaism ever gave to the riddle of God's cruelty. The religious Jew also held the inspired belief that God was compassionate and

PROBLEM OF GOD'S LOVE AND CRUELTY

infinitely patient; but this he kept in another compartment of his mind.

In the *Wisdom of Ben-Sira* we have a book written, Dr Oesterley tells us, " to combat Hellenic influences and to teach Jewish readers how they should live in relation to God and His law." It is thought to have been written about the beginning of the second century B.C. The writer holds strongly that rewards and punishments are meted out by God, not only in this life but in the next. He says:

> " Say not, ' I sinned, and what happened unto me ! '
>   For the Lord is long-suffering.
> Count not upon forgiveness,
>   By adding sin to sin.
> And say not, ' His mercies are great,
>   He will forgive the multitude of my sins ';
> For mercy and wrath are with Him,
>   And upon the wicked doth His anger abide.
> Delay not to turn unto Him,
>   And put it not off from day to day;
> For suddenly doth His indignation come forth,
>   And in the time of vengeance thou wilt perish.
> Trust not in unrighteous gains,
>   For they profit nothing in the day of wrath."
>   *Wisdom of Ben-Sira*, v. 4-8.

Yet this doctrine of vengeance does not appear to satisfy the writer. After extolling God's power, which no man can comprehend, he adds:

> " What is man, and what profit is there in him ?
>   What is the good of him, and what the evil ?
> The number of man's days
>   Is great if it reach an hundred years;
> As a drop of water from the sea, or as a grain of sand,
>   So are man's few years in the eternal day.

Man is a poor thing to excite divine wrath.

THE LORD OF THOUGHT

> Therefore is the Lord long-suffering toward them,
>   And poureth out His mercy upon them.
> He seeth and knoweth that their end is evil,
>   Therefore doth He increase His forgiveness."
> <div align="right"><i>Ibid.</i>, xviii. 8-12.</div>

Later on, just after a magnificent passage in which the forces of nature are described as God's instruments for the punishment of the wicked, we get this reflection upon the hard lot of humanity:

> "Much occupation hath God allotted,
>   And heavy is the yoke on the sons of men;
> From the day that he cometh forth from his mother's womb,
>   Until the day of his returning to the mother of all living.
> As for their thoughts, and fear of heart,
>   The idea of their expectation is the day of death.
> From him that sitteth upon a throne in exaltation,
>   To him that sitteth in dust and ashes;
> From him that weareth a diadem and crown,
>   To him that weareth a garment of hair,
> There is but anger and jealousy, anxiety and fear,
>   Terror of death, strife and contention.
> And when he resteth upon his bed,
>   The sleep of night doubleth his trouble.
> For a short time that he may rest for a moment, he is undisturbed,
>   And then by dreams is he disturbed.
> He is troubled by the vision of his soul,
>   He is like a fugitive fleeing before the pursuer."
> <div align="right"><i>Ibid.</i>, xl. 1-6.</div>

To this we may add a still later passage:

> "Ah, Death, how bitter is the remembrance of thee
>   To him that liveth in peace in his habitation;
> To him that is at ease, and prospereth in all,
>   And that still hath strength to enjoy luxury.

PROBLEM OF GOD'S LOVE AND CRUELTY

>   Hail, Death, how welcome is thy decree
>   To a luckless man, and that lacketh strength,
>   That stumbleth and trippeth in everything,
>   That is broken and hath lost hope."
>   *Ibid.*, xli. 1-2.

It is difficult to understand how any man who pitied his fellow-men in this way should think it just that their Creator should visit them with severe retribution. In several kindred passages, indeed, we almost see a doctrine of mere natural consequence as dogging the acts of man rather than the further punishments and rewards of a personal God.

The *Apocalypse of Baruch*, though written after the fall of Jerusalem, is believed to embody some earlier traditional matter. It comes in the unbroken line of Jewish eschatological teaching, and is related to the world of ideas in which Jesus Christ thought and worked as any book would be related to the ideas of a period forty or fifty years earlier. Few periods in world history have been so convulsive as the last fifty years in Western Europe; yet the young man of to-day has many more beliefs in common than at variance with the youth of his father's generation. The very contradictions we offer to the notions of our fathers grow out of the same background of ideas. William Penn and John Bunyan, in the last quarter of the seventeenth century, wrote out of a background of ideas very much the same as that which surrounded Milton's youth, although the Commonwealth and Restoration and the popularizing of Galileo's discoveries, had intervened. The world of intellectual assumptions and imaginative conceptions, take it all in all, moves very slowly. The author of *Baruch* was

_{Clearer expression of the problem in our Lord's century.}

THE LORD OF THOUGHT

probably in the formative period of his early manhood during the years of our Lord's ministry. There is no sign that he was influenced by that ministry; but he represents the world of Judaic ideas in which our Lord lived.

In this book the criticism of what was received as divine justice, although very timid, becomes explicit. What strikes us is the modernity of this criticism.

The author, writing ostensibly of a long-past period, is really discussing the destruction of Jerusalem, which has lately occurred. He complains to God that it is inconsistent to give His revelation to the Jewish nation and then destroy the nation. He asks what advantage it will be to God if the divine *cultur* is wiped out from the world.[1]

He feels assured that although Jerusalem has been punished by God for her sins, and Rome now triumphs, Rome in her day, as Babylon in hers and as all wicked nations on the face of the earth, will be visited by God's penal and destructive power.[2]

Baruch is more merciful than God.

But soon his mind recoils from this wholesale destruction. He challenges the apocalyptic tradition. He is more merciful than his God. "Those who have sinned"—*i.e.* the heathen—"are many," and when these are destroyed "few nations" will be left for God to admonish. He reflects that, even if the righteous Jews are secure of final good, they yet suffer much in attaining it, and that the righteous are few, even among the Jews. He protests, first, that it was not worth while creating the world for this general destruction of heathen nations, and secondly, that it was not worth while revealing the divine law to the Jews,

[1] *Apocalypse of Baruch*, III. 4-8, v. I.   [2] *Ibid*, XII. 1-4, XIII. 3-8

PROBLEM OF GOD'S LOVE AND CRUELTY

for if other nations suffer for oppressing the Jews, the Jews themselves as a nation suffer the same fate because they despise the law. What advantage was it, then, to the Jews to have a better religion ?[1]

Such protests appear at intervals in the earlier part of the book. He lays them all most candidly before the Almighty, who always replies that both the heathen and the Jews could have done right had they chosen: having done wrong they ought to be tormented.

The author has no original solution to offer, but he protests, precisely as the modern man protests, against an exaggerated view of human responsibility.

Baruch says to God :

" Be not therefore wroth with man ; for he is nothing.
And take no account of our works. For what are we ?
For lo ! by Thy gift do we come into the world,
And we depart not of our own will.
For we said not to our parents, ' Beget us.'
What, therefore, is our strength that we should bear Thy wrath ? "

Our author makes God answer :

" Thou hast prayed simply, O Baruch,
And all thy words have been heard.
But My judgment exacteth its own. . . .
For the Judge shall come and will not tarry,
Because each of the inhabitants of the earth knew when he was committing iniquity
And they have not known My Law by reason of their pride."
Apocalypse of Baruch, xlviii. 14-17, 25-26, 39-40.

There follows a description from the mouth of God of what will happen after the Great Judgment, and of the immortal glories of those who have kept the law (whose numbers both God and Baruch have

Baruch confounded by the prospect of doom.

[1] *Ibid*, xiv. 2-6.

admitted to be very few); together with a description of the just torments of the damned.¹

Baruch replies that in that case it is better not to weep for our friends when they die, but to reserve our tears till they come to God's judgment:

"Why therefore again do we mourn for those who die?
Or why do we weep for those who depart to Sheol?
Let lamentations be reserved for the beginning of that
    coming torment,
And let tears be laid up for the advent of the destruction
    of that time."—*Ibid.*, lii. 2-3.

There is no answer to this, even in heaven; the remark seems to pass as what goes without saying.

Baruch gives up; he accepts the inevitable; he tries to become enthusiastic about God's justice. But even then, in spite of humble prayers and praises which he offers to God, he betrays his dissatisfaction:

"And when I was pondering on these things and the like, lo! the angel Ramiel, who presideth over true visions, was sent to me, and he said unto me: 'Why doth thy heart trouble thee, Baruch, and why doth thy thought disturb thee? For if owing to the report which thou hast only heard of judgment thou art so moved, what wilt thou be when thou shalt see it manifestly with thine eyes? And if with the expectation wherewith thou dost expect the day of the Mighty One thou art so overcome, what wilt thou be when thou shalt come to its advent? And, if at the word of the announcement of the torment of those who have done foolishly thou art so wholly distraught, how much more when the event will reveal marvellous things? And if thou hast heard tidings of the good and evil things which are then coming, and art grieved, what wilt thou be when thou shalt behold what the majesty will reveal, which will convict these and cause those to rejoice?'"—*Ibid.*, lv. 3-8.

The *Apocalypse of Ezra* appears to belong to the

¹ *Ibid.*, l., li. 1.

PROBLEM OF GOD'S LOVE AND CRUELTY

same period as *Baruch*, though edited later. This book begins with Salathiel's deliberate accusation of God's justice. " O Lord, my Lord, didst Thou not speak from the beginning (*i.e.* in the creative fiat) and formedst the earth Thyself alone! (Responsibility is thus fixed on God.) And Thou didst command the dust and it gave the Adam a dead body. Thou didst breathe the breath of life into him. He transgressed and forthwith Thou didst decree upon him death." Salathiel indicts God. But before Adam died he had started humanity on the wrong track. " Peoples and tribes and nations and clans without number " had to be destroyed in the flood. Noah, however, was spared, but to what end ? " Children and peoples and many multitudes began again to be ungodly." Abraham was chosen, and the law given to Israel. " And yet "—here the accusation reaches its bitter point—" Thou didst not remove from them the evil heart ! " " Infirmity remained in them." " The law, together with this evil root," caused the Jews to be sinners and the nation to be destroyed. Jerusalem is destroyed ; but what of the sins of the nations that have triumphed over her ? They also must be destroyed by divine justice. Then he sums up : " When have the inhabitants of the earth not sinned before Thee ? " " Men who have names " —*i.e.* a few notable saints—" have kept Thy commandments, but a virtuous nation Thou shalt not find." [1]

What could be a stronger arraignment of Omnipotence taking vengeance upon human sin ?

An angel called Uriel was sent to convey the divine answer, the substance of which is simply that that

---

[1] *Apocalypse of Ezra (Salathiel)*, III. 4-5, 7-10, 12, 17, 19-20, 22, 27, 35-36.

THE LORD OF THOUGHT

is God's way, and the fact that it does not commend itself to man is of no importance. "Is it possible that one who is corruptible in a corruptible world should know the way of Him who is incorruptible?"[1] To which Salathiel answers: "It would have been better for us if we had not come than, having come, that we should live in sin and suffer, and know not why we suffer."[2] There is again an elaborate answer, the substance of which is again that what is of earth cannot understand the ways of heaven. Salathiel pertinently replies: "Wherefore, O my Lord, hath understanding been given me for thought? I have not desired to ask about the way of what is above, but about those things which pass over us daily,"[3] including the judgments of God upon us and our sins. The answer to this, given in a somewhat elaborate dialogue and vision, is simply that a new order of things, a new age, will come, in which all doubts will be removed. It is clear, however, that the author is not satisfied. This is seen in several later passages, but we may content ourselves with one. Salathiel speaks:

"And I answered and said: Oh, what hast thou done, O earth, that these have been born from thee and are going to perdition! If now the intelligence is from the dust like the rest of creation, it would have been better if also the dust had not been, in order that the intelligence might not have come into being from thence. Now, however, the intelligence groweth with us; and on this account we are tormented, because while we know it we are perishing.

> Let the race of men mourn,
>   but the beasts of the field rejoice!
> let all who are born lament,
>   but the cattle and the flock exult!

[1] *Ibid*, IV. 10-11. [2] *Ibid*, IV. 12. [3] *Ibid*, IV. 22-23

PROBLEM OF GOD'S LOVE AND CRUELTY

For it is far better for them than for us, because they do not expect the judgment, neither do they know torture, nor hath life after death been promised to them. For what do we profit that we live, but are to suffer torment? For all who are born are defiled with sins, and are full of iniquities."—*Ibid.*, vii. 62-68.

This bitter cry came out of the very world of thought in which Jesus moved. We shall need to inquire later whether he also acquiesced in this doctrine concerning God.

CHAPTER V

THE JEWISH IDEA OF MAN

Legal morality involves low view of humanity.

WE turn now to consider the contemporary Jewish conception of man. The general problem of evil was rendered insoluble for the Jew by the legal view of virtue as consisting in comparative innocence.[1] They looked for that innocence which involved having striven to keep the law from the youth up, or at least from some crisis of conscious repentance. Looking abroad upon humanity, they might, with St Paul,[2] have found a proportion of virtue in all men, for there is much natural virtue in men who are also evil and unrepentant; but this was hidden from them.

If we read through *The Book of Enoch*, *The Wisdom of Solomon*, *The Wisdom of Ben-Sira*, *The Third and Fourth Books of the Maccabees*, *The Apocalypse of Ezra* and *The Apocalypse of Baruch*, we shall not find, in any of them, the expression of the least doubt concerning the doctrine that all men are seen by God as either righteous or unrighteous, godly or ungodly. It is certainly acknowledged that before the final judgment of God a man may change from the class of the unrighteous to the class of the righteous by such a

---

[1] Innocence is a negative conception of virtue, the imbecile is innocent. The law-breaker is classed as evil whatever positive virtues may be his.
[2] Romans ii. 14-15.

THE JEWISH IDEA OF MAN

repentance as will mean the mending of his ways. God is merciful, and will meet him in this amendment; but this does not alter the fact that at any given time humanity falls into two classes. This doctrine was accepted as a revelation given in the law. It does not seem to have been questioned.

Many Christian theologians have also accepted this doctrine as revealed; but in more recent times, unlike the Jews of the apocalyptic period, they have spent much ingenuity in harmonizing it with the obvious fact that all men are mixed—both good and bad.

We are so accustomed to these arguments of Christian apology for the apocalyptic division of humanity that we do not realize how inadequate to the complexity of human nature was the idea of man in the minds of Judaic writers who could accept, without apology, the classification of all men into good and evil, saved and lost. Perhaps we find in the baptism of John the first suggestion that some outward sign or symbol was required to justify a division between the absolutely saved and the entirely unsaved, because in character men were not thus wholly different.

But let us examine the conception of mankind expressed in the quotations in the preceding chapters. In these we find that (1) all idolaters—that is, the great bulk of mankind; (2) all nations who had ever interfered with the Jews; and (3) all Jews who were indifferent to strict observation of the law, are classed as meet for destruction. Such a belief could only rest upon either a contemptuous view of humanity or a superficial view of righteousness: that is to say, those who held it cannot have really known and loved men and women in both opposing classes or they would have realized that they were one and all compact both of good and evil; or else they cannot have realized that natural goodness of heart is something more fundamental than ritual exactness. They allowed themselves to be misled by the notions of primitive taboo or the legal confusion of innocence and virtue.

<small>Higher Greek idea of humanity.</small>

The Hellenic world of their own day knew better. Bishop Butler, in the Introduction to his *Sermons on Human Nature*, tells us "That the ancient moralists had some inward feeling or other, which they chose to express in this manner, that man is born to virtue, that it consists in following nature, and that vice is more contrary to this nature than tortures or death, their works in our hands are instances." This expresses what Greek philosophy had taught the world long before the Jews of this period made their vehement classification. The doctrine that there is in man one principle of virtue which is more truly one with the self and centre than the various tendencies to evil which are all at variance with one another, was common in the prevalent Hellenic culture. The Apocalyptists, therefore, held their belief that man was naturally worthless, in face of a higher truth—for in their day they had much traffic with Hellenic civilization.

<small>Mr Montefiore on the Jewish indifference to the soul of good in things evil.</small>

Mr Claude Montefiore, in an article already quoted upon "Jewish Religion of the First Century," says:

"The difference between the religious, spiritual and ethical monotheism of the Jews and all surrounding 'idolatries' was in fact gigantic, though it was perhaps still more gigantic in the eyes of the Jews themselves. They heard and saw what was grossest and most outward in other religions: of any inward verities, of any esoteric excellences, of the spiritual achievements of the few, they knew little and suspected less.

THE JEWISH IDEA OF MAN

Religion was so real and deep a distinction between the Jew and the non-Jew that it tended to intoxicate: the Jews were in the right; the rest of the world was wrong."

This is in perfect harmony with the impression given by the Jewish writings which we are reviewing. It explains the belief that all members of the heathen world could be classed as ungodly, evil and unrighteous; but it does not explain the entire reprobation of that class of Jews—always a large class—who were not living in strict accordance with the law.

Mr Montefiore goes on to say:

"People (of Jewish race) who had fallen, or were falling, away from the ranks of those who honestly sought to observe the law, were neglected and shunned by the Teachers and by the law-abiding Jews. They were looked down upon and disliked as ignorant, as law-breakers, as unclean. And it was a marked weakness of this legal religion that, while it taught, and its votaries practised, compassion to the poor and the afflicted, if they sought to obey the law, it did not teach redemptive compassion and kindness to those who fell away."

He might have added that the acceptance of legal innocence as the test of virtue [1] produced entire failure of observation and reflection on the part of Jewish teachers and writers who could thus believe not only the heathen but their own brethren to be wholly bad.

The only extant explanation of this obstinate classification into righteous and unrighteous is given in the *Testaments of the Twelve Patriarchs*: *Judaic reprobation of partial virtue*

"If the soul take pleasure in the good inclination, all its actions are in righteousness; and if it sin it straightway repenteth. For, having its thoughts set upon righteousness, and

---

[1] Cf. "For whosoever shall keep the whole law, and yet offend in one point, he is guilty of all."—James ii. 10

THE LORD OF THOUGHT

casting away wickedness, it straightway overthroweth the evil, and uprooteth the sin. But if it incline to the evil inclination, all its actions are in wickedness, and it driveth away the good, and cleaveth to the evil, and is ruled by Beliar; even though it work what is good, he perverteth it to evil."—*Testaments of the Twelve Patriarchs—Asher*, i. 6-8.

So far this is an analysis that by a strict definition of "incline" might be correct; but see how it works out:

"There is a man that loveth him that worketh evil, because he would prefer even to die in evil for his sake; and concerning this it is clear that it hath two aspects, but the whole is an evil work. Though, indeed, he have love, yet is he wicked who concealeth what is evil for the sake of the good name, but the end of the action tendeth unto evil. Another stealeth, doeth unjustly, plundereth, defraudeth, and withal pitieth the poor: this too hath a twofold aspect, but the whole is evil."—*Ibid.*, ii. 3-5.

The passage is concluded with the statement that "the latter ends of men do show their righteousness (or unrighteousness) when (at death) they meet the angels of the Lord and of Satan."[1] This is equivalent to saying that whenever death may find a man he is either wholly worthless in God's sight or fit to enjoy the happiness of the good. It is not necessary further to insist that this involves a shallow conception by man of goodness and of God who is responsible for man.

<small>Low conception of human nature shown in estimate of women</small> From such legal morality a harsh view of women might be expected. A good wife—*i.e.* one useful to man—is certainly admitted to be "from the Lord"; for she is occasionally mentioned as a very excellent adjunct to a man's possessions; but she is never mentioned in any of the recurring descriptions of the

[1] *Ibid.*, vi. 4.

THE JEWISH IDEA OF MAN

resurrection of the elect. This can hardly be for lack of power to produce her as an imaginative detail. In the *Book of Ezra*, when the assembly of the people have been made to put away their heathen wives, it is distinctly stated that the women stood up with the men to hear the law; and in the *Apocalypse of Abraham*[1] it is distinctly said that " a great multitude, men, women and children," are seen in a terrestrial vision.

Against the passages in which women are recognized as very useful indeed to men when they are good—*i.e.* silent, diligent and not at all jealous—we get many passages in which they are mentioned as almost altogether vile. In the first place, in woman is the root of all human sin. The legend of Eve, in Genesis, gives a presentation of this idea, very noble and refined compared with the legend of the fall of the angels related in *Enoch* and in the *Twelve Patriarchs*, and assumed in other apocalypses, but only referred to in Genesis.[2] Without quoting these we proceed to other passages which are the more significant because there is never any effort to refute them in any of these books :

"Evil are women, my children; and since they have no power or strength over man, they use wiles by outward attractions that they may draw him to themselves; and when they cannot bewitch by outward attractions, him they overcome by craft. Moreover, concerning them, the angel of the Lord told me, and taught me, that women are overcome by the spirit of fornication more than men, and in their heart they plot against men. . . . Command the women likewise not to associate with men, that they also may be pure in mind. For constant meetings, even though the ungodly deed be not

Woman a source of evil

[1] Chapter xxi.   [2] Gen. vi. 2, 4.

wrought, are to them an irremediable disease, and to us a destruction of Beliar and an eternal reproach."—*Testaments of the Twelve Patriarchs—Reuben*, v. 1-3; vi. 2-4.

"The angel of God showed me that for ever do women bear rule over king and beggar alike. And from the king they take away his glory, and from the valiant man his might, and from the beggar even that little which is the stay of his poverty."—*Ibid.—Judah*, xv. 5-6.

In the *Wisdom of Solomon* there is much said concerning the conditions under which man may acquire Wisdom, and the character of those to whom God gives Wisdom; but there is not the slightest suggestion that a woman could ever obtain Wisdom. The *Wisdom of Ben-Sira*, Dr Oesterley tells us, "gives us such a clear glimpse of the social conditions, and of Jewish life of the period generally," as no other book does. "We get details of home life, the relations between husband and wife . . . and father and daughter."

Certainly in this book we get a little about the value of a wife, if she be beautiful, dutiful and silent:

"A woman will receive any man,
But one daughter is better than another daughter.
　The beauty of a woman maketh bright the countenance,
And excelleth every delight of the eye.
　And moreover, if there be in her a gentle tongue,
Her husband is not from among the sons of men.
　He that acquireth a wife hath the highest possession,
A helpmeet for him and a pillar of support."
　　　　　　Wisdom of Ben-Sira, xxxvi. 21-24.

Here is even a higher form of appreciation:

"The grace of a wife delighteth her husband,
　And her understanding fatteneth his bones.
A silent woman is a gift from the Lord,
　And a well-instructed soul is beyond worth."
　　　　　　Ibid., xxvi. 13-14.

THE JEWISH IDEA OF MAN

But we get much more about the faults of women:

"Any wound, only not a heart-wound!
    Any wickedness, only not the wickedness of a
        woman! . . .
There is no poison above the poison of a serpent,
    And there is no wrath above the wrath of a woman.
I would rather dwell with a lion and a dragon,
    Than keep house with a wicked woman.
The wickedness of a woman maketh black her look,
    And darkeneth her countenance like a bear's.
In the midst of his friends her husband sitteth,
    And involuntarily he sigheth bitterly.
There is little malice like the malice of a woman,
    May the lot of the wicked fall upon her.
As a sandy ascent to the feet of the aged,
    So is a woman of tongue to a quiet man. . . .
From a woman did sin originate,
    And because of her we all must die.
Give not water an outlet,
    Nor power to a wicked woman.
If she go not as thou would have her
    Cut her off from thy flesh. . . .
Grief of heart and sorrow is a wife jealous of another;
    The scourge of the tongue communicating to all.
Like a yoke of oxen shaken to and fro is a wicked
        woman,
    He that taketh hold of her is as one grasping a
        scorpion."—*Ibid.*, xxv. 13, 15-20, 24-26; xxvi. 6-7.

"Shame to the father that begetteth an uninstructed son,
    And a daughter is born to his loss."—*Ibid.*, xxii. 3.

"A daughter is to a father a deceptive treasure,
    And the care of her putteth away sleep;
In her youth lest she commit adultery,
    And when she is married lest she be hated; . . .
Keep a strict watch over a headstrong daughter
    Lest she make thee a laughing-stock.

THE LORD OF THOUGHT

In the place where she abideth let there be no lattice,
  And in the house where she sleepeth no entry round about.
Let her not display her beauty before any man,
  And in the house of women let her not gossip;
For from the garment cometh forth the moth,
  And from a woman a woman's wickedness.
Better the wickedness of a man than the goodness of a woman."—*Ibid.*, xlii. 9, 11-14.

In this whole book, which, we are told, reveals the domestic heart of Judaism, nothing good is said of a woman except as she is of value to husband or father; and there is a great deal said about her frequent lack of value in these relations. When women, considered merely *qua* woman, is spoken of, she is referred to as evil.

In the *Fourth Book of Maccabees* the mother of the seven martyrs stands out a heroic figure. About this Mr Emmet, in his Introduction to the S.P.C.K. edition, remarks:

" The point throughout is not the greatness but the weakness of womanhood. Reason triumphs even in her; it might naturally have been expected that it should fail; and the fact that it did not is a tribute to the power of reason rather than to the strength of woman. The closing chapter really supports the common view of the superiority of man. For the mother quotes the teaching of the father throughout. The story has made it impossible to introduce him directly, but in this rather roundabout way it is made clear that the heroism of the seven sons and of the mother is due to the man's influence. The boast of the mother is that she has confined herself to what were regarded as the essentially feminine duties of preserving her chastity and looking after the home in humility and subjection."

Servants mere chattels.

Another indication in *Ben-Sira* of the estimate of human beings *qua* human is furnished by the advice as

THE JEWISH IDEA OF MAN

to the right treatment of servants; in which self-interest appears the only principle of action:

" Fodder, and a stick, and burdens, for an ass;
    Bread, and chastisement, and work, for a servant.
Set thy servant to work, and thou wilt find rest,
    Leave his hands idle, and he will seek liberty.
Yoke and a thong will subdue the neck,
    And for an evil servant there are racks and tortures. . . .
Set him to such works as are suited for him,
    And if he obey not make his fetters heavy.
Be not excessive toward any creature,
    And do nothing without judgment."

Consideration is specially enjoined because it would be awkward to wait on oneself:

" If thou hast but one servant, treat him as thyself,
    For as thine own soul thou hast need of him;
If thou maltreat him, and he depart and run away,
    On what way wilt thou seek him?"
                              Ibid., xxxiii. 24-26, 28-31.

We get thus, in the books of this period, a conception of humanity which contains an extraordinary contradiction. A few human beings, always assumed to be masculine, were thought able to attain to sublime friendship and intelligent communion with the Most High God. On the other hand, the great majority of mankind were regarded as literally worthless, born only to be destroyed in the judgment of God. Women, who form half mankind, who are the mothers of all men, were thought of without respect; and servants and slaves were regarded as chattels.

Fundamental contradiction in Jewish idea of man.

Now the low estimate of women is significant in a nation which rose above surrounding nations in its thought of the height to which good men could attain.

71

THE LORD OF THOUGHT

Women have always had an instinctive perception of what modern psychology has made plain, that humanity is governed by attraction, not compulsion. Probably, without knowing why, the Jewish women took little interest in the thunders of the law. It may be that only in a religion that preaches the attraction of Infinite Love do women become saints.

The same, for another reason, may be said of the average serf or slave. He is too hard-worked to repent, too much accustomed to ill-treatment to care whether God ill-treats him or not.

CHAPTER VI

THE PROBLEM OF INADEQUATE SALVATION

EVEN if man's worthlessness in Jewish thought justified a final and wholesale destruction, there still remained the problem of God's failure to manage His creation.

If God created the world and sustains it, He is responsible for man's existence and his environment. The Jew of our period did not question this. He attributed to God entire authority and kingship over men, but was troubled because the divine authority and kingship had proved inadequate. The best that God could do was to show man what was right, *i.e.* He gave man a revealed law. Further, according to Jewish belief, He threatened, punished and, in the last resort, exterminated from the earth the disobedient. But all this was ineffective. The world—with the exception of a few comparatively righteous persons—went wrong. *[Human failure creates doubt of the Creator's success.]*

This lyric neatly sums up the Judaic view of the world :

> "Wisdom went forth to make her dwelling among the
>   children of men,
> And found no dwelling-place :
> Wisdom returned to her place,
> And took her seat among the angels.

THE LORD OF THOUGHT

And Unrighteousness went forth from her chambers:
Whom she sought not she found,
And dwelt with them,
As rain in a desert,
And dew on a thirsty land."—*Book of Enoch*, xlii. 2, 3.

<small>The perdition of nations.</small>

In that part of the *Book of Enoch* attributed to Noah we read:

"And then Michael, Uriel, Raphael, and Gabriel looked down from heaven and saw much blood being shed upon the earth, and all lawlessness being wrought upon the earth. And they said one to another: 'The earth, made without inhabitant, cries the voice of their crying up to the gates of heaven. And now to you, the holy ones of heaven, the souls of men make their suit, saying, " Bring our cause before the Most High."' And they said to the Lord of the ages: 'Lord of lords, God of gods, King of kings (and God of the ages), the throne of Thy glory standeth unto all the generations of the ages, and Thy name holy and glorious and blessed unto all the ages! Thou hast made all things, and power over all things hast Thou: and all things are naked and open in Thy sight, and all things Thou seest, and nothing can hide itself from Thee. . . .

And now, behold, the souls of those who have died are crying and making their suit to the gates of heaven, and their lamentations have ascended: and cannot cease because of the lawless deeds which are wrought on the earth. And Thou knowest all things before they come to pass, and Thou seest these things and Thou dost suffer them, and Thou dost not say to us what we are to do to them in regard to these.'"—*Book of Enoch*, ix. 1-11.

We must clearly realize that these Jews had no difficulty in believing that God forgave the repentant: their difficulty was that so few sinners cared to repent.

In the *Apocalypse of Ezra* the seer, Salathiel, complains of this to God:

PROBLEM OF INADEQUATE SALVATION

" Regard not the follies of the intrigues of the ungodly, . . .
   think not upon those that have behaved themselves badly before thee, . . .
and will not to destroy those that have become like the cattle, . . .
and be not angry against those who have behaved worse than the beasts. . . .
For what is man that thou shouldest be so angry with him,
or a corruptible race that thou shouldest be so hot against it?"
—*Apocalypse of Ezra*, viii. 27-34.

God answers him :

" As the husbandman who soweth many seeds and planteth many plants, but not all the seeds live in due season, nor indeed do all the plants strike root ; so also they who have come into the world do not all live" (*i.e.* "are not all saved").—*Ibid.*, viii. 41.

To which the seer replies :

" But man who hath been fashioned by thine own hands and is made like thine own image, for whose sake thou hast created all—hast thou likened him to the seed of the husbandman ? No ! "—*Ibid.*, viii. 44.

God then severely tells him to give up troubling about the lot of the wicked and to contemplate only the happy lot of the righteous, for :

" Now that men have been created upon the world that standeth firm, and upon a table that lacketh not, and upon a Law that is unsearchable, they are become corrupt in their deeds,
   and I regarded my world, and lo ! it was lost !
   and my cosmos, and lo ! it was in peril—
   on account of the manners of its inhabitants.
And I saw and spared a small few, and saved me a grape out of a cluster, and a plant out of a great forest. Let the multitude, therefore, perish because it hath come into being in vain."—*Ibid.*, ix. 19-22.

THE LORD OF THOUGHT

The obvious answer to this, which the human heart must always give, is that if in the heart of man there is no knowledge of what is right or wrong it is unjust of God to condemn him; and if man does know what is right and wrong he knows that God is unjust. Further, the logic of these apocalyptic seers drove them to perceive that if God had set Himself to make men good by offers of reward and threats of punishment or else quickly destroy them, then, if badness prevailed in the world, God's purpose in creation had surely failed. They were too reverent to more than hint at the inevitable conclusions—God was unjust; God Himself had failed. They did not dream that their premises might be false.

Salathiel thus broods over humanity on the scrap-heap:

"But ask the earth, and she shall tell thee; because she is bound to mourn . . ., because many are they who have come into being upon her, and from the beginning all who have come into being upon her, and the others who (are to) come, lo! they all go to perdition, and their multitude is for destruction."—*Ibid.*, x. 9, 10.

Again he complains that the divine and glorious law has only condemned men to perdition:

"And I said: O Lord (my Lord), thou didst verily reveal thyself to our fathers in the wilderness . . . and thou didst say (to them):
    Do thou, Israel, hear me,
    and, seed of Jacob, listen to my words!
    For behold, I sow in you my Law, and it shall produce in you fruits of righteousness, and ye shall be glorified in it for ever.
    But our fathers received the Law, and kept it not,
    and commandments, and did not perform them. . . .

PROBLEM OF INADEQUATE SALVATION

And this is the rule: that when the earth receiveth seed, or the sea a ship, or any other vessel what hath been put therein, viz. the food, or what hath been put, or what hath been kept—these are destroyed, but these that received them remain. But with us it hath not been so; but we who have received the Law and sin perish together with our heart which accepted it. Thy Law, however, perisheth not, but abideth in its glory."—*Ibid.*, ix. 29-37.

In the *Apocalypse of Baruch* the seer suggests to God that if men's lives were not so short more of them might seek the light. The conversation is a reflection upon God's power to save:

"And I answered and said: 'O Lord, my Lord, lo! the years of this time are few and evil, and who is able in his little time to acquire that which is measureless?'
And the Lord answered and said unto me: 'With the Most High account is not taken of much time nor of a few years. For what did it profit Adam that he lived nine hundred and thirty years, and transgressed that which he was commanded? Or wherein did Moses suffer loss in that he lived only one hundred and twenty years, and, inasmuch as he was subject to Him Who formed him, brought the Law to the seed of Jacob, and lighted a lamp for the nation of Israel?'
And I answered and said: 'He that lighted hath taken from the light, and there are but few that have imitated him. But those many whom He hath lighted have taken from the darkness of Adam, and have not rejoiced in the light of the lamp.'"—*Apocalypse of Baruch*, xvi.-xviii.

When we look at the case of the individual unrepentant sinner, the doctrine that instead of being made right he must in some way be got rid of, is as bad as the same doctrine when applied to multitudes. If it is inefficient for a potter to make a multitude of vessels that cannot resist the wear to which they must be put, it is inefficient for him to make one such vessel. If it

[sidenote: Perdition of the individual.]

displays weakness in a king to send an army on an expedition that must end in their destruction and disgrace, it would be a sign of weakness for him to send one soldier on such an errand. If it would show inefficiency in a schoolmaster for him to set his school a task beyond their years and then expel them all for not accomplishing it, it would be a mistake for him to treat one pupil in that way.

The seer, in this same apocalypse, classing himself with the sinful Jew, prays thus:

"For we have all been made like a breath. For as the breath ascends involuntarily, and again dies, so it is with the nature of men. . . . The righteous justly hope for the end, and without fear depart from this habitation, because they have with Thee a store of works preserved in treasuries. . . . But as for us,—woe to us, who also are now shamefully entreated, and at that time (the Judgment) look forward only to evils."
—*Ibid.*, xiv. 10-14.

In the *Apocalypse of Ezra*, again, we get a strong protest on behalf of the individual unrepentant sinner. The Almighty is thus addressed:

"For One art Thou, and one fashioning are we, the work of Thine hands, as Thou hast said. And Thou dost indeed quicken for us now in the womb the body which Thou hast fashioned. . . . And when the womb giveth again what has been therein, Thou hast commanded that out of the members should come milk, the fruit of the breasts, that what hath been fashioned may grow for a short time. And afterwards

Thou guidest it in Thy mercy,
and nourishest it in Thy righteousness;
and disciplinest it in Thy law,
and admonishest it in Thy wisdom—
and Thou killest it as Thy creature,
and quickenest it (in the Resurrection) as Thy work.

If, then, Thou suddenly and quickly destroyest this one who

PROBLEM OF INADEQUATE SALVATION

hath been fashioned with all this great labour, according to Thy command, for what purpose, then, came he into being ? "—*Apocalypse of Ezra*, viii. 7-14.

The problem of the government of free creatures is very old and very universal. It is expressed in the proverb, "One man can lead a horse to the river, but twenty men cannot make him drink." In this period no higher or more kingly way of governing had been thought of, the whole world over, than the power to threaten and punish.

The Jews had at least stated the problem with regard to God's government. They, in the whole world, were the only nation with the spiritual insight to perceive that threats and punishments had very little saving value. More than this, they had a very distinct idea of a better divine government, when free spirits could be given power to be righteous without loss of freedom. But this, they realized, could not be until the regime of threats and punishments was over. In this they were so far in advance of even Greek philosophy that it would seem that their genius for prayer and mystic adoration had resulted in true inspiration.

"I will put my law in their inward parts, and in their heart will I write it; and I will be their God, and they shall be my people."[1]

"Create in me a clean heart, O God; and renew a right spirit within me." "I will run the way of thy commandments, when thou shalt enlarge my heart."[2]

In a vision of that future Golden Age of God it is said :

[1] Jer xxxi. 33. Cf. Jer. xxiv. 7; xxxii. 40
[2] Psa. li. 10, cxix. 32.

THE LORD OF THOUGHT

" For wisdom is poured out like water,
And glory faileth not before him for evermore.
For he is mighty in all the secrets of righteousness,
And unrighteousness shall disappear as a shadow,
And have no continuance."—*Book of Enoch*, xlix. 1-2.

The inward compulsion to do right arising from the irresistible attraction of goodness is always shown to be a mark of the heavenly kingdom. It was therefore clearly imagined as the ideal government:

" And he said unto me:
' He proclaims unto thee peace in the name of the world to come;
For from hence has proceeded peace since the creation of the world,
And so shall it be unto thee for ever and for ever and ever.
And all shall walk in his ways, since righteousness never forsakes him:
With him will be their dwelling-places, and with him their heritage,
And they shall not be separated from him for ever and ever and ever.
And so there shall be length of days with that Son of Man,
And the righteous shall have peace and an upright way,
In the name of the Lord of Spirits for ever and ever.' "
Ibid., lxxi. 15-17.

" As the ruler of a people so are his officers,
And as the head of a city so are the inhabitants thereof."
Wisdom of Ben-Sira, x. 2.

Of the works of God's creation apart from man, Ben-Sira writes:

" When He commandeth them they rejoice,
And in their prescribed task they rebel not against Him.
Therefore from the beginning I stood firm,
And when I had considered it I set it down in writing:

PROBLEM OF INADEQUATE SALVATION

> The works of God are all good,
> > They supply every need in its season.
> None may say: This is worse than that,
> > For everything showeth its strength in its season."
> > > *Ibid.*, xxxix. 31-34.

It is evident that if this could be said of God's human creation God's power would be more glorious. Good government is thus described:

> "All these things live and abide for ever,
> > And for every need all are obedient to Him.
> All things are different, this from that,
> > And He made not one of them superfluous.
> One thing surpasseth another in its goodness,
> > And who shall be satiated in beholding their beauty?
> . . . .
> For His own sake He maketh His work to prosper,
> > And by His word He worketh His pleasure.
> Yet more things like these we will not add,
> > And the end of the matter is: He is all.
> We will still magnify, though we cannot fathom,
> > For greater is He than all His works."
> > > *Wisdom of Ben-Sira*, xlii. 23-25; xliii. 26-28.

They had no idea that God could work in the hearts of the unrepentant, or that God and the unrepentant could meet in love.

They could only conclude that God must "shatter to bits" this "sorry scheme of things entire," and "remould it nearer to the heart's desire." With their premisses it was the only reasonable conclusion.

The Narrative concerning John's Testimony to Jesus as given by Luke, the Q Passages in Italics.

And he (John) came into all the region round about Jordan, preaching the baptism of repentance unto remission of sins: as it is written in the book of the words of Isaiah the prophet, etc.

He said therefore to the multitudes that went out to be baptized of him, Ye offspring of vipers, who warned you to flee from the wrath to come? Bring forth therefore fruits worthy of repentance, and begin not to say within yourselves, We have Abraham to our father: for I say unto you, that God is able of these stones to raise up children unto Abraham. And even now is the axe also laid unto the root of the trees: every tree therefore that bringeth not forth good fruit is hewn down, and cast into the fire.

And the multitudes asked him, saying, What then must we do? And he answered and said unto them, He that hath two coats let him impart to him that hath none; and he that hath food, let him do likewise. And there came also publicans to be baptized, and they said unto him, Master, what must we do? And he said unto them, Extort no more than that which is appointed you. And soldiers also asked him, saying, And we, what must we do? And he said unto them, Do violence to no man, neither exact anything wrongfully; and be content with your wages. And as the people were in expectation, and all men reasoned in their hearts concerning John, whether haply he were the Christ; John answered, saying unto them all,

I indeed baptize you with water; but there cometh he that is mightier than I, the latchet of whose shoes I am not worthy to unloose: he shall baptize you with the Holy Ghost and with fire: whose fan is in his hand, throughly to cleanse his threshing-floor, and to gather the wheat into his garner; but the chaff he will burn up with unquenchable fire.

With many other exhortations therefore preached he good tidings unto the people; . . . Now it came to pass, when all the people were baptized, that Jesus also having been baptized, and praying, the heaven was opened, and the Holy Ghost descended in a bodily form, as a dove, upon him, and a voice came out of heaven, Thou art my beloved Son; in thee I am well pleased.—Luke iii. 3-22.

CHAPTER VII

JOHN THE BAPTIST

JOHN THE BAPTIST carried on the apocalyptic tradition; indeed, he harked back to a very early apocalyptic conception found in the *Book of Malachi*.

It may be well to recall some of the words of Malachi and compare them with the words of John, and see how both coincide with the fiercer strain of apocalyptic teaching. We may thus realize how perfectly the Baptist joined himself to his forerunners. The point is important in its bearing on the significance of Christ. *The messages of Malachi and John compared*

The passages in Malachi run thus:

(Jahveh speaks) "Behold, I send my messenger, and he shall prepare my way before me: the Lord in whom (ye think to) delight shall suddenly come to his temple. . . . But who may abide the day of his coming, and who shall stand when he appeareth? For he is like a refiner's fire. . . . Then shall ye return and discern between the righteous and the wicked, between him that serveth God and him that serveth him not. For, behold, the day cometh, it burneth as an oven; and all the proud, and all that work wickedness, shall be stubble; and the day that cometh shall burn them up, saith the Lord of Hosts. (The simile here is the old clay or brick oven, in which the fuel is all burned up before the bread is put in.) It shall leave them neither root nor branch. But unto you that fear my name shall the sun of righteousness arise with healing in his wings;

THE LORD OF THOUGHT

and ye shall go forth and gambol as calves of the stall, and ye shall tread down the wicked; for they shall be as ashes under the soles of your feet in the day that I shall do."—Mal. iii. 1, 2, 18; iv. 1-3.

The oldest account we have of John is in the brief Q passages[1] embedded in the narratives of both Matthew and Luke.[2]

The Q passages in Luke stand thus:

" Then said he (John) to the multitude that came forth to be baptized of him, Ye offspring of vipers, who warned you to flee from the wrath to come? Bring forth therefore fruits worthy of repentance, and begin not to say within yourselves, We have Abraham to our father: for I say unto you, that God is able of these stones to raise up children unto Abraham. And even now is the axe laid unto the root of the trees: every tree therefore that bringeth not forth good fruit is hewn down, and cast into the fire." . . . " John answered, saying unto them all, I indeed baptize you with water; but there cometh one that is mightier than I, the latchet of whose shoes I am not worthy to unloose; he shall baptize you (with the Holy Ghost and) with fire: whose fan is in his hand, throughly to cleanse his threshing-floor, and to gather the wheat into his garner; but the chaff he will burn up with unquenchable fire."[3]—Luke iii. 7-9, 16-17.

Later Jesus says (also a Q passage):

" But what went ye out to see? a prophet? Yea, I say unto you, and much more than a prophet. This is he of whom it is written, Behold, I send my messenger before thy face, who shall prepare thy way before thee. I say unto you, Among them that are born of women there is none greater than John: yet he that is but little in the kingdom of God is greater than he."—Luke vii. 26-28.

[1] "Q" is the technical name for a documentary source used by both Matthew and Luke.
[2] Cf. Matt. iii. 1-17 with Luke iii 3-22
[3] The corresponding Q passages in Matthew (chap. iii. 7-12) are so nearly the same that we need not quote them.

JOHN THE BAPTIST

It should be observed that in the Introduction to Mark's Gospel the quotation from Malachi, misquoted in the words attributed to Jesus by Matthew and Luke, is credited to Isaiah and combined with the passage from Isa. xl. 3, "The voice of one crying, Make straight in the wilderness the way of the Lord." Further, in Mark the doom of fire and the baptism of fire are left out, and only the baptism of the Holy Ghost is left in the narrative.[1] As the Jews understood the fire to be wholly destructive, and as Christians understood the Holy Ghost to be an influence of joy and comfort, they are alternative, and not compatible, prophecies: we must judge which we will accept as the authentic word of the Baptist.

Our contention is that John, carrying on the tradition of Malachi, was, like him, foretelling a destructive Agent of God who should appear on a day of doom. The earliest account of his preaching contains no suggestion that he regarded Jesus as this Agent.

In all the references to John in the Q passages common to both Matthew and Luke, the only suggestion that he heralded Jesus as the Messiah is made by Jesus in the passage cited, where Jesus is represented as misquoting Malachi in speaking to the multitude about John. "This is he of whom it is written, Behold, I send my messenger before thy face, who shall prepare thy way before *thee*."[2] *[Grounds for doubting that John announced the ministry of Jesus]*

In Malachi it is God who is represented as speaking, and the text runs: "Behold, I send my messenger, who shall prepare the way before *me*."[3]

---

[1] Mark i. 2-6. Fire was the symbol of destruction, not sanctification. "The Holy Ghost" was a Christian term, used by Mark and supposed to be an intrusion upon John's message as given in Q.
[2] Luke vii. 27.   [3] Mal. iii 1.

THE LORD OF THOUGHT

It is important here to observe that the narrative as it now stands in Matthew, Mark and Luke cannot with true reverence be accepted. We are shut up to one of four explanations: either Jesus misquoted Malachi out of ignorance—a mistake that the very bystanders would have detected; or he parodied Malachi to advance his own claims—an obviously absurd hypothesis; or the early compilers of Q put into his lips words he did not say; or the words of Q were altered to suit a later and mistaken tradition. It shows no true respect for the historicity of the records we have to withhold full investigation.

<small>Obvious inaccuracy in Q.</small>

We will here assume that Jesus quoted the text, and quoted it correctly; for it is natural enough that in the mind of Jesus, John should have been connected with Malachi. Knowing the Prophets, Jesus would know that John took upon himself the "burden of Malachi," and Jesus might, on that account, regard him as preparing the hearts of many for further revelation of God. In that case some tradition must have early altered the pronoun to make it appear that Jesus said that John was his forerunner.[1]

<small>The historic Baptist.</small>

From the Q passages it would seem that John saw all the world as coloured by the eschatological teaching of his period and of preceding centuries. We have the same lurid background—fear urged as the motive of righteousness; the vision of the goodly realm of heaven beyond, almost obscured by the intervening drama of the Judgment, through the terrors of which only a few, by repentance and ritual observance and good works, may

---

[1] The argument does not at all assume that Q is *always* older and more correct than other Sources, but in this narrative Q is the older and the more consistent.

JOHN THE BAPTIST

win their way. The fair realm is seen as a land or city drifting nearer as upon the clouds, and before it flies an all-powerful Being, an Agent of God in whose estimation an unreformed humanity is worthless. He comes among forests of living men like a giant woodman cutting down fruitless trees at a stroke and casting them into the fire. He is seen, in the Resurrection, among multitudes of prostrate human beings destroyed like crops when death has cut them down as the reaper cuts the wheat; among them he works like a ruthless husbandman, to winnow and garner and burn, and there is all the cruelty of a vengeful eschatological fantasy in that finishing touch, "with unquenchable fire." Clearly, the symbol of this fierce and majestic Angel of destruction cannot be a dove! To meet him is a baptism of fire: yes, but hardly a baptism of the Holy Spirit as exemplified in Jesus of Nazareth. This both superhuman and inhuman Angel of the threshing-floor and the unquenchable fire, whom John foretold, could not, at the time of John's preaching, have been a rational designation of the man Jesus, whose baptism of the Holy Spirit was figured forth by the bird that represented gentleness and peace. John would have had to be familiar with the whole system of Church Christology to have so mixed his symbolic images.

Let us see the close connection between the *Book of Malachi* and the Baptist's preaching. The word "Malachi" itself means "messenger," and we remember that the Baptist calls himself "a messenger." The writer of the *Book of Malachi* is filled with indignation at the sins of Israel; Jahveh is represented as comforting the righteous remnant in Israel by immediate

The Baptist takes up the burden of Malachi.

intervention and judgment upon the wicked; and with Malachi the " day of the Lord " is a day of fire. The Baptist's first simile for the sinners of Israel is the viper—" the most secret and skulking denizen of the desert, that would only come into the open to escape the peril of an approaching bush fire." Again, Malachi, instead of promising Israel a triumph over other nations in the day of judgment—as earlier prophets had done—insists that the judgment will come upon disobedient Israel. He contrasts the base offerings of the Hebrews to God, and their disobedience, with the worship of Gentiles in all parts of the world (Mal. i. 11). John preaches that to be of the chosen race will not suffice to enable one to escape the doom of the day of fire; and, like Malachi, insists that a radical reformation of life is necessary; God, he says, could turn stones into better Jews. The judgment of Malachi is not to be a mere triumph for righteous Israel as such: it is to be " as a refiner's fire " for the sins and blemishes of those who are good enough to be saved, and a destructive fire for the wicked. In Mal. iv. 1-3 it is said that the trees are to be burned " root and branch ": the Baptist cries that " the axe " of judgment " is even now laid to the root of the trees " that are to be cast into the fire. The agent of destruction in Malachi (iii. 1-3) is " the Lord . . . even the angel of the covenant," not a Messiah or saviour. We find the Baptist announcing that he is only the messenger of someone surpassingly great, who will baptize Israel with destroying fire. The threshing-floor, where all the wheat is winnowed, corresponds with Malachi's conception of the crucible out of which the righteous will emerge untarnished. The chaff, which always bulks

JOHN THE BAPTIST

the greater, and is entirely destroyed, is like the stubble thrown into Malachi's oven or furnace, and afterwards cast out as ashes to be trodden under foot.[1]

We cannot doubt that the Baptist, in seeking to solve the problem of Israel's redemption, took up the message of Malachi. He seems to have adopted a substantially identical view of the character of God and of the sins of his own generation—with this difference, that the strict observance of the ritual law, which the *Book of Malachi* preaches as the only way to escape destruction in that day, had, by the time of the Baptist, proved inadequate, so John preaches a stricter ethic and a new ritual exaction—baptism.

If the character of John's message makes it difficult to believe he was foretelling the coming of Jesus as Messiah, the historic facts concerning John's end go to confirm this doubt.

The three Synoptic Gospels all agree that Herod imprisoned John at or soon after the beginning of the public ministry of Jesus; but they do not give the proclamation of a Messiah as the reason for this action of Herod. Further, the reason Josephus assigns for the murder of John—that Herod only suspected that John might in the future make some seditious move—does not corroborate the Evangelist's story that John made a definite Messianic prediction, for had he done so and named anyone as the deliverer of the nation, it would have been a sufficient reason.

Concerning John we have in *Josephus* a brief statement, evidently untouched by Christian editors, as follows : " John was a good man, and commanded

[1] On many of these points I am indebted privately to Dr B W. Bacon.

the Jews to exercise virtue, both as to righteousness toward one another, and piety toward God, and so come to baptism; for that the washing would be acceptable to him, if they made use of it, not in order to the putting away of some sins, but for the purification of the body; supposing still that the soul was thoroughly purified beforehand by righteousness." [1]

It is difficult to consider the whole matter candidly and believe either that John heralded the ministry of Jesus or that Jesus regarded himself as carrying to completion the ministry of John.

Underlying any man's teaching is his conception or idea of God, which includes not only the character of God but what that character involves—His relation to man.

We note the harshness of John's doctrine that God could more easily make new Israelites out of stones than bear with inexhaustible patience the waywardness of a race whom He had hitherto regarded as His children;

---

[1] This account of John's baptism is neither the Christian view of baptism, nor does it suggest that John proclaimed God's friendliness to men while they were yet sinners. Josephus tells us why Herod murdered John. "Herod, who feared lest the great influence John had over the people might put it into his power and inclination to raise rebellion (for they seemed to do anything he should advise) thought it best, by putting him to death, to prevent any mischief he might cause, and not bring himself into difficulties by sparing a man who might make him repent of it when it should be too late." Josephus hated Herod, and in the context shows a deep interest in the double crime of this Herod, who set aside his lawful wife—that indignant princess from "the rose-red city half as old as time"—and married his half-brother's wife, Herodias, who was also his niece. So it would seem that Josephus would have been glad to make the murder of John more heinous by adding the motive of personal spite, had that sensational story been current in his lifetime As he does not assign this motive to Herod, we may take it that this whole passage about John is not modified by Christian editors.—*Josephus*, Book XXIII chap v. § 2.

JOHN THE BAPTIST

and comparing this with the teaching of Jesus concerning God's tender Fatherhood, we are impressed by the sharp contrast—a contrast we must develop later.

The Baptist's God is not the Father preached by Jesus.

From the dawn of human intelligence until the preaching of John men had thought of the unseen, divine Power as favourable to those who pleased Him and hostile to those who did not. It is very important to realize clearly that in no religion, least of all in Judaism, had God been thought of as the friend of sinners. Whatever name or form divine Power received among the nations; whatever the notion of what constituted disobedience or disrespect to Divinity; in one belief all religions agree—that God was hostile to sinners. "Until John" the development of religion had consisted only in the gradual elevation of the conception of God, and hence of what was pleasing to God. Men's earliest notions of what pleased the divine Power expressed themselves in magical ceremonies and taboo. There was also the qualification of racial or political birthright; and added to these came the notion of personal self-discipline.

The Law and the Prophets until John.

In every advanced religion all these ways of seeking divine favour have been welded together with varying emphasis. It was the distinction of the Jewish race to have added to these qualifications for divine favour a very lofty ethical ideal. Although, among them, with the elevation of the idea of God's ethical requirements came the idea of the joy of disinterested love to Him, the necessity of fulfilling conditions to obtain His favour was still uppermost, and dominated the conception of the divine character. Without some fulfilment there was no mercy. We have to bear in mind that in the Law and the Prophets

THE LORD OF THOUGHT

God's mercy only consisted in giving sinners a long chance to reform themselves: if they did not do so, all mercy towards them was at an end:

" Woe to you, ye sinners, when ye have died,
If ye die in the wealth of your sins;
And those who are like you say regarding you:
' Blessed are the sinners: they have seen all their days.
And now they have died in prosperity and in wealth,
And have not seen tribulation or murder in their life;
And they have died in honour,
And judgment has not been executed on them during their life.'
Know ye that their souls will be made to descend into Sheol,
And they shall be wretched in their great tribulation.
And into darkness and chains and a burning flame where there is grievous judgment shall your spirits enter."
Book of Enoch, ciii. 5-8.

" God, merciful and gracious, slow to anger . . . that will by no means clear (the guilty), visiting the iniquity of the fathers upon the children, and upon the children's children, upon the third and upon the fourth generation."—Exodus xxxiv. 6-7.

Across this long line of unbroken belief in God's penal hostility to sinners I believe that Jesus of Nazareth broke with a new idea of God. The evidence for this belief has next to be considered.

CHAPTER VIII

THE *DIES IRÆ* AND THE GOSPEL OF THE KINGDOM

In the light of preceding chapters we come now to consider whether the new tidings of the Kingdom [1] which Jesus gave forth summed up and developed the teaching of the Baptist and his forerunners, or contradicted and superseded that teaching.

"John came neither eating nor drinking"; and in the pleasureless wilderness he stood and cried to the men of his generation to come out from all their common avocations, from their homes and their markets, and avoid the fire of God's destruction by baptism and renunciation of their sins. Sin and condemnation and the "wrath to come" were the themes of his fierce eloquence. This is what the Gospels tell of him. Was such a message "good news"? *The prophet of the pleasureless wilderness*

The same Gospels tell of Jesus coming among the homes and markets of the common people, the very incarnation of abundant life and joy. Mark begins his narrative with the attraction Jesus exercised over Simon and Andrew, James and John. They were to go with him to "catch men" for God; and they saw that his way of catching men was to heal the suffering

---

[1] The phrase "Kingdom of God" or "of heaven" does not appear to be used in any pre-Christian apocalypse, and there is no good reason to suppose that John the Baptist used it. See Chap. xxi.

THE LORD OF THOUGHT

demoniacs and the sick. Immediately after we are told that the people brought him " all that were diseased and oppressed with devils." We get a reference to the prayers that Jesus prayed; going alone into rural places at the hour of the morning star, he seems to have felt himself akin to the daybreak. Then we come to the healings of the leper and the paralytic, and the loosing of the paralytic from his sins. Then follows the call of the outcast Levi; the feasting with publicans and sinners; the defence of his disciples, when the religious leaders chid them for not fasting, with the words, " Can the children of the bride-chamber fast while the bridegroom is with them ? " Bridegrooms in our modern days are comparatively sombre creatures, but in those days a bridegroom was borne by his friends to the wedding, the central delight of the gayest of human festivities, the very symbol of pleasure and rejoicing. All this comes before Mark has got well under weigh with the story he has to tell. Religion thus restated would be indeed good news !

Jesus the incarnation of life and joy.

Matthew and Luke reinforce this general impression. Matthew begins his prelude by quoting from Isaiah, " The people that sat in darkness saw a great light, and to them that sat in the region and shadow of death light is sprung up." Matthew collects early in his narrative a great deal of the teaching of Jesus. Besides Q, he apparently had another, and certainly not less original, compilation of the sayings of Jesus.[1] Luke begins his story of the ministry by telling us that Jesus took to himself the words of Isaiah : " The Spirit of the Lord is upon me, because he hath anointed me to preach the gospel to the poor ; he hath sent me to heal the broken-

[1] Compare forthcoming book, *The Four Gospels*, by Canon Streeter.

THE *DIES IRÆ* AND THE GOSPEL

hearted, to preach deliverance to the captives, and recovering of sight to the blind, to set at liberty them that are bruised, to preach the acceptable year of the Lord. . . ." There Jesus stopped, but the Second Isaiah did not stop. With him " the acceptable year of the Lord " is explained to be " the day of vengeance of our God." In Isaiah the beautiful words about " beauty for ashes, the oil of joy for mourning, the garment of praise for the spirit of heaviness " immediately follow. These words must have fascinated anyone who desired to bring salvation to the oppressed, but they are omitted—may we surmise because they could not be quoted without quoting with them the expectation of the divine vengeance ? Luke tells us that the people were astonished at his graciousness, at the doctrine he taught, and at the power with which he brought well-being to the devil-tossed and the sick. They were all convinced that from his early ministry there was a great effulgence of the light of joy shed upon the common life of common men. It was in these days that he came through all the villages preaching the Kingdom.

Can the Kingdom preached by Jesus in his early ministry have been developed from, or associated with, the apocalyptic predictions of the Baptist and his forerunners ? In the apocalyptic view the reign of God was associated with terrible woes and the day of doom : these woes, this judgment, were God's way with man. A few lines of description will suffice to enable us to realize that it would not have been human to herald with joy the near approach of the apocalyptic " day of the Lord."

" And there shall be a time of trouble, such as never

THE LORD OF THOUGHT

The birth-pangs of the Messianic reign. was since there was a nation, and at that time my people shall be delivered" (Daniel xii. 1). And again (Daniel vii. 9-14) we have the picture of the Ancient of Days appearing in fiery flame and the destruction of the mighty by sword and fire connected with the appearance of the Son of Man—*i.e.* the personification of the redeemed nation [1]—in the clouds. Then, also, there is Isaiah xiii. 9: "Behold the day of the Lord cometh, cruel with wrath and fierce anger; to lay the land desolate, and to destroy the sinners thereof out of it," and Joel ii. 30-31: "I will show wonders . . . blood and fire and pillars of smoke. The sun shall be turned into darkness, and the moon into blood, before the great and terrible day. . . ."

Enoch's description of woe is a growth from these Old Testament passages: perhaps part of it even preceded Daniel:

"Concerning the elect I said, and took up my parable concerning them:
>The Holy Great One will come forth from His dwelling, . . .
>And all shall be smitten with fear,
>And the Watchers shall quake,
>And great fear and trembling shall seize them unto the ends of the earth . . .;
>And the earth shall be wholly rent in sunder,
>And all that is upon the earth shall perish,
>And there shall be a judgment upon all men.
>But with the righteous He will make peace,
>And will protect the elect,
>And mercy shall be upon them. . . .

[1] "The title 'Son of Man' in Enoch was undoubtedly derived from Dan. vii, but a whole world of thought lies between the suggestive words in Daniel and the definite rounded conception as it appears in Enoch. In Daniel the phrase seems merely symbolical of Israel, but in Enoch it denotes a supernatural person"—*The Book of Enoch*, by Dr Charles, Appendix II.

THE *DIES IRÆ* AND THE GOSPEL

And behold! He cometh with ten thousands of His holy ones
To execute judgment upon all,
And to destroy all the ungodly:
And to convict all flesh
Of all the works of their ungodliness which they have ungodly committed,
And of all the hard things which ungodly sinners have spoken against Him. . . .
And for all of you sinners there shall be no salvation,
But on you all shall abide a curse."
Book of Enoch, i. 3-8; v. 6.

That the message of Enoch, first circulated some one hundred and fifty years before Christ, had not been modified in the time of Jesus is proved by similar ideas in the *Apocalypse of Ezra*, written at the end of the first century A.D.:

" Behold the days come when the inhabitants of the world shall be seized with great panic. . . .
And suddenly shall the sun appear by night,
and the moon by day;
and the wood shall distil blood,
and the stone utter its voice;
and the peoples shall be in commotion;
and the air shall be changed."
Apocalypse of Ezra, v. 1, 4-5.

" And it came to pass that when I heard I stood upon my feet, and I heard, and lo! a voice of one speaking, and his voice was as the voice of many waters. And he said:
Behold the days come, and it shall be,
when I am drawing nigh to visit the dwellers upon earth,
and when I am about to require at the hands of evil-doers,
and when the humiliation of Zion shall be complete;
and when this world is about to be sealed, which is about to pass away . . ."—*Ibid.*, vi. 17-20.

THE LORD OF THOUGHT

In the *Apocalypse of Baruch*, also written at the end of the first century A.D., we read:

> "Thou, too, shalt be preserved till that time, till that sign which the Most High will work for the inhabitants of the earth in the end of days. This, therefore, shall be the sign. When a stupor shall seize the inhabitants of the earth, and they shall fall into many tribulations, and again, when they shall fall into great torments. And it shall come to pass when they say in their thoughts by reason of their much tribulation: 'The Mighty One doth no longer remember the earth'—yea, it will come to pass when they abandon hope, that the time will then awake."
> —*Apocalypse of Baruch*, xxv.

If Jesus piped as for a dance, he could not have announced the judgment of the apocalyptic seers.

Such was the *dies iræ* of contemporary apocalyptic and of John the Baptist. But John, we are told, emphasized the fact that the descent from Abraham—which no doubt the majority of Jews felt to be the bark that would carry them through the storm of judgment—was entirely insufficient. Could this be, in any sense, "good news"?

It is true that there was a conventional aspiration, a verbal desire, rife among the Jews for the coming end of the age. This appears to resemble closely the aspiration for death and heaven which we find in many Christian hymns of the eighteenth and nineteenth centuries. But even to a Victorian congregation lustily singing such a hymn the announcement that all would soon die would not have been congenial. It is certain that the announcement that the cataclysm of apocalyptic vision was near at hand would be, to all classes of Jews, a message fraught with terror.

If "the common people heard him gladly" the Kingdom that Jesus preached was surely not the

THE *DIES IRÆ* AND THE GOSPEL

goal of apocalyptic eschatology.[1] He must have re-associated the word with a new idea. He must have made the difference very clear. He himself says that he piped as if for a dance, while John mourned as if for a funeral. Perhaps he referred to the world's funeral which John had predicted and to the festal dance at which, in the great day for which he hoped, the world should be reconciled to God.

[1] Cf. Chap xxi, by C. W Emmet.

CHAPTER IX

THE SON OF MAN AND THE OFFER OF ESCAPE

IN earlier chapters, when we were considering the Judaic idea of God and the problem of God's cruelty, we saw that the discussion of the character of God must include that of the supernatural agents of His condemnation or salvation. In this period the idea was common to Jew and Gentile that the Most High acted upon the worlds of matter and spirit through agencies variously conceived. The divine Logos, the divine Wisdom, the Angel of the Covenant, etc., were thought of as manifestations of God. Such an agent was the Son of Man of the *Book of Enoch*.

The apocalyptic Son of Man portrayed as cruel and ruthless.

The character of the Almighty and of His agent, the Son of Man, is thus portrayed in that book:

" And thus the Lord commanded the kings and the mighty and the exalted, and those who dwell on the earth, and said, ' Open your eyes and lift up your horns if ye are able to recognize the Elect One.'

> And the Lord of Spirits seated him on the throne of His glory,
> And the spirit of righteousness was poured out upon him,
> And the word of his mouth slays all the sinners,
> And all the unrighteous are destroyed from before his face.
> And there shall stand up in that day all the kings and the mighty,
> And the exalted and those who hold the earth,

THE SON OF MAN AND OFFER OF ESCAPE

> And they shall see and recognize
> How he sits on the throne of his glory,
> And righteousness is judged before him,
> And no lying word is spoken before him.
> Then shall pain come upon them as on a woman in travail,
> And she has pain in bringing forth
> When her child enters the mouth of the womb,
> And she has pain in bringing forth.
> And one portion of them shall look on the other,
> And they shall be terrified,
> And they shall be downcast of countenance,
> And pain shall seize them,
> When they see that Son of Man
> Sitting on the throne of his glory."

But repentance is unavailing :

> " And the kings and the mighty and the exalted and those who rule the earth
> Shall fall down before him on their faces,
> And worship and set their hope upon that Son of Man,
> And petition him and supplicate for mercy at his hands.
> Nevertheless that Lord of Spirits will so press them
> That they shall hastily go forth from His presence,
> And their faces shall be filled with shame,
> And the darkness shall grow deeper on their faces.
> And He will deliver them to the angels for punishment,
> To execute vengeance on them because they have oppressed His children and His elect :
> They (the elect) shall rejoice over them,
> Because the wrath of the Lord of Spirits resteth upon them,
> And His sword is drunk with their blood."
> Book of Enoch, lxii. 1-5, 9-12.

The Church has commonly believed that Jesus accepted the rôle of apocalyptic Son of Man as his own, adopting with it that of the Suffering Servant of Isaiah liii. The two were conceived as combined in this way—that Jesus on earth was the Suffering Servant, and became, through the grave and gate of death, the triumphant Judge. This is not really to combine these characters, or to qualify one with the other; and the notion that one being could be first one and then, transformed by death, become the other, was not original to Christianity. Jewish literature of our period —300 B.C. to 100 A.D.—is full of this same notion of transformation applied to the ideal Israel. In a large number of Jewish sayings, "the poor," "the oppressed," "the suffering," "the righteous" are interchangeable terms. The Suffering Servant of Isaiah was accepted as a personification of this ideal Israel. They were poor in this life, and the character of Jahveh was to be vindicated by transforming them in glory to participate in the judgment of "the rich," "the full," "the mighty," "the unrighteous." Israel from being a Suffering Servant on earth was to sit on the throne of judgment:

"And grieve not if your soul into Sheol has descended in grief,
   And that in your life your body fared not according to your goodness,
But wait for the day of the judgment of sinners,
And for the day of cursing and chastisement."
Ibid., cii. 5.

"The Most High God, the Eternal, the Only God shall arise,
And manifest Himself to punish the nations, . . .
Then shalt thou be happy, thou, O Israel. . . .
God shall exalt thee. . . .
   Thou shalt look from on high, and behold thy adversaries on the earth,
And shalt know them and rejoice."
Assumption of Moses, x. 7-10.

THE SON OF MAN AND OFFER OF ESCAPE

The idea that the righteous remnant, the ideal Israel, was itself to become Judge of the Gentiles was not uncommon, and is seen in *Daniel*, where the ideal Israel is identified with the apocalyptic Son of Man, and in the *Wisdom of Solomon*, where the souls of righteous persons are said to become judges of nations and to rule over peoples.[1]

When raised to this supernatural level and acting with God as vindictive Judge, Israel, or the Son of Man, must have been regarded as in union with the divine character. It must therefore have been part of the Judaic idea of God, and we may assume that if Jesus did not exemplify and extol such a character in his life, he could not have thought it God-like; and, *vice versa*, if he did not believe this implacable Judge to portray the character of God the Father, he could not have accepted the rôle of apocalyptic Son of Man.

Let us examine the ideal of Enoch more fully:

" In those days shall the mighty and the kings who possess the earth implore Him (the Son of Man) to grant them a little respite from His angels of punishment to whom they were delivered, that they might fall down and worship before the Lord of Spirits, and confess their sins before Him. And they shall say : . . .
    Would that we had rest to glorify and give thanks
    And confess our faith before His glory!
    And now we long for a little rest, but find it not:
    We follow hard upon it and obtain it not:
    And light has vanished from before us,
    And darkness is our dwelling-place for ever and ever:
    For we have not believed before Him,
    Nor glorified the name of the Lord of Spirits, nor glorified
        our Lord,
    But our hope was in the sceptre of our kingdom,
    And in our glory.

---

[1] *Wisdom of Solomon*, iii. 8.

THE LORD OF THOUGHT

> And in the day of our suffering and tribulation He saves us not ;
> And we find no respite for confession. . . .
> And after that their faces shall be filled with darkness
> And shame before that Son of Man,
> And they shall be driven from His presence,
> And the sword shall abide before His face in their midst."
> *Book of Enoch*, lxiii. 1, 5-8, 11.

The character of Jesus contradicts, rather than resembles, the Son of Man of apocalyptic.

There is nothing in other apocalypses to contradict this idea of God : compare it with the character of the All-Father as drawn by Jesus, and with his own character as the Son of Man as seen in the Gospel story :

" But Jesus called them to him, and saith unto them, Ye know that they which are accounted to rule over the Gentiles exercise lordship over them ; and their great ones exercise authority upon them. But so it shall not be among you : but whosoever will be great among you, shall be your minister : and whosoever of you will be the chiefest, shall be servant of all. For even the Son of Man came not to be ministered unto, but to minister, and to give his life a ransom for many."—Mark x. 42-45.

" It hath been said, Thou shalt love thy neighbour and hate thine enemy. But I say unto you, Love your enemies . . . that ye may be the children of your Father which is in heaven : for he maketh his sun to rise on the evil and on the good, and sendeth rain on the just and on the unjust. . . . Be ye therefore perfect, even as your Father which is in heaven is perfect."—Matthew v. 43-48.

" For the Son of Man came to seek and to save that which was lost."—Luke xix. 10.

" What man of you, having a hundred sheep, and having lost one of them, doth not leave the ninety and nine in the wilderness, and go after that which is lost, *until he find it* ? And when he hath found it, he layeth it on his shoulders, rejoicing. And when he cometh home he calleth together his friends and his

THE SON OF MAN AND OFFER OF ESCAPE

neighbours, saying unto them, Rejoice with me, for I have found my sheep which was lost. I say unto you, that even so there shall be joy in heaven over one sinner that repenteth, more than over ninety and nine righteous persons, which need no repentance."—Luke xv. 4-7.

We must remember that the brief allusion to the Son of Man conceived as this regenerate *nation* in Daniel had little to rouse the imagination compared with the gorgeous descriptions of the supernatural *individual* called the Son of Man in the *Book of Enoch*. The Jews were an imaginative people. This book, with its images and rhythmic phrases, had passed into the common speech and common mental scenery of the nation at the time of Jesus. All other apocalypses assumed its cruel ideals. But the history of the Wisdom literature, its staunch morality, its love of God and its repudiation of all extravagance, taken together with the history of Judaism after the fall of Jerusalem, makes it clear that there must have been a strong godly minority who through all this period had centred their minds on what was essential in the religion of Jahveh, and were able to adapt this to a cosmopolitan outlook and the synagogue worship of the Dispersion. To which of these classes are we to believe Jesus belonged ?[1]

We have seen how clearly sensitive souls in Judaism apprehended and stated the difficulty of reconciling the kindness and the cruelty of God.[2] That problem has become for the Christian Church the problem of the love and cruelty of Jesus Christ. Confronted with the facts, we are bound to ask whether Jesus could have

---
[1] Cf. Part III chap. xxii, by C. W. Emmet.
[2] See Chapter iv.

THE LORD OF THOUGHT

believed that his own character was, or could after death develop into, that of the implacable Judge who consigned sinners to age-long torture, and before whom repentance was unavailing. This question can only be answered by an appeal to what is most essential in his own teaching, to the character of his own actions and the calibre of his understanding.

Fear of universal doom makes salvation equivalent to escape.

Closely connected with this problem is the question whether Jesus preached the doctrine of individual escape from a doomed world. If the speedy doom and final judgment of the world as administered by himself were to be such as all the apocryphal books described, escape was the only hope. A terrible doom awaited the majority. But within the enclosure of Jewish thought this escape was never individual: it was the escape of the righteous part of the nation, held to be the true, spiritual nation. For the Jew *the righteous unit was the nation*, of which righteous individuals were only fractions.

The Jew sought national escape.

In the Gentile world it was very different. The supremacy of Rome had killed, or was killing, the patriotism of small subject races, sublimating it in the pride of Rome. The small national religions were losing their prestige. In the flux of such conditions under the Empire, the chief notion of personal religion was "Every man for himself"; and very literally the devils were believed to take the laggards. Like the Jews they wanted escape from a power outside themselves that worked for destruction; but with them each fugitive soul was independent of its earthly neighbours. The loosely constructed brotherhood of the Mystery Religions was a refuge for such individual ugitives.

THE SON OF MAN AND OFFER OF ESCAPE

These current Gentile religions furnished a quite different conception of the character of God, which Christian thought has freely used in constructing its Christology. This conception, like that of the *Enoch* Son of Man, was very prevalent, not among the Jews—unless, indeed, the baptism of John shows some trace of it—but among the class of heathen converts that flocked into the Church before the Gospels in their present form were written. This was the character of the god of saved individuals that, under very different names and symbols, was the object of adoration in the Mystery Religions. This god—or sometimes goddess—offered to individual souls escape from the common lot, and when these religions rose to some moral height, purity of life and a certain standard of good neighbourliness were demanded of the initiates. What was *not* demanded of them was that they should save the world in which they lived. Their religion consisted in a plan of escape from that world and from the doom that was conceived to attend the average person after death. *The Gentile sought individual escape.*

Mr Edwyn Bevan thus describes the perhaps nobler side of this desire for escape:

"Stoicism of the high and dry scholastic kind, although it purported to give men the key of the universe and human life, left many of their natural desires unsatisfied . . . and this kind of defect was, one must believe, more generally felt at the time of the Christian era than in the days when Stoicism was first instituted. For some reason or other, men apparently had come to feel more keenly the inadequacy of a life limited by our bodily senses, to strain more and more, in tedium or disgust, or in some craving for a larger life, away from this world to the Unexplored beyond. Of course, the feeling had always existed to some extent: the old Bacchic and Orphic sects centuries before had borne witness to it among the Greeks: but in the

THE LORD OF THOUGHT

later world the feeling had become more general. ... A feeling came over men, and suddenly the familiar Universe seemed a strange place, terrifying in its enormous magnitude—the earth stretching into regions of unexplored possibilities, moved and shaken by inhuman forces, and over all the silent enigma of the wheeling stars. They awoke, as it were, to find themselves lost in the streets of a huge, strange city." [1]

Professor H. A. A. Kennedy gives us this phase of religion :

" It is not difficult to give a rough account of the chief aims of the Mystery Religions. They may be said to offer salvation (σωτηρία) to those who have been duly initiated. And salvation means primarily deliverance from the tyranny of an omnipotent Fate, which may crush a human life at any moment. Death, with its unknown terrors, will be Fate's most appalling visitation. Hence the element prized above all others in σωτηρία is the assurance of a life which death cannot quench, a victorious immortality. This boon is reached by the process of regeneration. A genuinely Divine life is imparted to the initiate. ... The full significance of the process becomes clear from its being frequently described as deification (θεωθῆναι) and it always seems to depend on some kind of contact with Deity." [2]

He goes on to speak of the mystical eating of the god Dionysus, of the states of enthusiasm and ecstasy produced in the mystic cults both of Dionysus and Cybele, the ecstasy producing the saving contact with the god. In the worship of Hermes and of Mithra it is pointed out that we get symbolized the same conception of saving contact :

" One of the most arresting aspects of the idea of regeneration in the Mystery Religions is that which is associated with the death and restoration to life of a Divine person, a process

---

[1] *Stoics and Sceptics* (Oxford Clarendon Press,) pp 96-97
[2] *St Paul and the Mystery Religions* (Hodder & Stoughton), pp. 199-200

THE SON OF MAN AND OFFER OF ESCAPE

through which, by a mystic sympathy, the initiate obtains the guarantee of undying life for himself." [1]

The point that is important for us is the individual nature of salvation thus conceived. Of Orphism Professor Kennedy says:

"Orphic theology had been specially concerned with the salvation, by rites of purification, of the individual soul. As this individualism became more pronounced, the Orphic could no longer find a complete satisfaction in the immediate union with his God in orgiastic ecstasy.... Pythagoras rekindled the mystic faith inherent in Orphism by transforming the cult into a way of life. He substituted for ritual cleansing a purification by means of the 'pursuit of wisdom' ($\phi\iota\lambda o\sigma o\phi\iota a$)." [2]

Later on he says:

"One effect of this individualistic appeal is very suggestive. Many devout people, not content with a single initiation, embraced every fresh opportunity that came to them of using this means of communion with deity.... The truth which they would feign grasp was presented to them in the guise of Divine revelations, esoteric doctrines to be carefully concealed from the gaze of the profane, doctrines which placed in their hands a powerful apparatus for gaining deliverance from the assaults of malicious demonic influences, and above all, for overcoming the relentless tyranny of Fate." [3]

We have here another problem of great magnitude: Did Jesus think of himself as saving individual souls from a future doom that would fall on the human race at large, or did he believe that the intense long-nurtured patriotism of Israel was of God, and could be sublimated into a world-saving agency? [4]

Did Jesus address himself to patriots?

Again the appeal must be to his own teaching.

[1] *Ibid*, p 206   [2] *Ibid*, p. 13.   [3] *Ibid*, pp. 22, 23.
[4] Compared with this question, the question as to whether the Church took over the symbols and ritual of the Mystery cults is unimportant, as are all questions of ritual as compared with questions of ethics.

PART II
THE GENIUS OF JESUS

CHAPTER X

THE SYNOPTIC PORTRAIT

BY the providence of God or by the culpable neglect of men, we are left with only such record of the teaching of Jesus as must make all interpretation of him speculative in the first essay. We propose to try to discover what was original to him by first distinguishing and setting aside those elements of the teaching as recorded which, whether actually part of his message or not, certainly did not originate with him, and which, being characteristic of the religion of the first Christians at the time the Synoptic Gospels were written, may possibly have filtered into the record from contemporary thought and be no part of the teaching of the Master. *No literal and exact history of the sayings of Jesus has been given us.*

As we have seen, a great number of those Jews who embraced Christianity had their minds filled with apocalyptic teaching. It was in the figures and terms of this teaching that, immediately upon the death of Jesus, they explained his life and death and resurrection. Their legal minds felt the need of a supreme sin-offering to account for his teaching of God's free forgiveness. A despised sect, they wanted an avenger to come quickly to destroy his enemies and theirs. *Jewish converts liable to mix apocalyptic doctrine with the first oral tradition.*

Again, the Gospels were not written until after the influx of Gentiles into the Church, and the greater

THE LORD OF THOUGHT

<small>The notion of a private salvation common among Greek converts.</small> number of those Gentiles who embraced Christianity had their minds filled with the salvation set forth in the imagery and phrases of the various Mystery Religions that offered a personal refuge from the common condition of men who were the prey of supernatural terrors and the fear of death. They knew little of Israel, or of that long history which had raised brutal instinct into *esprit de corps* for the living God. Their own salvation had been sought by initiation into an exclusive society through ceremonies which led to ecstatic adoration of a Saviour-God, who was the private property of his initiates.

We are, therefore, justified in believing that if in the Gospels as we have them there is some infiltration of matter extraneous to the thought of Jesus, the elements most likely to be thus intruded would be those beliefs concerning the end of the world characteristic of the Jewish thought of the period, and the beliefs connected with individual escape from a lost world characteristic <small>If these are eliminated the bulk of the teaching is consistent.</small> of those Gentiles who accepted Christianity. If, by way of experiment, we eliminate these ideas from the Synoptic record, what have we left?

We have the portrait of a prophet with a new vision of God and man, a thinker with a new philosophy of salvation, a poet with a transcendent gift of condensed and picturesque expression.

Jesus grew to full vigour of manhood in Galilee at the time of the Baptist's revival preaching. Tradition tells us that he had early shown most remarkable intellectual powers, and as all religious Jews went when possible to the Temple feasts, he would have travelled sometimes to Jerusalem and would have met upon the road not only Jewish fanatics, but educated Jews

THE SYNOPTIC PORTRAIT

from all the cities of the Empire. He was not among the disciples who assisted John in the enormous work of baptizing the multitudes that flocked to Jordan[1]; and later he proclaimed publicly that John belonged to a superseded school of thought; so that it is fair to infer that from the first he doubted the complete inspiration of John's message. Yet John's teaching was, at that hour, perhaps the purest and best the world had seen. Luke tells us that he proclaimed a humanitarian ethic[2] as the first essential of the religious life. Jesus submitted himself to John's baptism, perhaps as publicly taking the side of the best that then was, perhaps in youthful doubt as to whether his own solitary convictions reflected the mind of God. In the hour of his baptism he had a sudden experience of communion with God in which he attained the perfect conviction that he, and not John, had the message of salvation for his people, and, through them, for the world. This conviction drove him at once away from the scenes of John's ministry. He went into another part of the wilderness, probably to think out further the expression of the inward knowledge to which he had attained by years of thought and which he now felt sure was according to the mind of God. He felt himself at one with God as against the world, and to hold in the hollow of his hand that for which the whole world craved.

Jesus did not help the Baptist.

There is evidence that he had the world-outlook but that his first and most special thought was for his nation.[3] The whole framework of Jewish thought demanded that the Gentile world, if saved at all, should be saved by, or through, the Jews. His fellow-

[1] See Chap viii   [2] Luke iii 11, 14   [3] Cf. Chap xii

THE LORD OF THOUGHT

The temptation of solitude is the call of the herd.
countrymen were divided roughly into three classes, with each of whom he must from boyhood have had much to do. Sympathetic and large-hearted as he was, he must have felt great natural sympathy for each. First, he loved the common people who would not take the ritual laws of their religion very seriously, because with them, as with all poor men the world over, the mere business of getting a living absorbed all thought. The ground out of which the poor produce their bread is always stony: with his genius and power to influence men, he could do much to better their material conditions; was it right to devote his life only to giving them the word of God? Again, he must have had great sympathy with the faith and self-devotion of the Pharisees, and with the hot advocates of revolt who later were called Zealots. Both alike believed that if they gave themselves, though in very different ways, with sufficient devotion to God's service, God would interfere with a miraculous salvation on behalf of their nation; but both conceived that service as something that could not, apart from miracle, forward the end in view. The scrupulous keeping of the law could not naturally dethrone the Cæsars; the puny armies of Israel could not naturally vanquish the armies of the Empire. On the best estimate they were wasting time, waiting for a miracle: they were seeking, as it were, to cast the whole nation down from the pinnacle of the Temple, believing that God would bear it up. Was he quite sure that it was never God's way to save by such miraculous interference? And there was a third class—the godly Hellenizers [1]—who

[1] The author or authors of the *Wisdom of Solomon* are good examples of this class.

THE SYNOPTIC PORTRAIT

saw quite clearly that there was so much that was good in the culture of the Gentile world that many of the Gentiles, even as they were, were worthy to sit down in the kingdom of God. All the kingdoms of the world and the glory of them were open to those who transcended national prejudices and accepted the culture of the Empire. There was so much that he saw to be wrong in national prejudices; was compromise with the worship of the Hellenic culture on the whole the better way?

At this juncture it seems almost inevitable that it would be a great temptation to Jesus to ally himself with one of these classes rather than start out upon a task of such tremendous difficulty all alone. In any case, the conversion of these three classes of his people must have bulked large in the task he saw before him, and in some way shaped the parable of the Temptation. He did not compromise his message by alliance with any class.

After long meditation, in which, contending with the evils that possessed the world, he conferred not with man but with God alone, Jesus at last came forth, comforted with divine comfort, with the joyous conviction of divine inspiration. He decided to go first to his own people in the northern province, to go to them in their own towns and villages and, as God's representative, preach to them new truth about God and His kingdom. It was a message of great joy; it was to say that God was among them as one who served [1]; that, unjust and unthankful as they might be, they were secure of God's abounding favour and kindness; that they must turn their minds from all hostility because,

Jesus decided that he must formulate a new message

[1] Matt vii 7-11 (and parallels), xviii 19   Luke xii. 37, xxii 26-27

THE LORD OF THOUGHT

evil as they were, God was friendly to them.[1] He assured them that God liked them, as a father likes his children, doing them good always,[2] welcoming them into His kingdom.[3] The kingdom was not a future event, to be presaged by dire distress, but a spiritual reality to be more and more fully accepted, to have cumulative power for the world.

The belief that some time in the future God would reign on earth over a people thoroughly converted to His service was a common belief; but, as we have seen, the blessing of this reign was always in the future. It was associated with the lurid terrors of preceding judgment, and would only be enjoyed by thoroughly reformed people.[4]

Jesus regards the divine energy in nation and man as natural, not abnormal.

Instead of this, as I hope to show, the teaching of Jesus was that God, here and now, is ruling in all that is kindly and compassionate, beautiful and good,[5] that He does not ask for reformation before admitting men and nations to His kingdom, but only for a change of mind—a recognition of His own surpassing goodness, which, when recognized, will convert and reform.[6] Instead of divine inspiration being an odd and rare thing, God is indeed as willing to inspire men as they are to give bread to their little children; and it is well known that no good father feeds his little ones with reference to their deserts. He spoke very simply to the common people, with many figures and illustrations. Instead of rating them for not keeping the law, he taught them that they had already many virtues which God approved, and many misfortunes which

---
[1] Matt v 45 [2] Luke vi 35
[3] Luke xi 13 [4] See Chap viii pp 96-98
[5] See Chap xiii p 164 ff., xvi p. 204 ff [6] See Chap xiii

THE SYNOPTIC PORTRAIT

would draw from God compassionate compensations; but that the depth, width and simplicity of God's requirements they had yet to learn.

We shall find that he set forth to them the way of life, which was to draw from God inspiration that they might see, simply, the right from the wrong, and to draw from Him, too, the power to lead beneficent lives. He bade them, as a nation and each in the name of the national God, give spiritual hospitality to the inimical world. To this end they must be clothed in the beauty of divine humility and readiness to serve, care-free because secure of God's loving-kindness in life and death, and inspired by the new social purpose of welcoming all men to the inexhaustible riches of God. His method of saving the world was that men should save each other, the joy and power spreading as leaven spreads in meal, as seed naturally increases with sure and rapid multiplication.

There can be no question but that Jesus preached as one whose thoughts and dreams were full of the love and joy of God. He spoke with evident inspiration; the power of his preaching was observed by all. He taught about a God whose glory it was to be fatherly to every living creature, whose holiness consisted in overcoming hatred by love. *[sidenote: Jesus was filled with joy, recognizing God in all good;]*

The announcement or gospel of Jesus was also terrible in its imagery of the natural consequences of sin.¹ The result of neglecting to learn the craft of generously carrying to all men the beneficent love of God would be a national destruction that would engulf them all. Great would be the fall of the house in which they trusted if built upon the sands of the *[sidenote: but earth as an austere school of cause and consequence.]*

---
¹ See Chap. XIII.

present hostile morality and apocalyptic expectation. Merely to fail to accept and act on his words was to build upon these sands. There would be no pretence of justice in the doom of consequence: the well-intentioned and ill-intentioned would alike perish in the destructive wars which their present revolutionary attitude was bound to provoke, and the fate of the Jewish state would typify the fate of all who trusted in privilege and sought to save their souls from the common doom. If Jewish tradition caused his disciples to transform the foresight of inevitable consequence into the picturesque prophecy of apocalyptic judgment, it is only what we should expect.

Jesus certainly held that God had made the austere world of sowing and reaping, in which a wrong choice wrought disaster and through which each soul must make dangerous pilgrimage; but God did not stand outside, like a master with hire in one hand and a whip in the other. He journeyed with each soul, making common cause with it to fend off trouble and increase delight. It was no dualistic scheme; for while the system of causation, tending to vaster good, could not be adapted to individual ends, yet God was all and in all. The innocent sparrow must fall, yet God was with it, and God Himself the sum of all delight.

His hope for his nation, and its frustration

It would seem that the splendid simplification of religion at which Jesus had arrived was so clear to his genius and so attractive to his generous character that he thought it had only to be suggested to his people to be accepted; but he found that on the whole it was rejected without being understood. The people were drunk with the old wine of a theology that

THE SYNOPTIC PORTRAIT

counted their national grudge and national selfishness, their personal indignations and superiorities, God-like. They could not taste the exquisite new wine of liberty and power that he offered. In his urgency to persuade his nation to be the light of the world, the salt that could disinfect humanity, he seems to have realized more and more the unique and supreme importance of his message. He alone had the vision of truth. If "No man knoweth the Father but the Son" became a reflection of bitter experience, "No man knoweth the Son but the Father" asserted a renewed conviction that God alone knew what he strove to express. His mission was to make Jerusalem [1] an impregnable base for a mission of God's truth to the world. Even if his people received him, it would take many years to educate them in the truth, for they were so slow to learn. But if they would not take upon them the yoke of national forgiveness and the mission of revealing God's love to the world, he saw all too clearly that they would kill him and that there would be no time for another prophet to arise. The hour was ominous. With his clear insight into the only way of national salvation, he was ready to be called by any name that meant "Saviour" if thereby he could arrest the attention of his people and turn their hearts. They must accept him or their Church-State would perish, and with it the hope of any orderly and undeviating progress in the salvation of the world.

His identification of himself with his divine message.

The fever of apocalyptic expectation which had long been burning in the veins of the nation was most acute in bands of fanatical Jews who assembled at the

[1] See Chap xii p. 146.

THE LORD OF THOUGHT

feasts in Jerusalem. The delirium that prated of God as about to destroy the order of the world and give the sceptre of empire to Jerusalem was there clamant. It was obvious that frenzy and national suicide would soon result. In Jerusalem, also, the subnormal temperature, the cynical lack of enthusiasm, of the Herodians was more apparent. The leaders of this party appeared willing to trade what was sacred in the national Church for worldly ends. The petty traders in the Temple were but symbols and symptoms of this political barter in the things of God. Jesus must have known Jerusalem well. His action in clearing the Father's house of sacrificial animals and all that made priestcraft lucrative, must have been premeditated and symbolic. He shrank from death with a terrible shrinking because his death meant the downfall of Jerusalem, that sacred city set upon the hill of all the highest that the world had yet conceived concerning God. Had he been able to teach in Jerusalem with acceptance, in a few years he might have been able to make them understand the fulness of God's truth, and thus have set in this old candlestick of divine workmanship a light that would reach to the darkest places of the earth. The immeasurable loss to the world broke his heart.

His death meant national catastrophe.

Yet the chief characteristic of his life was trust in God, whose way with men he alone understood. As he himself had received in personal communion the confirmation of all his most daring hopes and speculations concerning the free kindness of God, he was sure that God would impart this revelation of Himself sooner or later to the world. He could declare to the priests, his official murderers, that his message would

THE SYNOPTIC PORTRAIT

be justified in the ultimate dominion of the divine wisdom.[1]

The power of his presence was great. He seems to have radiated the health of God. His enthusiastic love for God and for men, his serenity in danger, his wit in dispute, his friendliness, his insight and power of quick decision, and that something of majesty which grew upon him as, by his continual rejection, he more and more realized that to him alone was committed the full knowledge of God—all combined to create a profound impression of ideal manhood, of God-likeness, of God manifested in a human life. This, at the least, is what stands out as the story of the Synoptic Gospels, if we set aside the current beliefs of the age. We must seek further for its corroboration.

Let us, however, immediately note how inevitable was misinterpretation. The apostles had expected for him, who was all in all to them, visible success and prestige as a great teacher: they found themselves suddenly in a world where he was numbered with the malefactors and his memory scorned. They had a secret knowledge of his continued presence with them. They alone knew that death had not ended his ministry. They could not express, even to themselves, the spiritual power which had transcended death except by giving him a place in the popularly accepted drama of the end of the world and the day of judgment. Any application of the Messianic doctrine which the apostles at first made would probably be at once exaggerated on popular lines. The character of " judge or divider " amongst them, which we are told Jesus had rejected in his lifetime, seemed now the only appro-

His disciples lacked new language to express a new certainty.

[1] See C W Emmet, Chap xxiii

priate one. The expectation that an Agent of God was coming to divide the inheritance of the universe, giving all that was good of it to the righteous, elect, or initiated Jews, fitted in with Christian beliefs, the only change being that the division was now to be made between the Jews who accepted and those who rejected the initiation or baptism of the Christian Church. The wave of baptismal enthusiasm set in motion by the Baptist rose again, and at once lifted the name of Jesus into comparative popularity. Jesus and John had both preached a humanitarian ethic: the likeness seemed to justify the amalgamation of the character of Jesus with that of the destroying agent of God whose approach John had foretold.

<small>Christians participate with Jews in the desire to do away with Jesus.</small> The Jews had to let the Romans execute him; they were not free to stone him to death, but in the desire of their hearts that was the way they killed him. And those of them who pressed into the Church after his death combined to build him a magnificent sepulchre by insisting that he was himself that implacable Being who would soon come to destroy his enemies and theirs, that condemning Judge whom they so desired to see in the heavens. Do we not whiten that sepulchre to this day?

The sepulchre is empty: he was never held by the tomb. His transcendent genius has been the truth that, in spite of all attempts at rejection, has vitalized the Christian centuries, that will more and more vitalize the future for us.

But the causes of his rejection were such that we can easily understand and participate in the desire of his generation to qualify his message by the intrusion of their own hostilities. We ourselves do not wish to

THE SYNOPTIC PORTRAIT

forgive our national enemies,[1] or to find our own salvation in saving the world. We are apt to ascribe to his opponents—Pharisees and Scribes—the misunderstanding of his message: we easily forget that it was his closest followers to whom he said, " Ye know not what spirit ye are of " ; " Get thee behind me, Satan." " Ye know not what ye ask : can ye drink of the cup that I drink of and be baptized with the baptism wherewith I am baptized ? "

We have, then, the corroboration of our own firsthand knowledge of human nature to the naturalness of this misinterpretation. Let us see what further corroboration we find in the records to the accuracy of our interpretation.

[1] Cf. Chap. xii. p 143 ff

CHAPTER XI

NEW IDEAS OF GOD AND MAN

It has now become necessary to make a careful examination of the historic evidence in order to ascertain what grounds there may be for regarding the historic Jesus as great in power of thought, pre-eminent in genius, and able to transform the religious thought of the world.

To this end we have, for the time, set aside all traditional interpretation of the great Personality who is the subject of our inquiry. Even if, on other grounds, we accept the fact of the divinity of Jesus, we must proceed upon the tentative hypothesis that this was not manifested in miraculous endowments, but in human greatness. We need not be convinced that this hypothesis represents the truth, but it is the only one upon which we can proceed.

First, we have to recognize that every genius must begin life as the child of his place and time; what is original to a great thinker is always produced in reaction to the thought in his environment. Another brief survey of the environment of Jesus of Nazareth may help us to see how natural to his genius it was to transcend that environment. If this procedure be felt unsuitable by some who believe that he was the " super-natural," perfect, and final revelation of God,

NEW IDEAS OF GOD AND MAN

let it be remembered that we assume that God is Truth, that all discovery is also God's revelation, that the discovery of God's true character, *i.e.* His true relation to man's moral need, would be of supreme value to man, and when once made would be so far final.

We may take it as certain that in the small land of Palestine, while John was accepting the traditional message of the wrath of God towards sinners, Jesus, in his northern home, was pondering deeply the problem of Israel's redemption.

As we have seen, the time was critical; the situation demanded the earnest consideration of every thinker in Israel. Here was this small nation, standing against the world for its belief in God, beset by military despotism from without and by irreligion and superstition within. These foes were not new, but never since the Jewish nation had begun to realize its national importance had the theocratic conception of Jahveh, which was the very centre of the nation's belief, been so imperilled as by the obvious insignificance of Jahveh's nation in comparison with the world-wide power and justice of Pagan Rome. The Roman law and Roman peace were in many aspects salutary; the philosophy and ethics of Greece in her highest period had gradually become so diffused through the Empire that every educated Jew knew something of their value. And the Jews were intelligent; education was more advanced among them than Christian commentators have been accustomed to allow. How should Jewish culture and Jewish law triumph over Roman power and Hellenic culture? Then, also, the tiny nation was racked with the inward dissensions of

<small>The crisis in which the Baptist and Jesus appeared</small>

THE LORD OF THOUGHT

those who sought in different ways to secure national independence. The party afterwards called Zealots, whose creed was literally militarism *in excelsis*, preached that if they went out and died fighting, God, a military power, would send forth His angels to fill up their ranks and bring their foes to naught. The Pharisees and Scribes believed that God would bring about a miraculous turning of the tables if only the exactions of the law were scrupulously respected. The godly Hellenists and worldly Herodians were for admitting the culture of the Empire and making peace with it. And between all these sects the masses of the people were indifferent to high endeavour; while the very symbol and centre of the pure worship of Jahveh—the Temple—was controlled by the vested interests of greedy officials and their sycophants.

As we have seen, the *Book of Malachi* set forth the great hope which Pharisaism had afterwards embodied, that if the ritual exactions of the Levitical law were kept, Jahveh would certainly show Himself strong on behalf of His people. But it was long since Malachi wrote, and his plan of salvation had failed: the law had not been kept except by a few, and the keeping of it had not made those few into ideal characters. The Baptist seems to have thought that if the humanitarian side of the law [1] were emphasized and obeyed, God would rise in His power for His own honour and the deliverance of His people. There was no better opinion than this. Its substance had come down through all the apocalyptic writings, and is made especially attractive in the *Testaments of the Twelve Patriarchs*. It is also seen in the *Wisdom of Ben-Sira*

[1] Luke iii 11-14.

NEW IDEAS OF GOD AND MAN

and the *Wisdom of Solomon*. John stood out as the very incarnation of the best that Judaism had yet produced: and while he preached, Jesus seems to have remained quite quiet, no doubt thinking, thinking with all the human power with which he was endowed.

What he must have thought about we know in part from the doubts and questions that beset other thoughtful Jews of this century. We know how inadequate the law seemed to young Saul the Pharisee in his quest of salvation by its means. We have seen how faulty God's justice appeared to the writer of the *Apocalypse of Ezra*, and how the writer of the *Apocalypse of Baruch* points out the natural frailty and hard life of the common people, in surprise that God should exact from them the keeping of the law. We have seen that they were impressed by the inadequacy of God's power to save the world. And these men must have represented the thoughts of hundreds. *What any thoughtful Jew might have felt in this crisis.*

Any earnest-minded Jew of the period would have been apt to argue in this way: If, as the prophets had long ago said, the humanitarian requirements of the law were far more important than all its ritual, it was impossible that God should ever divide the righteous from the unrighteous on the ground of ritual observance and non-observance—certainly not by such a new ritual test as the baptism of John. But if no ritual observance could secure salvation, salvation must involve something more than mere outward action. All the best passages in the Psalms and prophets said this. If, then, humanitarian requirements must be carried into the inmost thoughts of the heart, all its imaginations and impulses tested by them, who would be found amongst the righteous?

THE LORD OF THOUGHT

If none were good but all evil, it would be no longer suitable to look round and divide men into godly and ungodly—to judge and to condemn; no longer meritorious to go about correcting the errors of others, for this very attitude would imply a worse error—the assumption of goodness and conscious superiority. In that case even the best sort of Pharisaism stood condemned. But the best, as well as the worst, of Judaic moral teaching had always consisted largely of throwing stones at those taken in transgression or neglect of the law. If none were without sin, this whole attitude of stone-throwing, of denunciation, was wrong.

Still—such a Jew would argue—between right and wrong there must always be the difference between light and darkness, between pleasing and displeasing God, between attaining His reward or being punished by Him. But, on the other hand, these rewards and these punishments had been set forth very clearly now for many centuries; and their object must be to make the people good. But the people were not good; nor was goodness even increasing. The fear of punishment did not seem to do people much good.

Such a Jew might then ask himself: Did the law, and all the belief that had grown up around it, truly represent God? In human relationships one could see that the best results on character were not brought about by rules and threats. The best things blossomed where, between man and man, between child and father, there was a relation of mutual trust; where nothing was said about obedience, but where the good in one attracted and developed good in the other. But the average mind would recoil from doubt. No,

NEW IDEAS OF GOD AND MAN

the law was revealed; it was too dangerous to criticize it. God's ways were inscrutable. It was necessary to bow before them in humble submission; but, alas for man! the law is spiritual, but he is carnal, sold under sin; for in his flesh dwelleth no good thing. The good which he would he does not, and the evil which he wills not to do, that he does. "What advantage is there that there is promised to us an immortal time, whereas we have done the works that bring death? And that there hath been made known to us an imperishable hope, whereas we miserably are brought to futility? And that the glory of the Most High is destined to protect them who have lived chastely, whereas we proceed in wicked ways?"[1] So lamented Salathiel. So Saul, the ardent Jew, seems to have felt before he found the light.

These reasonings were in the thought of the age. The objection that we modernize Jesus when we seek in his teaching an answer to these questions is absurd: on all sides of him people were crying out for an answer. What answer did Jesus give?

In his mature teaching we may find suggestions as to what he thought before he realized the full message that he had to bring to the world. What was his attitude as a boy to the birds and the flowers in the country about him? Many boys with atavistic impulse go about killing and crushing living things, heedless of their beauty; but evidently Jesus possessed the highly developed humane temperament of the artist and poet. He had watched wild things with delight and felt reverence for their careless perfection. He had seen them struck down and felt tender compassion.

What Jesus may have thought in his youth.

[1] *Apocalypse of Ezra*, VII. 119-120.

THE LORD OF THOUGHT

He had taken a dead sparrow in his hand—its little song just over; its little eye just dimmed; all the beautiful order and iridescence of its feathers still warm and perfect. What was God's relation to it? Was it struck down as a punishment for some fault? No, that was not the explanation. Was it God's will, then, that it should die? One thing was at least certain: that its beauty and life were of God, that it must be dear to Him as a part of His creation; for His interest, His compassion, could not fail. When the scythe cut down the lovely field lilies with the grass, when they became withered and unsightly, and were stuffed into the earthen ovens to be burned, what was God's relation to that? Certainly he cared for their beauty. Certainly they were not struck down for any fault of theirs; their fate was no punishment. And God must also pity the poor who needed them for fuel. Yet in some way the life of the lily must be dear to Him who clothed it in its transient beauty. There was another crop more beautiful than the lilies, another race of living things more precious than birds. It grew up in every village—the children, in whose joyous, innocent eyes one seemed to catch a glimpse of angels beholding the face of God. As they grew up they lost the innocence, and often the joy. Some of them succumbed to sudden temptation and never regained the power to look honestly in the face of a friend. And some gradually hardened, becoming more and more remote from what had seemed the holy possibilities of their childhood. What was God's relation to this? If a friend went ever so kindly and spoke to such men and women, what was their reply? They did not seem able to cope with the evil without them

NEW IDEAS OF GOD AND MAN

and within, or they did not seem able to want to cope with it, which was the same thing. But if the character had been built better from the first this downfall would not have happened. The ruin of the child-nature was like the ruin of a badly built house in a spring flood. Was not the downfall itself perdition? And were the forces that brought it about of God? Did God, even then, hate the thing that He had made, wicked and unrepentant as it was? Or did He feel for it the infinite compassion with which He must encompass the withered lilies and the dead birds?

There were others who kept the childlike sincerity in their eyes, and added to it the virtues of mature life. Was their best characteristic innocence? Most of them had many faults and failings; yet though neither scrupulous for legal exactions nor ethically faultless, they were forces for good in the community. The two or three men and women in the village who really helped most to make other people good helped them in all sorts of earthly ways, little and big, and were themselves very good company and light-hearted. Their natures were such that they never even noticed small affronts or injuries; they were not quick to mark what was amiss; they never harboured a grievance. Yet such men and women were the cheer and the wit that kept the village life from being insipid, the light that showed the groping souls about them how better to live. What was God's attitude? Were the faults and failings and even the brutalities of the community of much importance compared with the cultivation of that something which helped people to rise out of them, helped the young men to keep the look of sincerity in their faces in spite of disobedience to

A new value for man involved a new valuation of women.

parents and times of riotous living, something that could reinstate young women, even when they had wandered far in wrong ways ? If this was true in village life, was it not true also in national life ? The best of the prophets, in their highest hours, had taught that the Jewish nation was to save the other nations and bring them to God. Not by legal innocence or scrupulousness could this be done, still less by a vindictive temper or the temper that is quick to mark what is amiss. Only by an outgoing of forgiving generosity, only by inspired wit, and a hold upon the joy and power of God such as nothing can dismay, could a nation serve the world. If that were the only policy that could save the world, must not that be the policy of God towards men ?

If this were true God could not be a legal judge. He could not be seeking innocence as the sign of human worth, but rather that strength of character, that quality of discernment, which grew in the conflict of life. He would not undervalue the wheat of virtue because mingled with the tares of fault and failing. He must mark all that was wrong—that was true; but not with intention of vengeance, only with the will to help the wrong-doer. And mankind must be of great value to God, costing so much patience. All men and women must have great possibilities in them if thus by God's patience they could be made great.[1]

Such thoughts of God's infinite compassion towards His righteous favourites had been expressed by prophets and psalmists. If the mind of Jesus leaped to the belief that all men equally shared the appreciative and patient love of the Father of all; if he believed that

[1] Psa. xviii. 35.

NEW IDEAS OF GOD AND MAN

no man was righteous, for none could compare with God in love of right; that no man was ever godless in the sense of being abandoned by God, he was only carrying forward the best thought of his race, adding to it conclusions for which the village life around him could have afforded him the data; how much he could add to earlier doctrine is seen in his new valuation of women.[1] If, as an inference from this thought of God and man, he believed it to be the mission of his nation, by being as the God-like friend of all, to bring about for itself and the world an international salvation, he was only finding a rational path to the goal already seen by the greatest prophets of his race.

[1] Chap v p 66 ff

CHAPTER XII

SALVATION INTERNATIONAL BECAUSE NATIONAL

IT must always be remembered that God, to the people to whom Jesus preached, meant the God of the Jews, not Zeus or the God of any other nation. They believed their God to be the God of all the earth, and that the divinities of the Gentiles were not true gods. This great God was their own national God, unrecognized as yet by any but Jews, proselytes and God-fearers.

We shall now seek to justify the statement that the repentance preached by Jesus was a national change of mental attitude and of conduct. He foretold a universal salvation, allying himself with the great prophets [1]; and the reformation he preached was to be an international salvation because it was first national. In the same sense his reformation was intended to be national because it was first individual. The individual was to win his soul by acting always as it behoved a member of the nation to act—acting as he told them their God acted. A nation of men thus acting was to win the world, to be the stone that "cut without hands" would smite and change the world-order.

[1] E g Isa. xi. 10, xix. 23-25; xlix. 6, Zech viii 20-23

SALVATION INTERNATIONAL

We miss the tremendous force of the contrast between Jesus and John, and all the apocalyptic teachers who were the forerunners of John, if we do not realize that it was the salvation of the nation—or what in this instance is the same thing, the Jewish Church—with which they were all concerned. John taught that the Jews had only to be forgiven by God to be saved: Jesus taught that salvation consisted in forgiving and blessing the inimical world. *Jewish state akin to a national Church.*

The distinction between individual and national morality, so much considered since nationalism came to its present emphasis in Western Christendom, was not a possible thought to a Jew of that time. To attribute it to Jesus is to make him modern indeed. The relation was more like that later relationship of the individual Christian to the Church or to his branch of the Church. Thus, in the Middle Ages, when heretics were persecuted by the Church, there was no difference recognized between the attitude and temper of the Church and what ought to be the attitude and temper of the ideal Catholic towards the heretic. If it was the duty of the Church to torture and burn, it was the duty of the Christian, high or low, to become informer and approve the execution. Also let us note that there could be no possible enlightenment for the Catholic Church on this subject except by the cumulative enlightenment of individuals. When a sufficient number of Catholics—priests and laymen—gained another outlook, the change of the Church's attitude became ideally at once the duty of every individual. But it is doubtful whether, after the size of the Church became unwieldy, the ideal of duty for individual Catholic and Church was ever as fully realized as, in the

THE LORD OF THOUGHT

Palestine of our epoch, was this identity of duty between Jew and Jewish nation. No Jewish prophet or seer ever preached an individual morality that was not also a national morality, or a national duty of which the obligation did not fall on every Jew.

Certainly at this time the claims of Imperial Rome were such as to force on the serious-minded Jew the problem of the relation of Jahveh to the whole world. The home-keeping Jew might consign the whole foreign world to destruction, but the Hellenic Jew was less fanatical. Through Galilee, where Jesus lived, Jews of the Dispersion streamed to Jerusalem with offerings for the Temple. Going and returning, wherever they halted they must have talked much of the world-outlook to their fellow Jews. Men delegated to carry the offerings of foreign communities to Jerusalem would be persons of intelligence and weight. Such men from Rome, Syracuse, Byzantium, Corinth, Ephesus, could have had no illusions about any triumph of Jewish arms or any world-wide political authority of the Jewish state, and it is likely that to most of them the supernatural scene-shifting of apocalyptic was not a belief of practical application. Such travellers must have been keenly anxious for their nation's safety when they came in contact with the ominous temper of the home-staying Pharisees and the Siccarii who made for armed revolt. The Pharisees harboured a sullen expectation of God's vengeance on Rome, a temper not compatible with conciliation. The Siccarii, maddened perhaps by news of fresh divine honours paid to Augustus, were even now reviving and augmenting all the national and religious antagonisms against the Gentiles, which a few years later were to bring about

<small>The Judaic Church was undergoing a crisis in the first century.</small>

SALVATION INTERNATIONAL

the destruction of the state with the suicide of their own sect. The warning, "except ye experience a change of mind ye shall all perish," must have been frequently spoken by the wise Jews from overseas to their brothers in Jerusalem who looked out on all the kingdoms of the world and the glory of them believing that God would give them to the Jews if only He were properly worshipped through obedience to the law or in the heroism of battle. The young Jesus, going and coming from the great yearly feast at Jerusalem, would not have been intelligent had he failed to master the outlook of these travellers.

"The Jew of that time, indeed, knew no distinction between national and individual salvation. The law and the prophets had merged individual in national welfare; and it is only necessary to read the Jewish literature of the two centuries preceding, and of the time contemporary with, the life of Jesus to be assured that the national ideal and interest was still the main thing emphasized. The salvation of the whole world, if it was to be saved, or of such part of it as might be saved, depended, according to the Jewish seers, upon submission to the divine Law that governed the Jewish state. The salvation of the Jewish nation itself depended upon the zealous loyalty of its members to the national king, who was none other than Jehovah." [1]

I quote from Mr Montefiore upon the state of the Jewish mind in the first century :

"The laws of the nation were also its religious doctrines and its ceremonial rites. Politics and religion were closely blended. The greatest religious hope was also the greatest political hope, the greatest national hope. . . . But though the God whom the Jews worshipped was in a special sense *their* God, their national God, he was also much more. He was the only God ; the one and unique God ; the God of the whole world. But such a

[1] The present writer in *Hibbert Journal*, October 1921, p. 114

universal God required a universal cult. . . . There is evidence that outside Palestine, and to some extent also within it, there was a considerable amount of propagandist fervour, crowned with a considerable amount of success. . . . Yet there was always a certain difficulty about proselytes, and a school of thought existed which was opposed to them, for the convert had not only to adopt a new religion, but a new nationality. The Jews were proud of their monotheistic religion. In a sense they were keen to push it and to proclaim its merits, but they were hampered by their nationalist Law. They wanted to stand high in the opinion of outsiders, but their Law to a considerable degree made them hostile to foreigners, and unable and unwilling to associate with them. To this Josephus bears abundant witness. The proselytism which many of them attempted was often, as it would seem, undertaken less for the benefit of the heathen than for the glory of their nation or the glorification of their creed and Law. . . ."[1]

The false hope of the destruction of the Roman Empire. The kingdom of God, as understood by most Jews of that day, was a kingdom based upon the downfall and destruction of the Roman Empire. The destruction of that Empire was foretold or assumed in many Messianic predictions. Even when the final conversion and salvation of the Gentiles was coupled with the coming of the kingdom, it was only a faithful remnant of the Gentiles that were thought of as saved, after all who represented the power of the oppressor had been destroyed. The hope of the kingdom rested upon the conviction that it was God's intention to avenge the wrongs of His people and destroy their enemies and His. They had not conceived of a God who could forgive His enemies and theirs; whose very nature it was to be forgiving; whose power was not the futile power of punishment, but the supreme power of irresistible attraction.

[1] *The Synoptic Gospels*, Introd § 36

SALVATION INTERNATIONAL

When Jesus in his preaching of the kingdom said, "Love your enemies, that ye may be the children of your Father which is in heaven," his words must be taken as in antithesis to many other words on which the pious soul of the nation was feeding—such words as : *The only real hope lay in the conversion of Rome*

"Then shall the great kingdom of the immortal king appear among men, and a holy king shall come who shall have rule over the whole earth for all ages of the course of time. Then shall implacable wrath fall upon the men of Latium ; three men shall ravage Rome with pitiable affliction ; and all men shall perish beneath their own roof-tree, when the torrent of fire shall flow down from heaven. Ah, wretched me, when shall that day come, and the judgment of immortal God, the great king ? "—*Sibylline Oracles*, Book III. 46-56 (a Jewish section).

They could not forgive while God would deal thus with their oppressors :

" I beheld till the thrones were cast down and the Ancient of Days did sit. . . . The Judgment was set and the books were opened. . . . I beheld even till the beast was slain, and his body destroyed and given to the burning flame. As concerning the rest of the beasts, their dominion was taken away."—Daniel vii. 9-12.

It is true that several writers had taught that as brethren the Israelites should live at perfect peace with one another [1] ; but the reason given was not that forgiveness in the abstract was higher than avenging justice ; nor were they asked to forgive that wicked world which God was bound to punish.[2]

There were, perhaps, three minds in the nation at the time of Christ. Some—the large sect of the Pharisees—said, Be patient with your national enemies

[1] E g *Testaments of the Twelve Patriarchs—Gad.* vi 3-7
[2] E g *Apocalypse of Ezra,* viii 35 ff.

THE LORD OF THOUGHT

because God will not forgive but will avenge. In the light of psychological fact this attitude is not an attitude of forgiveness at all, but only of peaceable conduct and ominous resignation. Others—the small and scattered Hellenist party—said, There is so much good in the religion of your enemies: come to a compromise with them because God has evidently done so. Others —afterwards called the Zealots—said, No compromise; no waiting for God to act; up! and punish your enemies, and God will punish them through you. They could not understand how it might be possible to be friendly with the ungodly without compromising divine righteousness.

If we take what is most distinctive and salient in such teaching of Jesus as comes down to us, is it not clear that he superseded all these doctrines by a new teaching concerning God's holiness and the universal duty of mankind? He also said, No compromise; for "salvation is of the Jews." He also said, No waiting for God to act; there is not an hour to be lost. The note of urgency is in all his ministry. The thing to be done, he said, is to forgive your enemies because God forgives them. To forgive, to serve and by serving to reinstate, is divine righteousness. Forgiveness means beneficent action: go out to your enemies with generous gifts and service; share your spiritual and worldly goods with them to the utmost because God gives without measure to them and to you. This is what the records say that Jesus said [1]; and if he had great insight he must have said these things, for

Conversion of enemies can only be wrought by love.

---

[1] Matt v 38-48 Luke vi 27-38 Matt xviii 21-34 In this last parable the Jews, because they know God's will, are clearly represented as owing more to God than their oppressors owe to them. verse 35 is a later addition in Matthew's style

SALVATION INTERNATIONAL

we can all see now, indeed, that only thus could the theocratic state of the Jews be established on earth, and only thus could the Jewish nation keep, in the city of the true God, the home base of their great missionary work. I hope to make this clearer in detail.

Dr Burkitt says:

"In Jeremiah and Ezekiel we have announcements of divine vengeance upon the enemies of Israel, but it is all piecemeal and detached. In Daniel, on the other hand, there is a philosophy of universal history: 'The great Gentile kingdoms, like the Greek supremacy of the Seleucids and Ptolemies, which seemed so overwhelming and terrible, are shown as phases in a world-process whose end is the kingdom of God' [Bevan]. Even now 'the Most High ruleth in the kingdom of men, and giveth it to whomsoever He will' (Dan. iv. 17). Intensely patriotic as was the author of the *Book of Daniel*, there is something cosmopolitan about his outlook on the world. The stone cut out without hands does not merely claim the right to exist: it is the conscious rival of the Imperial Statue. In other words, Judaism is to the author of Daniel a cosmic world-religion, and that not merely by detached and occasional glimpses, but consciously and all the time."[1]

We thus see that Judaism was conceived as including both the state and also the Church of God. "If I forget thee, O Jerusalem, let my right hand forget her cunning" was equivalent to ardour for God and God's cause. In the minds of the crowds that gathered round Jesus to hear him there was one question, one desire, How shall we, as God's nation, be saved? God grant salvation to Israel! Each man, each woman, felt his own, her own, salvation to be bound up in that of Israel.

If we think of eager groups in this temper surround-

[1] *Jewish and Christian Apocalypses*, p. 7

ing Jesus, and read the Sermon on the Mount and other teaching as addressed to their state of mind, we shall see how gratuitous is the assertion of later times that it is the preaching of an individual escape, a setting up of a spiritual community without reference to the hopes and cherished nationalism of Israel. With the magnificent history of their Church-State behind them, men who at this juncture would have given it up for lost could not have been addressed as " the salt of the earth." If their concern was for Judaism they could only be addressed collectively as representing it. Thus read, the Sermon, omitting Matt. v. 18, a text of doubtful authenticity, is a collection of campaigning orders.

The crowds that gather round an evangelist in Hyde Park come with some more or less distinct desire for personal safety, just as the wistful Gentiles of the first century gathered round the Jewish synagogue or round the preachers of the Mystery cults. But the recent war has taught us that crowds can gather round a preacher of religion in a very different temper. In those gloomiest moments of the late war when the enemy seemed within easy reach of Calais and thence of Kent, London crowds, in churches and outside of them, were eager to know what they, as part of the nation, could do to move God to intervene on their behalf. We all know, because we have witnessed it, that in time of national danger, even in Western Europe and in the twentieth century, religion and patriotism are merged in one another.

The crowds to which Jesus preached were concerned for the national peril.

Let us remind ourselves here that from the Jewish race all unpatriotic stock had been sifted again and again. In the Babylonian exile it was only ardent patriotism that caused Jews to remain—to their own

SALVATION INTERNATIONAL

detriment—Jews. In the persecution under Antiochus; in the Hellenizing influences that surrounded Jerusalem under the High Priests; in the many beguilements that encompassed the Jews of the Dispersion in all parts; it was only those men in whom race and religion had become one loyalty who resisted the steady pull of surrounding influences. For we must remember that their nation was very insignificant and despised in the eyes of the world; all that belonged to the pride of life was always enticing their young men and their maidens to marry as did pretty Jessica, and cease to be Jews. Therefore the Jews who for generations, in Babylon and elsewhere, had resisted this pressure were by inheritance intense nationalists. With such peculiar inheritance, would Belgians when Germans occupied their land, would members of Sinn Fein before Ireland was a Free State, have hung upon the words of a prophet who did not tell them how to set their nation free?

As a nation the Jews were poor, peaceable because it was not safe to be otherwise, despised, rejected, hungry and thirsty for justice on earth, holding fast to the vision of the one righteous Judge. They looked forward to being in the future blessed, filled, satisfied with all that was good. Jesus told them that here and now all they desired was theirs by the blessing of God in pure, spiritual possession. If, as a nation, they would practise not only a universal generosity but a high inward morality, they would be as " the stone cut out without hands "—a new civilization supplanting the Roman civilization. They were now the salt of the earth, the light of the human household, the city of God upon the hill of truth;

THE LORD OF THOUGHT

but they could only become so effectually by accepting a new mission of great generosity and purer life.

We have seen that Jewish thought stated clearly the problems of divine power and justice; and though it failed to reach the solution which Jesus presented, it is but one step in thought from the lamentations over the miscarriage of God's supposed justice and the inadequacy of God's power, which we find in these Jewish writers, to the solution: God is not like that. Jesus perceived that the adverse criticism of what from time immemorial had been called " divine justice " came from the best that is in man, and was in harmony with that vision of infinite compassion and goodwill which intense communion with God has always given. It belongs to the genius of all true mystic experience to perceive by direct intuition that God is love. It belonged to the genius of Jesus alone to perceive what that truth implies.

The answer of Jesus to the problem raised by apocalyptic.

Jerusalem, had she grasped the universal grace of God as embodied in the highest hopes of Jeremiah, the Second Isaiah and the *Book of Jonah*, or more fully in the teaching of Jesus, would have been a centre of missionary light which the scattered and ill-educated Church of the first Christian centuries sadly lacked.[1] We cannot doubt that the salvation of the Jewish Church from false doctrine and irrelevant ritual, which knowledge of God's true character alone could give, was at first the hope, and always the passionate desire, of Jesus of Nazareth. But knowing—as the fanatical mind never does—what is in men, he knew that the expression of the national religious mind could only

---

[1] Cf essay by Canon Streeter, "Christ the Constructive Revolutionary," in *The Spirit*

SALVATION INTERNATIONAL

be changed by the conversion of individuals, singly and in groups. All permanent reforms in the world have come about in this way. The conversion of the individual soul is of supreme importance; but not simply as an end, rather as a means to the conversion of the community, for only in a converted community can the individual find the full expression of heavenly life. When, therefore, Jesus taught the forgiveness of enemies, the iniquity of judging one's fellow-men,[1] the absurdity of trying to correct their vision when the vision of the would-be correctors was obscured by conceited ignorance of the true character of God,[2] he was not mainly teaching what ought to happen between brother and brother in one nation or between friend and friend in some isolated assembly of the elect —that peaceable conduct was a duty in such cases had already been amply taught among the Jews—he was teaching the right individual attitude towards every enemy, personal or national, and the right national attitude towards an enemy nation. *Charitable discernment an international necessity.*

"Agree with thine adversary quickly whiles thou art in the way with him, lest at any time thine adversary deliver thee to the judge and the judge deliver thee to the officer and thou be cast into prison. Verily I say unto thee, thou shalt not come out thence till thou hast paid the uttermost farthing."[3] This quick agreement with Rome was the only policy by which the Jewish state could have escaped destruction; but it is a parable that, on the face of it, would be immoral if it related merely to avoiding suffering under some penal code, for to submit to organized injustice out of fear is base. Nothing is

[1] Matt vii 1-5 [2] Matt. xv. 14 [3] Matt. v. 25-26. Cf. Luke xii 58-59.

THE LORD OF THOUGHT

better known about adversaries than that they always suppose themselves entitled to more than they ought to have; and the judge here, like the potentate of other parables, represents *ex hypothesi* the law of consequence, in which the idea of justice does not enter.[1] On the other hand, it is heroic to submit to wrong in order to overcome the wrong with good, because God also submits to wrong for this purpose. The above passage, taken as referring to a national forgiveness of the Roman power, both shows moral insight and points to the only way in which the Jews could fulfil their divine destiny. Thus, and thus only, could the ethical requirements of the Jewish law—a law on its ethical side at that time supremely good—be fulfilled. There was only one way for the Jews to show forth the goodness of God to the surrounding nations and to the Roman power, and that was by such a generous outflow of benevolence that friendliness could not incur the reproach of cowardice or servility. Peace[2] was a political necessity, but to be a peacemaker simply because it was the best policy would be to endeavour to serve both God and Mammon. To make peace even with the unjust from the splendid motive embodied in the prayer, "Thy kingdom come; thy will be done in earth as it is in heaven; give us only the material things we need; forgive us our sins as we

[1] The usual assumption of Christian commentators, that the adversary can appeal successfully to divine justice, is one of those large assumptions for which there is no evidence, still less is there any reference to punishments to be endured after death in a Purgatory in which the debt of sin is to be paid off

[2] The modern use of the term "pacificism," i e the doctrine that it is always wrong to fight, is not relevant here To fight may conceivably be a duty of love owed to an irrational opponent · it is ill-temper, individual or national, that the doctrine of forgiveness invariably opposes

SALVATION INTERNATIONAL

whole-heartedly forgive those who sin against us"—this is a position of the greatest dignity and moral strength. "I say unto you, Love your enemies. Bless them that curse you. Do good to them that hate you, and pray for them that despitefully use you and persecute you, that you may be seen to be the children of God who acts in this way"[1]—that was the distinctive teaching of Jesus, the law of the theocracy in which his nation must find its national salvation. The argument is: if God does not destroy evil but only seeks to overcome it with good, then only in that way can the ultimate good come about.

Man, after all, is instinctively godly. He can never whole-heartedly seek to be what he does not believe that God is. It is only lack of knowledge of human nature that has allowed any religious teacher to assume that man could be taught to forgive where God did not forgive, or to refrain from cursing in his heart those accursed of God, or to fail, whenever he had the power, to lift his hand to smite those whom God intended to smite. In that part of the Synoptic Gospels which represents the earliest teaching, Jesus couples with the command to exercise a universal, generous benevolence involving complete forgiveness of all injury, the reiterated statement that this is the very glory or "perfection" of God.[2]

Man will always imitate his God.

It is a fact of history that all wars, all oppressions of race by race, of class by class, all acts of legal cruelty and false justice, have been done by men who believed that God is the God of war, the God who takes sides with one nation against another or of one class against another, the God who metes out legal pains and penalties.

[1] Matt. v. 44 [2] Matt. v. 45. Luke vi. 35-36.

THE LORD OF THOUGHT

That man has always fought with, or tyrannized over, his fellow-man in the name of justice is a mere matter of history, and may be most clearly seen in the fact that religious wars or oppressions or persecutions or penal codes have always been the most cruel. The political wolf must always persuade his following that the political lamb has muddied the stream and thus defied the powers of good. No war could be begun unless God, or whatever in the community embodies the idea of supreme right, were invoked: war can never cease until men cease to think of God as a man of war and a legal judge—*i.e.* as a Being who, sooner or later, will vindicate right by using *force majeure*.

<small>International love would bring about the end of the present world-order.</small>

If the genius of Jesus, working up through rational inference from the best that is in man, on through clear-eyed, mystic vision, to the knowledge of God's free and universal forgiveness, had in that vision received from God confirmation of that knowledge, he would be sure, with an absolute conviction, that all civilization founded on force and oppression must be temporary, that God's way with men must be the best way of government, that man can only deal satisfactorily with man by the divine method, that only by the attraction of goodness, the persuasion of suggestion and the education of good example, could men be thoroughly and permanently civilized. The world-civilization, as it then was, must pass away; a new order based on the persuading power of reason and fellowship take its place.

If the Jewish nation, the Church-State of the true God, was to be saved, if indeed it was not, like other ancient civilizations, to be broken up because of its long-harboured appeal to that divine vengeance which

SALVATION INTERNATIONAL

was only a figment of the human brain, it must be the first to enter the kingdom of a forgiveness universally received and given.

Wrong-doing produces dreadful results. The argument of Jesus, as all the Gospel parables show, was not that injurious acts, whether of men or nations, were unimportant, but that such acts, in a moral universe, entail such terrible natural consequences upon the injurious persons that they ought to excite compassion and the desire to save the wrong-doer. This compassion must be reinforced by recognizing that the injured is never guiltless—all men, all nations have injured, or sought to injure, some foe. The good news of Jesus is the offer of escape from the universal Nemesis of sin that threatens alike forgiver and forgiven.

The doom of consequence comes swift and sure. It is necessary always to hasten to do such good deeds that evil may be swallowed up of good—but how ? Only out of the good heart can good come. Evil has come, therefore the heart has not been good: the tree is not good that is producing evil fruit ; only the good tree can produce good fruit. A new birth, a complete change of disposition, is necessary. How attain it when, the world over, it is always true that the good men will to do, they do not, and the evil they have grown to despise, that they do ? The secret of power lies in the realization of God as near and dear ; not angry with the past or impatient in the present ; not annoyed by failures and falls ; never reproachful ; always encouraging ; offering always to exorcise the inward evil, to heal the hearts of the discouraged, to deliver from the train of habit, to give new vision of what ought to be done and new and secret incentive

Urgency to forestall the doom of ill-consequence

to effort in the certainty of divine approval; to open the eyes of the blind individual and the blind nation to a higher ideal of love as the only true justice and the only true patriotism.

The good activity, which it was then necessary the Jewish nation should initiate with haste, was to consist in care for the enemy's welfare as evinced in whatever particular neighbourly work came to hand—care for human welfare without regard to human desert, because God does not regard desert; without regard to nationality, because God does not regard nationality. Other nations would press into the kingdom if the Jews refused to enter.

Man cannot serve two masters—mercy and retributive justice.

The contrast between the single eye and the evil eye [1] would thus seem to refer to the contrast between the unified sense of duty, that sees in merciful love the only real justice, and the ethical confusion that has always existed when justice and mercy are looked upon as opposing duties, and opposing natures in the Deity. The lesson that follows in Luke's account is obvious. When judgment and love are seen to be the same thing both in God and man, then, and only then, all ritual, all sacrifice, all other doctrine, will take its proportionate place.

The units of the thought of Jesus were communities rather than individuals. Jerusalem, Tyre, Sidon, Capernahum, Chorazim are spoken of as having sinned as a man might sin. Such sayings as " Salvation is of the Jews," [2] taken along with the lesson of the widow of Sarepta and Naaman the Syrian, or the noting of

---

[1] Luke xi 34. Cf Matt vi 22-23

[2] This sentiment appears even where most unlikely, in the Fourth Gospel, which seeks to individualize the message with the intention of making it more spiritual and more widely applicable

SALVATION INTERNATIONAL

the superior faith of the centurion, show a mind alert to the relation of Jew and Gentile. The command to render to Cæsar what belongs to Cæsar suggests an international outlook. An imaginative grasp of the known world is implied in " What shall it profit a man if he gain the whole world?" " I am come to send fire on the earth," " This gospel which shall be preached to the whole earth," " As the lightning cometh out of the east, and shineth even unto the west." This last may easily be an anticipation of the universal acceptance of the light he had to give although he must confine his ministry to the saving of one nation, captive and blind and bruised, whose deliverance would make it the deliverer of the world. The conversion of his most intimate friends is openly explained to be a means for the conversion of the community. The early vision [1] of " all the kingdoms of the world and the glory of them " as gathered into the kingdom of his Father seems to hover over all his teaching.

All the kingdoms of the world in the mind of Jesus.

[1] In the Temptation, which was the prelude to his work

CHAPTER XIII

TEACHING CONCERNING CONSEQUENCE

IN dealing with men whose minds are steeped in the belief that all misfortunes come about by the direct will of God, it is impossible to affirm that God does not punish sin without appearing to them to say that sin has no torturing and deadly consequence. This must be kept in mind in examining the teaching of Jesus.[1]

<small>Consequence distinguished from punishment.</small>

In this universe, so far as we know, the consequences of wrong-doing are, sooner or later, very terrible. In the soul the wrong intention has withering result ; and in the world the wrong action produces misery ; and if human life is projected beyond death, the sequence of spiritual cause and effect must, surely, go on while the self retains its identity and any social relations.

But it is often urged : What is the difference between saying that God punishes sin and saying that God is responsible for a moral universe in which sin is a cause of which the effect is misery ? That there is a difference is indicated by the fact that many causes beside sin bring about misery, for misery existed before moral

---

[1] Even now, in a Christendom where there is no such definite doctrine of providence, if anyone questions the belief in divine punishments he will find himself pilloried as teaching an easy-going and immoral doctrine. How much more difficult must it have been in the time of Jesus!

TEACHING CONCERNING CONSEQUENCE

responsibility was developed in man; and also that sin in this life brings about more misery for the innocent than for the sinner.[1] Again, as we can only think of God under some figure borrowed from humanity, and have chosen that of "father," we are able to see that there is a real difference between a God who might be likened to a father who would break his son's ankle because he played football clumsily and a father who would let his son take his chance in the game. The first we all recognize as a man of inhuman temper; the second we call a good father. Nor would it make any difference to this distinction if the father had devised the game himself to educate and invigorate his son.

Two considerations must always be kept in mind along with the thought of the painful consequences of wrong action. One is that faith can descry a moral universe by seeing the inevitable spiritual deterioration resulting from the lower choice and the material ill-consequence of wrong actions. The other is that the system of causation is evidently on a vaster scale, tending to vaster ends, than any system that could be exactly adapted in detail to the desert of each individual or group. Evil consequences must therefore be sharply distinguished from punishment, which implies the infliction by a moral intelligence of pain upon the wrong-doer on account of his evil intent.

But because Jesus was speaking to a generation to whom this distinction was unknown he would find no channels of human thought through which he could pour the full truth concerning God's attitude to sinners; and even that measure of the truth that the

Need for parable

[1] See *Concerning Prayer*, where the point is fully discussed by the present writer in essay on "Repentance and Hope"

best minds of his time were ready to receive would, if expressed literally, have confused, perhaps confounded, the common mind. Had he plainly said that God was incapable of wrath, most of his hearers would have thought that he taught indifference to evil. However clearly he apprehended and rejoiced in his own conception of God's character, he could only exemplify it in action and resort to parable in his verbal teaching.

A doctrine essential to complete joy in God

Yet in this idea of God we seem to touch the spring of the unruffled peace and joy of Jesus and of those disciples who best understood him. To conceive God as having in His heart " no condemnation"; as liking His children in spite of their failings and sins; as compassionate, beneficent and affectionate, even when disapproving; as pardoning all because knowing all, is something which must make the heart of the humble leap for joy. With such belief the heaven is for ever clear of all cloud: no ominous shadow or dismal storm can veil the zenith. The soul that experiences perfect joy in God while believing in His punishment of the damned, evinces either mental confusion or lack of imagination, which we hesitate to attribute to Jesus. But the soul who has once realized such love in God may have a clear, rational and imaginative grasp of all there is to know and at the same time be invulnerable. "Neither death nor life," nor present nor future, nor ecstasies of the height, nor depth of sin, can ever again separate it from God's joy.

It is, no doubt, difficult to think of God as the supreme Power and at the same time regard any happenings as other than His direct will. Yet, difficult as it may be, the religious mind has always made this distinction in

TEACHING CONCERNING CONSEQUENCE

the case of *sin*—saying that all is of God except sin. To make all the *consequence* of sin also foreign to God's will is only logical. Yet as the whole system of the universe is of God's ordinance, we are compelled to say that not only all evil *consequences* of sin, but all sin itself, are, *in that sense*, of God. Also, when we reflect what the only inevitable consequences of sin are—more sinfulness and more degraded spiritual conditions—we find it impossible to attribute these to a good God's will in any sense in which sin is not His will. Reflection shows that a plurality of wills has always been accepted, though not explained, by the adherents of all ethical religions and philosophies that admit man's moral responsibility; for these have taught that a large proportion of the actions of a very numerous and widespread class of living creatures are, and always have been, at variance with the divine government of the world, and that such actions are not only causes of evil, but themselves the effect of a cause working from the beginning of the race. So familiar is this view that the ordinary religious mind does not recognize that the existence of these God-defying activities constitutes a problem which, as commonly stated, is insoluble—God, on the one hand, as Creator, Sustainer, and omnipotent Governor of the world, and, on the other, the mass of sinful, human activities which do not in any way represent His will or manifest His character or purpose —a dualism of good and evil, God and the devil.

<small>The answer to the Jewish problem of God's cruelty</small>

The Jewish and Christian defence of this position has taken the form of asserting: (1) that sin is something different from any other form of evil; (2) that it is something entirely alien to the true nature of man and the purpose of God; and (3) that it is something quite separable from the good life, and is proved to be subordinate to God by the final segregation of impenitent rebels.

<small>Sin is not a solitary factor in human life.</small> But sin can no longer be thought of as an element separable from the mass of evil. The systematized study of human development, biological and psychological, the study of the human soul and of human societies, have taught us that any act to which the theological definition of "sin" is applicable is only one element in a certain condition of soul, and has no actual existence except as an integral part of that condition. The quality of human sinfulness attaches only to such conditions of soul as are also characterized by defect and failing and mistaken ideal. And these three have their tap-roots in the far animal ancestry of savage man, and their fibrous roots in millenniums of faulty social environment, and they spread their branches of human suffering into an interminable future. If, then, we must say that sin is not God's will, what of these? As easily could we eliminate wetness from water as these attendant conditions from sin: except in a most artificial way of thinking, sin cannot be conceived as separate from the other imperfections of life.

Further, we cannot think of sin as eradicable by punishment, just because that would not be appropriate to those other flaws of existence from which sin cannot, except in theological imagination, be eliminated. The legal fiction by which pain is supposed to cancel sin is not applicable to the complexity of life. Life suffers, not because of what comes to it from without, but because of, or according to, its own

TEACHING CONCERNING CONSEQUENCE

character. Pain cannot be inflicted on stones, or acute pain on lower forms of life. Suffering, like sin, comes from within; they both develop as man develops; and it is noteworthy that the nobler man is more sensitive to suffering than the ignoble. Our first point, then, is that those who affirm that sin is contrary to the divine will for the world cannot accuse those who hold all evil and degrading misery to be contrary to the divine will of creating a new problem or a dualism that did not already exist in orthodox religious thought.

The old problem is always there, but arises in acute form if we use language which would seem to make the whole system of causation in which we live independent of or separate from the will of God. Such independence is virtually admitted by those who would solve the riddle by talking of the natural order and the spiritual order as distinct. No such language is used in this book. In maintaining that the system of causation has a larger scope and wider import than can be brought at any point to coincide in detail with individual desert, it is also maintained that this system is the divine method of continuously creating a living universe of which what we call spirit and matter are only different aspects. The whence and whither of this system are beyond our ken. What we do know is that life on this earth develops only as it adapts itself to such trends of circumstance as it may discover in this system, and only acquires power to enjoy and to suffer as it develops. Faith in God implies the belief that perfect correspondence with this spiritual universe is, when attained, the perfect human life. We see causation in spiritual

If spiritual at all, the universe must be spiritual throughout

things—so far as we can discern them—even more clearly than in material things; the results upon the soul of the higher or the lower choice are visible. To believe that God moves freely within this universal system of causation, as man feels himself to move, is not to believe that He moves to do the impossible—as was thought of old. The word "impossible" simply means "impossible within the system of causation as we know it." To say that more things are possible to God than to man is not to say that God does the impossible. (What are called "miracles" may or may not be possible; that is not the point here.) The point is that while all that man can know of the physical and spiritual order is too great to be fitted into any tidy human system of religious or moral justice, reason catches sight of indications in the world of fact that support the moral and theistic inferences drawn from human experience. It is more in keeping with the intuitions of faith, which are part of human experience, to believe that the system of causation is tending to good, and that God, in teaching men to have truer perceptions of good and evil, is adapting man to a perfect correspondence with that system, than to believe that every circumstance is exactly adapted to the moral desert of the individual or community.

When it is said that the degrading and miserable consequences of sin—psychic degradation is the inevitable consequence of sin—are not punishments of God's infliction, it may appear to the religious mind at first sight equivalent to saying that we live under a godless fate or necessity, that the happenings of this life are not under God's government, that we

TEACHING CONCERNING CONSEQUENCE

can no longer appeal to the care of God's providence or hope that prayer may affect the course of events. But that difficulty may arise largely from mistaken notions of " government " and " providence," and of the way in which we may expect God to affect the course of events. These notions come from symbolic pictures taken chiefly from Jewish eschatology and literature written when men lacked the conception of an ordered universe.

Let us, for a moment, symbolize the system of the universe as a loom, of which what we call " inanimate nature " is the frame. The predisposing causes of human actions would be the threads of the warp, fixed in an immemorial past, ending in an unthought-of future. The actions of free intelligence—man's and God's—would be live woof threads, ineffective unless they moved in and out of the warp, but, as they moved, changing the colour and consistency of the whole web. Moral theology has always insisted that the purpose of the universe was to be a training school for free intelligences. It is obvious that it could not be such a school unless all life and its environment were conditioned by dependable characteristics. The frame and the warp fitly figure the system of causation; but if we can think of the woof threads as endowed with personal life, we must note, first, that the weaver could not control these living threads except by personal influence; secondly, that his own activity is conditioned by the limitations of the web. It will be evident that this figure is quite inadequate, for each free action starts its own thread of inevitable consequence, each movement of the woof would set up a new strand of warp into

The universe symbolized as a loom

which all future movements must fit. Yet if this figure has served to take our minds one degree away from the old chess-board notion of life it may not be useless.

<small>A living universe</small>

It is life, and life alone, that is ever producing new buds or life germs, each of which sets forth upon its own path of existence; therefore the universe can only be adequately conceived by us as a living whole, each action of living beings bringing forth a train of appropriate consequence. Life, whether thought of as spiritual or physical, is lived by its own dependable characteristics. It differentiates itself from chaos or death by the abiding character or law of its being. A living universe can produce free intelligences because the law of its life is that good and evil reliably produce each after its kind. If it were not so, intelligence would be impossible and freedom meaningless. There could be no choice where means could not be used to an end.

We are, then, stating any problem of God's government wrongly if we think of the world as a " kingdom " in the ancient political sense in which static regions were owned, and armies and toiling millions controlled, by the will of an unconstitutional sovereign.

The fall of Jerusalem, deplored by Jesus Christ, may illustrate this. The siege, the fall, with all their worse than brutal horrors, were the consequences of the national ill-temper, consequences which,—given the continuance of the temper,—it was not possible to avert. The ill-temper, again, was a natural consequence of past events and past religious mistakes. Both belonged—as all good and evil events belong— to that system of cause and effect that is the law of

TEACHING CONCERNING CONSEQUENCE

life for a living universe in which a group of men are but as a grain in the multitude of free spirits passing through the process or school of creation. Faith in a good God must accept the school as God's, and believe the ill-temper to be contrary to His good pleasure; but if so, the causes and consequences of the ill-temper also belong to the category of the disapproved, are a part of that chaos that is partially resisting organization. To believe that the whole is good, and that each soul can ultimately so adapt itself to this environment of pulsing causation as to make good all its losses, does not necessitate the superstitious belief that whatever is is right. The prayer "Lead us not into temptation" would in this case apply to the events and theories which were the natural causes of the rebellion; the deliverance from evil would refer to its appalling results. If these were of God's devising and infliction it would be blasphemous to call them evil. It is interesting to note that the group of Jews that embraced Christianity were in this historic instance led out of temptation and delivered from the evil. If we believe that this living universe is constantly created or upheld by God, the other term of our problem—divine power—must be an activity adapted to the material in which He has chosen to work His purpose. Our present position is that if Jesus taught a distinction between the consequence of evil and the divine infliction of punishment, the doctrine is not incompatible with a single divine purpose great enough to contain and gradually train the separate wills of countless souls. It is therefore possible to hold that God may be all-powerful while He trains developing wills to adapt themselves to a

A school that is of God's devising, not so the faults of the scholars and their consequences.

developing universe which does not harmonize with man's notions of poetic justice. We have now seen that the divine government of man must be thought of as a dealing with growing life in the midst of growing life. It is not within the scope of this book to discuss the problem except as it is dealt with in the teaching of Jesus Christ. Jesus said, " Not a bird dies without God." " Not a hair on the head of man but is counted by God." " The flowers are clothed in beauty by God." " The birds are fed by God." Is it not obvious that we have here the thought of a nature-mystic conceiving of divine activity as " something far more deeply interfused " than man has words to express ? This thought of God at work through nature is perhaps a further development of such reflection on personal religion as " He restoreth my soul ; he maketh me to walk in the paths of righteousness " ; but it is as the poles asunder from the apocalyptic conception of God's activity.

<small>Divine immanence.</small>

" Your own faith has made you whole." " I by the finger of God cast out devils." In this apparent opposition, reiterated or implied in all his works of mercy, we have what may be called the immanent and transcendent activities of God seen by faith at work in perfect unity.

" All sins and blasphemies shall be forgiven unto men, except the blasphemy against the Spirit." There are here two thoughts—the direct denial of the eschatological doctrine that God, from a distant throne, was ever ready to adapt calamity to rebellion, and the assertion that irreverence for the in-dwelling God effectually hinders salvation. Yet we must take this call to reverence for the divine within as recon-

TEACHING CONCERNING CONSEQUENCE

ciled, in the mind of Christ, with the complete assurance that God is able ultimately to answer every prayer. " Fear not; it is your Father's good pleasure to give you the kingdom."

What were the symbols Jesus used for God's transcendent power? The husbandman; the shepherd; the father. Malachi can speak of God as a refiner of metal; and even St Paul can still think of Him as a potter turning his clay; but Jesus knows that God is dealing with life—life wayward and ignorant, that by the very character of its existence must suffer blight and disaster as a consequence of failure to respond to the law of its well-being. Husbandman, shepherd and father—all alike can only find their own well-being in that of their living charge. They cannot but suffer in the failure of that charge to respond to their nurture. The shepherd trudges painful paths after the wanderer; the father of the prodigal waits, straining his eyes upon the distance; and Jesus, representing the attitude of God, endures all possible grief. Symbols of divine power used by Jesus.

In the interpretation we suggest of the teaching in the Synoptic Gospels, Jesus does not speak of the activity of the Father or the Spirit as producing anything but well-being—wisdom, truth, or beauty. The Spirit teaches; the Father cares for the needs of the body, and for apparel, which is an aspect of beauty. It is to be noted that in no authentic discourse does Jesus speak of the pruning-knife of the husbandman. His husbandman suffers the tares to grow with the wheat, and continues the cultivation of the fruitless tree. Nor is there, in his reference to fatherhood, any suggestion of the rod or any other symbol of the severity which figured so largely in the

Judaic conception of God. The father gives to the asking child and loads benefits upon the returned profligate.

Within the sphere of power thus conceived, the sin incidental to freedom—thought of as so far like good as reliably to produce consequence of its own nature—might still be conceived as an integral part of the woe which it produced, the whole being alien to God who cherishes all life, the whole system of causation still being thought of as held in the power of an eternal will that can overcome evil by good because its character is love.

We have seen what the prayer, " Lead us not into temptation; deliver us from evil," may mean as applied to the fall of Jerusalem. The popular philosophy of the Jews gave the arch-devil, for the time being, almost as much, if not more, power than God in the world. He it was who would lead into temptation. Yet this dual authority does not explain the prayer, for, as we have seen, in Judaic philosophy the evil consequences of yielding to temptation were not conceived as inflicted by the power of evil, but by the power of good. God could not lead into temptation, but He could deliver from evil. It was, in fact, a confused state of thought. If we hesitate to attribute this confusion to Jesus we shall see that in his teaching it is remarkable how very often he recurs to the idea of natural consequence as an explanation of temptation and evil result. These come as a consequence of the refusal of the good; and he takes pains to point out that, however hard or unjust the school of the world may be, within it God works as a Saviour, manifesting His direct will in leading His chil-

TEACHING CONCERNING CONSEQUENCE

dren aright and thus saving them from harm. If God leads us out of temptation it would not seem that the temptation could have been of His devising. If He delivers us from evil the evil cannot be of His infliction.

Side by side with the older doctrine of retributive justice there runs, through the whole of the New Testament, the implicit notion that God's universe of natural sequence is a school for souls through which God is Himself always passing as the friend of the school children, suffering with them the pains they bring upon themselves, and saving them only by the attraction of His own goodness. If we possess any true history of Jesus it is certainly the God of this latter belief of whom he in his earthly life claimed to be the representative. Yet if we take the Gospels, written and edited as we now have them, there can be no doubt that the writers—as would be natural to members of a persecuted sect—accepted without question the apocalyptic notions born under a similar persecution [1]—the notions that all calamities in both worlds fitted into a scheme of human poetic justice, that God would be especially manifest as a severe father disciplining imperfect sons, as a judge executing criminals. It is therefore very remarkable that so many of the sayings and doings of Jesus which these writers record appear to show that Jesus himself thought otherwise. Such sayings show one test mark of authenticity in that they run counter to the presuppositions of the Evangelists.

Evidence in the Synoptic Gospels of the older doctrine of providence.

The men on whom the tower of Siloam fell, the Galileans slain at the altar, are brought forward as examples of the working of good and evil consequence. They did not suffer as exemplary sinners; and yet the

[1] See Chapter 11.

THE LORD OF THOUGHT

whole nation would suffer in like manner if it could not change its vengeful and sullen attitude towards hostile powers, and seek, with generous benevolence, the salvation of the world. Jerusalem must be left desolate, as it will not heed the call to a better mind; but its desolation is not the will of Jesus, who wept over its fate, and cannot be thought of as the will of the God whom he represented. "It is impossible but that offences will come." How deep is the sense of the inevitable working of evil in such a word! The offences are not brought about by God. "The blood of all the prophets shall be required of this generation." There is no justice in this, as men count righteous justice; yet it was absolutely true; evil consequences are cumulative; but Jesus carefully does not say that God's part was more than the sending of the prophets. When Jesus says that his teaching shall result in strife, even between men and women of the same household, he certainly does not mean that the strife is God's will; it is the inevitable consequence of the fact that many "that have drunk old wine do not desire new, for they say the old is better."

Jesus teaches the natural results of good and evil

In the parable of the sower,[1] the seed is the word of God, and the divine Father, described as Jesus always describes Him, cannot desire other than a hundredfold harvest in every heart; but the results are strictly according to earthly conditions.[2] The saying about the weather and the signs of the times,[3] if it be a

---

[1] Luke viii. 5-8
[2] It is, of course, a question whether the explanation of this parable is not, like the explanation of some other parables, a later addition. The style would suggest this—the parable exquisite word-painting, the explanation prosy.
[3] Luke xii 54-56.

TEACHING CONCERNING CONSEQUENCE

warning concerning the critical position of the Jewish Church-State, is a distinct command to look to the working of cause and effect rather than to miraculous deliverance.

As we have just seen, if God clothed the lilies and fed the birds,[1] it surely must have been obvious to all that in such cases God worked through the ordinary processes of nature and did not interfere with them. Indeed, Jesus seems consistently to have discouraged the conception of God's magical interference. Both the militants and the Pharisees, in their outlook upon the national future, were expecting a divine deliverance for the nation to result from a course of conduct which, in the nature of things, could not be expected to bring it about. As we have seen, they were casting the nation down from the pinnacle of the Temple, believing that God would bear it up. Jesus, on the other hand, remarks that the men of his generation are ready to enter the kingdom in crowds if rightly taught, but only by human prayer and human faith can God work to send labourers into the harvest.[2]

If we now turn to the distinctive teaching in Matthew, which apparently records the early Jerusalem tradition, we find, if we subtract the additional editorial touches which are recognized as "Matthew's style," that we have a teaching about God and nature which is not the teaching of Jewish eschatology. In the remarkable parable of the hiring of the husbandmen at a penny a day,[3] the husbandman here is certainly not the judge of legal equity. Nature often deals like this with men, disregarding any human notion of justice; or a God whose method of education was

[1] Matt. vi. 25-29. [2] Luke x. 1-2 [3] Matt xx. 1-16.

always to give good things to His children irrespective of their deserts might be so typified ; but certainly not the God of Jewish eschatology. In the parable of the wise and foolish virgins [1]—that poignant story of lost opportunity—the foolish virgins have the best intentions. Folly, not sin, is consigned to outer darkness. But the bridegroom cannot typify the shepherd of lost sheep, the All-Father. In the parable of the sheep and the goats,[2] whatever may be our final conclusion concerning it, we should remember that the reward and punishment, all the picturesque details and many of the most quoted phrases, are taken from the *Book of Enoch* and the *Testaments of the Twelve Patriarchs*.[3] All that is original to Jesus in the parable is the conception of virtue as a course of conduct that cannot be measured by legal innocence, and the suggestion of the universal divine in-dwelling—God suffering in unfortunate men, and in men of all nations. In the parable of the wheat and the tares [4] the teaching appears to be that ideas and institutions, however inferior, cannot be suddenly brought to an end without also rendering abortive much good. For example, such things as slavery or militarism or penal codes cannot be uprooted until by slow growth something better has come to growth. Or again, a false conception of God or of worship or of moral obligation, if suddenly removed leaves an unready individual or community a prey to atheism or irreligion or immorality. Or again, the

---

[1] Matt. xxv. 1-13.
[2] Matt xxv. 31-46
[3] See C W Emmet, essay on "The Bible and Hell" in *Immortality* (Macmillan), note on p 197.
[4] Matt xiii. 24-30

TEACHING CONCERNING CONSEQUENCE

strongest characters are formed by the cultivation of virtues that will outgrow faults rather than by first endeavouring to eradicate the faults. The "explanation" of the parable, furnished later in the chapter in Matthew's characteristic way, is improbable; for in the parable of the sower, where the same figure is used, Jesus is said to explain that the "seed" is "the word of God"[1] or truth: the sower going forth to sow does not sow men but ideas. The same use of the figure in the parable of the wheat and the tares would make the "good seed" stand for truth and the "tares" for falsehood; but, in order to make this parable conform to eschatological belief, Matthew inconsistently tells us that the "good seed are the children of the kingdom" and "the tares are the children of the wicked one."

All the parables of the kingdom in Matthew xiii. are very intelligible as illustrating how what is true and what is good in human society is hidden by, or mixed with, what is inferior, until by a development of what is most wholesome in the community, the good becomes apparent and the bad is cast off. In the parable of the drag-net,[2] as in that of the tares, it is the eschatological addition only that makes the parable seem to apply exclusively to the fate of individual souls, asserting that at death each man will be found either wholly worthless or wholly good—a doctrine that no experience appears to corroborate. Elsewhere it will be shown that it is quite in Matthew's style to give "explanations" which are peculiar to him.

The authors of both Matthew and Luke seem to

[1] Luke viii 11.   [2] Matt xiii 47-50

THE LORD OF THOUGHT

think that certain parables represent a miserable destiny as fixed by the fiat of God for those who displease Him. But, placing this interpretation side by side with the character of God as depicted by Jesus in all that he taught, as represented by him in all that he did, we see that it presents an unthinkable contradiction. If, however, these parables, common to both Gospels, represent the law of cause and consequence,[1] both in the moral and physical spheres, they are extraordinarily suggestive of the ills from which the truth of God " as it is in Jesus " would save us. Take the parable of the wedding garment[2] : is it not a wonderful picture of the way nature treats the well-intentioned but mistaken man or sect or nation dehumanized by religion, zealous without the wisdom of God ? The parable of the talents,[3] too—" whosoever hath to him it shall be given, and from him that hath not shall be taken away even that which he hath "—displays what is certainly the law of natural psychological sequence, both for individuals and for nations ; but it cannot display the immediate will of a Saviour-God. We have also the parable of the consequential man who takes the seat of honour at his friend's feast and is put to shame.[4] It is a perfect description of the place the Jews were seeking to take as a nation at the feast of nations, with the natural result of their national vanity pointed out. In all the feast stories, the potentate of the feast is much more like a personified principle of consequence than like the God who has a right to demand from His children inexhaustible compassion for one another and unending fellow-feeling because He

The despot of the parables symbolizes natural consequence.

---

[1] See C W. Emmet, Chap xix [2] Matt xxii 11-14
[3] Matt. xxv 14-30 [4] Luke xiv 7-11

TEACHING CONCERNING CONSEQUENCE

Himself, their Father, has infinite compassion and a holy and glorious way of doing good to the unthankful and the evil.

A text often cited as proving divine punishment is that in which the Father in heaven is supposed to be shown as killing men, soul and body.[1] When so much of our Lord's teaching clearly indicates that, while a right course of action leads naturally to life, a wrong course of action leads naturally to perdition, it is hard to understand why the power who "after he hath killed hath power to cast into hell" should be identified with God, especially as that saying, in the Q passage in which it appears in both Gospels, is the preface to a statement of God's most tender and minute care for all His creatures. The downfall of the house built on the sand [2] has a distinct cause, but that cause is not God's power, which, if arbitrary in the matter, would surely have been exerted to cause the builder—whether individual or nation—to found his dwelling on rock. As we have already seen,[3] Jesus does not suggest that God's punitive power was behind Pilate when he slew some Galileans at the altar, or that the tower in Siloam fell by punitive fiat of God.[4] Yet the lesson Jesus draws is that if the nation will not take up the right attitude to its enemies, all its members will meet with consequent destruction. But again there is no hint that such destruction will be by the action of the Father. Why, then, should we assume that he who "has power to cast into hell" is other than that power of evil—whether conceived as an arch-demon

---

[1] Luke xii 4-9. Matt x 28-31.
[2] Matt vii 24-27   Luke vii. 47-49
[3] Pp 139, 167   [4] Luke xiii 1-5

or as personified consequence—constantly seen in the parables of Jesus ? The whole drift of his ethical teaching goes to show that the soul, by neglecting the good, casts itself into evil conditions. The " power " that " casts into hell," into all the " hells " there are, is sin, *i.e.* the law of consequence working through sin.

CHAPTER XIV

TEACHING CONCERNING PUNISHMENT

"HE that hath seen me hath seen the Father." These words in the Fourth Gospel sum up a belief about Jesus that has been accepted by the Christian Church—that Jesus is a perfect and living symbol of God. At the least estimate it points to the fact that the character and ethics of Jesus appeal to the highest ideal of Christian men, and that man, if he believes God to be good, must of necessity attribute to God this, his highest ideal of good.

Thus it is evident that if we are seeking the teaching of the Synoptic Gospels regarding God's reaction to man's sin, we must discover it in the way Jesus reacted to sin quite as much as in his verbal teaching.

It was no new idea that a prophet must act out a message too great and important to be adequately expressed in words. Jesus had a message concerning a divine love before which all notions of human justice faded and fell away—a message which, as we have seen, must have been disastrously misunderstood by multitudes if expressed in words. It is not unlikely that he would adopt Hosea's way of using his own actions as parables of God's actions towards Israel. The fact that Jesus quoted Hosea's words, "I will have mercy and not sacrifice," suggests that he had Hosea in mind.

Jesus, like other prophets, needs must act out his message as well as preach it.

THE LORD OF THOUGHT

<small>God eternally acts as Jesus acted.</small>   It has, in fact, always been recognized that Jesus did give his teaching about God in this way; but the full implication of this has not been accepted, for the Church, hampered by having adopted the apocalyptic visions of Jewish seers, has not been able to teach that God acts eternally as Jesus acted. Jesus was the friend of open sinners, the companion of their joys as well as of their griefs. He gave them relief from sickness and disability without asking if they were deserving of good fortune. He told them that their sins were forgiven without inquiring what those sins were. He remonstrated with sinners and warned them of the results of <small>Attitude of Jesus towards sin.</small> their conduct; but he did not punish. "In all their afflictions he was afflicted," even sharing the extremest earthly penalties that could accrue to human guilt. He submitted to every indignity men put upon him. He won them, in so far as he won them, by the sheer attraction of the beauty of goodness. Jesus did not punish anyone: his character is not that of a destroying angel or avenging judge or implacable God. As the Church has always acknowledged—in words at least—that Jesus had a knowledge of God which he could not put into speech but could only exemplify in action, it is inconsistent to accept quotations from apocalypses which have found their way into the records when they contradict the whole tenor of his life.

<small>Analysis of "righteous anger."</small>   In what is commonly called "righteous anger" or "indignation" there are two distinct elements. The first is passionate disapproval of the wrong-doing, which, in pure, *unsophisticated* family affection, is entirely consistent with as strong a desire to shield the culprit from punishment and to trust him to reform himself. The second is the more primitive desire that

TEACHING CONCERNING PUNISHMENT

the culprit should suffer—a partial sublimation of the instinct of revenge on which all our penal systems and moral dissertations are founded. These two are quite separable. The first Jesus certainly exemplified. But of the second we have no certain trace in him, for this distinction was not commonly made in the time of Jesus, and men who witnessed his passionate disapproval of wrong would be likely to interpret it as the anger they themselves would associate with it.

In the light of this distinction the appeal made by Jesus to the *Book of Jonah* is noteworthy.[1] The Jewish nation, fixing all its hopes upon a miraculous deliverance and the destruction of other nations, was an " evil generation " that sought after " a sign " ; and the reference to " the sign of the prophet Jonah " is significant, for Jonah despaired because God could take Israel's worst national enemy to His merciful heart.[2] Nineveh at that time typified such a national enemy as was Imperial Rome in our Lord's day. The reference to Jonah carries the same lesson as does the parable of the prodigal son and the parable of the penny a day—that they who look for God's free bounty to be in any way conditioned by desert will not themselves participate in the joy God would give them, and will quarrel with Him for His goodness to sinners. <small>God's bounty not conditioned by desert</small>

By the help of the analysis recent psychology has made of human character the doctrine of forgiveness becomes more explicable. That analysis, freed from some mistaken assumptions made by early expounders and based on a too exclusive dealing with unhealthy minds, amounts to this : in each of us to-day the habits practised by our progenitors are latent ; and habits

[1] Luke xi. 29-32, and parallels.   [2] Cf. Chap. iv. p. 46

practised for three million years are naturally stronger than those civilized habits only practised for three thousand years. Animal habits, habits necessary to primitive human life, exist in strong tendencies at variance with the character required by a rational civilization. Two cheerful facts are to be noticed. First, our animal ancestors were comparatively cleanly and temperate in greed, revenge and sexual indulgence as compared with degraded humanity, so that the child of the most degraded, in reverting to type, tends to comparative decency. Secondly, there is in humanity an unexplained assurance of the superiority of the more recently acquired power of reason and hence of the power to perceive truth, beauty and moral grandeur. This unexplained assurance, lacking only in the degenerate, may well be considered the divine spark or conscience in man; it affords a strong presumption for the existence of a divine mind in creative evolution. The effort to bring the instinctive and impulsive life into harmony with these high perceptions and the dictates of reason is always, everywhere and at all times recognized by normal men as virtue.

Psychological confirmation of this position

It does not follow, except in unsubstantiated theory, that that effort can always be made successful. There is much true devotional reflection that admits that man—as our collect has it—is unable " to stand upright." [1] What does follow from the universal belief that man's effort to moralize himself is virtue is that to relapse is to suffer the natural consequence of failure— for the individual it is to miss the prize, to fail in the race; for the community it is to be dominated by the more progressive community. For every forward step

[1] Collect for fourth Sunday after Epiphany.

TEACHING CONCERNING PUNISHMENT

is a new power. In the teaching of Jesus the success of effort to make the life beautiful and true and temperate is blessed; the failure is not cursed but pitiful. He says in effect: " Blessed indeed are those who have not given way to selfishness or avarice or pride or lust or frivolity; but with regard to those who have yielded, they will have woe. Pity them, for you also are imperfect. Do not condemn them, for God Himself does not condemn. Be merciful as your Father in heaven is merciful. Judge not." [1]

Now this is quite in harmony with psychological law. Man is like a baby learning to walk. Every parent will encourage the effort, although in falling he must hurt himself; no sane parent would whip him for falling.

To relapse from the higher perception of good to a lower practice is what religion has called " sin." It is " original " certainly; it is " inbred " certainly; it is " universal " certainly; it is productive of woe. All these affirmations of religion lie in the heart of truth; but when the inference is made that a good God must condemn and add punishment to conse-·quence, Christians state a thing for which there is no evidence, and which is denied by the main part of the recorded teaching of Jesus, and by his very character and life.

As a matter of historic fact, the dynamic of the Christian religion everywhere has been St Paul's joyful cry, " There is therefore now no condemnation to them that are in Christ Jesus." It is remarkable that this shout of St Paul's comes after his masterly analysis of the helplessness of the human soul in the grip of tendencies not yet habitually governed:

[1] Luke vi. 36-37.

THE LORD OF THOUGHT

"That which I do I allow not: for what I would, that do I not; but what I hate, that do I. If then I do that which I would not, I consent unto the law that it is good. Now then it is no more I that do it, but sin that dwelleth in me. For I know that in me (that is, in my flesh) dwelleth no good thing: for to will is present with me; but how to perform that which is good I find not. For the good that I would I do not: but the evil that I would not, that I do. . . . I find then a law, that, when I would do good, evil is present with me. For I delight in the law of God after the inward man: but I see another law in my members, warring against the law of my mind, and bringing me into captivity to the law of sin which is in my members."—Romans vii. 15-33.

God's forgiveness of sin as inevitable as natural ill-consequence

Man is not free to do right, because the old Adam, the age-long growth of instinctive animal life, is not wholly under the control of the newer growth of reason. The knowledge of right, the sense of " ought," the threat of penalty, the offer of reward—all these have proved, through the ages, to be too weak to govern primitive cravings the yielding to which, in the higher development of life, is sin. What releases the galley slave of sin is the realization that God, who can never be alienated, offers Himself as the in-dwelling power that gives freedom.

Contrast of this with Greek, Roman and Jewish ideas of God.

In the early Church the inspiration of Jesus was found to have convinced believers that God's forgiveness was an inevitable consequence of the sense of sin. "He is faithful and just to forgive us our sins."[1] How would such a community be likely to rationalize this novel and joyful doctrine, so astonishing to the legal mind? Would not the Jew naturally suppose that God's attitude had changed since the time when a different "infallible revelation" was given to his forefathers,

[1] 1 John i. 9.

TEACHING CONCERNING PUNISHMENT

and that the change must have been effected by some supreme sin-offering ? Would not the Greek, deeply imbued with Orphic ideas, suppose that the new relationship to God must depend upon some initiatory rite and the partaking of some sacramental food ? No generation can shift all the scenery in its mental theatre of life.

To realize the contrast between the old scenery and the new we must call to mind the beliefs about divine punishment which the Jews of our Lord's day had in mind :

" For their names shall be blotted out of the book of life and out of the holy books, and their seed shall be destroyed for ever, and their spirits shall be slain, and they shall cry and make lamentation in a place that is a chaotic wildnerness, and in the fire shall they burn."—*Book of Enoch*, cviii. 3.

Providence is represented as even smoothing the way to the pit :

" Like tow wrapped together is the gathering of the ungodly,
  And their end is a flame of fire.
The way of sinners is made smooth, without stones,
  And at the end thereof is the pit of Hades."
                              Wisdom of Ben-Sira, xxi. 9-10.

When we realize that one chief ground for such punishment as this mentioned in many places is simply *lèse-majesté*, we see how far it is from the thought of Jesus :

" But ye have turned away and spoken proud and hard words
With your impure mouths against His greatness.
Oh, ye hard-hearted, ye shall find no peace.
Therefore shall ye execrate your days
And the years of your life shall perish."
                              Book of Enoch, v. 4-5.

THE LORD OF THOUGHT

" Refrain your tongue from blasphemy ;
For even the secret utterance goeth not forth unnoticed (by God)."—*Wisdom of Solomon,* i. 11.

These passages are only a few out of many. They show us God concerned for His own dignity, exacting under the lash not only legal obedience but homage.

In contrast with this conception of an all-mighty Creator, disposing of all things in His vast creation as He would, whose holiness demanded the ruthless punishment of all rebels and disrespectful persons, consider the conception of God out of which grew the idea of the Incarnation. To our ears, dulled by the din of theological controversy, or perhaps merely by the drone of oft-repeated doctrines, the words " God became man in Jesus of Nazareth " do not suggest the extraordinary revolution in the thought concerning God which underlies them. Whatever interpretation or value we may give to the traditional creeds of Christianity, we must, if candid, admit that down all the Christian generations for two thousand years there has come—side by side with the more primitive strain—a stream of thought concerning the true nature of God's grandeur and holiness which, somehow, had its source in the life and teaching of Jesus, and which is quite different from the thought of God most prominent in the Old Testament and apocryphal writings, although it is a development of a certain nobler strain in those writings, and is the answer to the problem of the combination in God of goodness and omnipotence which those writings present.[1]

Striking originality of the teaching of Jesus.

We get the vivid mental scenery of the Jewish religion in the *Apocalypses of Ezra* and *Baruch,* which

[1] Compare Chap. xvi.

TEACHING CONCERNING PUNISHMENT

grew out of the period in which Jesus lived. Here is the seer's prayer for the divine compassion and God's reply:

> " O Lord that dwellest for ever, . . .
> whose look drieth up the deep,
> and whose rebuke melteth the mountains . . .
> think not upon those that have behaved themselves badly before thee,
> but remember them that with good will have recognized thy fear ! . . .
> and be not angry against those who have behaved worse than the beasts,
> but love them that have always put their trust in thy glory. . . .

And God answered and said to me : . . . In truth I take no thought about the fashioning of the evil-doers, or about their death, or about their judgment, or about their perdition; but I delight rather over the fashioning of the righteous, and over their life, and over the recompense of their reward."—*Apocalypse of Ezra*, viii. 20, 23, 28, 30, 37-39.

Compare the attitude of God in such a passage as :

"God so loved the world that he gave his only begotten Son, etc.," or this : " He took a little child and set him by his side, and said unto them, Whoever shall receive this little child in my name receiveth me : and whoever shall receive me receiveth him that sent me"; or again : "I am in the midst of you as he that serveth."—John iii. 16, Luke ix. 47-48 ; xxii. 27.

Such difference in the whole atmosphere of thought and feeling is revealed in this comparison that we know it could not have been effected by a mere verbal or doctrinal contradiction of the older doctrine, even if Jesus could have found words to make it. The perception of beauty in art or in nature cannot be conveyed in plain words to a people who have it not;

nor can the value of truth be taught in phrases and precepts to communities who have not learned to distinguish between fact and fancy. To teach an ideal of God and goodness hitherto undreamed of, Jesus could only exemplify it in action and seek by parable to create an atmosphere in which the new thought could grow.

No sense of fear in Jesus. An outstanding point of contrast between the mind of Jesus and the mind of the age is seen in his entire freedom from any sense of fear; while " a certain fearful looking for judgment," a fear of God that was the fear of deadly punishment, darkened the heaven of Jewish thought.

Here are the words of Salathiel, the Jewish seer, who is said to have lived a righteous life:

" For what advantage is there . . . that the glory of the Most High is destined to protect those who have lived chastely, whereas we proceed in wicked ways? And that Paradise, whose fruit withereth not, wherein is delight and healing, is manifested, whereas we do not enter in, because we have served evil places? And that the faces of the holy ones are destined to shine above the stars, while our faces shall be blacker than darkness? For we did not consider in our life time, while we were committing iniquity, that we were destined to suffer after our death."—*Apocalypse of Ezra*, vii. 119-126.

So Paul, who was " as touching the law blameless," thinking of his former life under the law, writes:

" The commandment which was unto life this I found to be unto death. . . . Who shall deliver me out of the body of this death? "—Romans vii. 10-24.

In the Gospels we breathe a new religious atmosphere, because we find them dominated by a new idea of God. If anyone will take the trouble to read the

TEACHING CONCERNING PUNISHMENT

story of judgment in the *Books of Joel, Zechariah, Malachi, Daniel* and *Enoch,* and the doctrine of judgment in the *Wisdom of Solomon* and the *Wisdom of Ben-Sira,* and then turn and read the Synoptic Gospels, he will recognize the dramatic transition from fear of punishment to freedom from fear. In closing the Judaic writings he leaves behind a complex structure of thought like a vast, dark, insanitary temple, magnificent and richly adorned but polluted by the blood of countless human victims, filled with rolling vapours of incense which, however, cannot disguise the stench of the shambles, and he goes out into a place of great, simple ideas, where he seems to see the blue sky overhead and to meet the sweet wind of the morning.

We may believe that there has never been a great temple in which God was not found, none but has been built by the spirit of worship. Where God and worship meet there is always something of truth and love and beauty; but in these matters there have been differences between temple and temple, between the practices of one religion and those of another. It is both the great achievement and the unique privilege of the Jews that their popular religious thought and practices better bear the scrutiny of ages than those of other nations, that their psalter has still such value for needy souls that it ranks as the great classic of the spiritual life. Yet, taken together, Law and Prophets, and the apocryphal visions of all their seers, and the Wisdom writings, present us with such thoughts of heaven and earth, of God and man, as oppress and dismay. Of this oppression and dismay the *Apocalypses of Ezra* and *Baruch* are a lasting record.

This great difference between the mental atmosphere

of Jewish literature and the Gospels is the more remarkable because the writers of the Gospels as we now have them certainly believed that they ought to make the one correspond with the other. The Synoptic writers themselves seem hardly aware of any incompatibility between the apocalyptic books in which they believed and the teaching of Jesus in which also they believed. They certainly seem blinded to the contradiction in the case already noticed, where they couple as compatible the eschatological baptism of deadly fire with the baptism of that Spirit whose emblem is the dove and who conveys power " to heal the broken-hearted and bring deliverance to those who mourn." [1]

<small>The Synoptists unconscious of difference between teaching of Jesus and apocalyptic.</small>

The great difference of fragrance and illumination that one experiences in passing from the eschatology of the day to the life of Jesus is indeed the transition from the shadows of a complex theology to the sunlight of divine simplicity. The completeness of the transition, even though not clear to the Gospel narrators, is obvious to us because their subject overmasters their theory. Jesus seems to be a character of whom it is impossible to write, whom it is impossible to quote, without bringing the soul of man out from under dark, ornate theological architecture into the sunny, open spaces where it may be " true to the kindred points of heaven and home."

<small>Analysis of the difference between Jesus and apocalyptic.</small>

When we try to analyze the difference of which we are speaking we find that the central idea of that eschatology identifies God with the power of " the hidden hand," a hidden but external and compelling

---

[1] In the middle and end of the first century A D , as in succeeding centuries, we find in the Christian Church the wheat and the tares, truths and errors, growing lustily together, but the change that even a partial understanding of the new truth makes is as light in darkness.

TEACHING CONCERNING PUNISHMENT

power. This "hand" works, now in afflicting the obedient to the end of their purification, and now the wicked by way of warning; but ultimately—and this is the expected triumph of faith and hope—ultimately the "hand" will be revealed in the punitive uprooting, not of sin from the heart, but of sinners from the society of the righteous. These writers are divided as to whether in the end the righteous remnants of all nations will submit to the law and worship the God of Israel. There is division, again, as to whether all sinners, or only a multitude of arch-sinners, shall be quickened from death to be condemned to torment. There is vast difference among them as to whether deliverance for Israel shall be wrought directly by God, or by God through some destroying agent, or through Messiah; vast difference also as to the character and work of Messiah, and as to whether deliverance shall come long before, or after, the final judgment. But all unite in leading us through the events of human history, past and future, to the day when the "hidden hand" shall strike in the open, "when the wrath of God shall be revealed." In all of them faith and hope are nobly sustained by an assured certainty of the perfect life beyond *that day*, that great and dreadful day. But the light of that future is always obscured by the lurid picture of judgment; and the life of the present is robbed of all peace, except for those complaisant souls who believe that they have laid up "such treasury of good works" that they may pass scathless through the lightnings that surround the awful throne. Under this regime of prophets and seers the true and worthy soul could not look up except to a firmament in which clouds of fate and fear were rolling up in ominous and cumulative volume between him and the face of God. Visions and revelations without number had curtained heaven with fire and vapour of smoke.

Any religion can be made workable by men who give themselves to the assimilation of its practice with the necessities of the life of their time, either by cutting off the common life and making religion their one business, or by a careful modification and adjustment of the claims of the Deity to the market and the home. But these two classes of men, taken together, are a small minority of mankind. The common man, whose best is a rueful feeling that he does not want to be evil but that the claims of God are much more than he can meet—what of him? Whenever his salvation is provided for by the fulfilment of some slight ritual exaction, he can be easy in his mind—easy, but never progressively good. But whenever his salvation is made to depend upon elaborate ritual exactions or the realization of high ethical aims, this common man has, in general, lapsed into comparative irreligion. For, after all, in the world as it is, it is a hard enough struggle to support one's wife and children, a hard enough struggle to get on in decent relation with one's fellow-men. Judaism, especially the Judaism of the first century, with its fulminations against sin and its looming Day of Judgment and scrap-heap of hopeless punishments, had no place for the common man. The prophets and the apocalyptic books are full of talk concerning the multitudes of " unrighteous " and " ungodly " among the Chosen People.

Moreover, this Judaism had no place for the sensitively moral man like Salathiel or for the author of *Baruch* or for Paul. " What the law could not do " was

TEACHING CONCERNING PUNISHMENT

to rid them of their fear of judgment and unify their natures by divine grace.

Paul's great discovery, "There is therefore now no condemnation to them that are in Christ Jesus," was a truth that we may believe Jesus had seen to apply to all men. All had their being in the inexhaustible generosity of God: all were, by the divine standard, unrighteous: no man was under sentence of divine punishment: all had their place in the divine purpose.

He went about preaching to the common, indifferent multitude and gathered round him sensitive, earnest souls from all classes. He taught them all. He did not say, "Be good, and then you shall be blest by God"; he said, "Here and now, in your common ways of life, you are blest." Probably they all felt that they were "poor in spirit"; they all knew what it was to "mourn"; they all "hungered" for a better state of things. They were often "persecuted" and reviled. The doctrine was not, "Be good and you shall be loved of God," but "Here and now, poor Galileans as you are, God likes and loves you; therefore you can be good." He told them that they had heard the humanitarian requirements of the law—that was true; they had heard them often and found them very hard to obey. But he went on to tell them that the requirements of duty were more exacting than they had thought. He traced duty back into the region of motive, so that it would be impossible to say, "That man keeps the law, and that man does not." Judged by such a standard everyone falls short; there are no longer two classes, righteous and unrighteous, justified and condemned; and God the Father, as a fact, does not condemn, but, by the infinite attraction of His own goodness to "the unthankful and the evil," encourages His children to be like Himself.

The problem of the punitive character ascribed to God in the Gospels.   If we set before us the seventeen or eighteen passages in the Synoptic Gospels that appear to teach the punitive character of God's attitude to men, we find that they are couched in the imagery of Jewish eschatology, and we may accept one of three conclusions concerning them. (*a*) We may believe that many of these sayings are additions to the true tradition, and that those few which seem most authentic Jesus used pictorially to exemplify the doctrine of consequence, which we have seen he otherwise taught, while any explanation he may have given with them has, like many other sayings of Jesus, been lost.[1] (*b*) Or we may believe that Jesus, like the average man, had a confused mind, in which traditional beliefs existed unchallenged side by side with newer and more vital ideals which, in the course of centuries, are found to contradict them. (*c*) Or we may believe that Jesus endorsed the conception of God which the acceptance of Jewish eschatology implies. We have seen what that belief was. We have seen how sensitive and holy souls not possessing the originality or independence of mind to reject it still shrank from it. Let us mark this: if Jesus endorsed the apocalyptic fantasy regarding divine punishments he endorsed it wholly. There is no sign in the use of eschatological phrases by Jesus, as reported by the Synoptics, that he taught a modified doctrine of divine punishment—quite the reverse. Such phrases would clearly refer his hearers to lurid and detailed passages familiar to them.

[1] Cf. C W. Emmet, Chap. xix.

CHAPTER XV

TEACHING ON FORGIVENESS

FORGIVENESS is a necessary element in every friendship between two personal intelligences, but it is never the most important element. It is true of every genuine friendship between brother and brother, friend and friend; but especially is it true of the friendship between a loving parent and his child; but the chief function of a parent is not to forgive: the chief joy of a child in his parent's society is not the sense of being forgiven. In any case where the friendship is between superior and inferior, forgiveness will be a constant and natural action of the superior; that is to say, all faults of taste, negligences, ignorances and ill-tempers on the part of the inferior or less disciplined character will be accepted with generous forbearance, and overlooked except in so far as the influence of the superior is directed towards their correction.

<small>Forgiveness is an element in all human associations, but not the most important element</small>

When Jesus taught the common people around him to argue from human fatherhood to God's, he must have implied that God delighted in them as growing things, that the element of transgression and forgiveness between them and God would have the same emphasis that it naturally has in the happy family relation, and no more. In addition to this we have those cases where he confidently assured depressed souls that their

<small>Jesus teaches that God's forgiveness may be judged by human analogy.</small>

THE LORD OF THOUGHT

sins were forgiven, without apparently inquiring as to the degree of sin or its cause or consequence, or as to the depth or validity of the repentance. Unless he was a wholly miraculous person, exercising on earth divine powers, omniscient with regard to the lives of those with whom he came in contact, this quiet and ready assertion that the sins of these sufferers were forgiven implied his belief that God always forgave fully and freely. The simple inference from his words and conduct is that they must get the consciousness of guilt and worry off their minds before they could realize their right relation to God.

<small>The evil of sin is not minimized.</small> This was not to minimize the evil of sin. The soul that builds upon the sand finds its shelter in ruins: " Except ye repent ye shall all perish "—*i.e.* the nation must perish unless it repented of its hostile behaviour. Nor was it to minimize the natural gratitude of the soul for God's generous compassion: he who is forgiven much loves much.

The prayer, " Forgive us, as we forgive," again implies the argument from human relations to the relation of God to man. How do we forgive ? For the most part, if the injury be a real one we do not really forgive at all; but that state of mind cannot be analyzed here. We do forgive quite constantly and habitually all sorts of little failings and stupidities in those we like ; that is, we like them in spite of these. Our pleasure in them and kindness to them do not vary because of their misdemeanours. The greatest need of human beings is the need of each other, and that is why, when any two people satisfy each other's need, forgiveness is a matter of course. Then again, when an injury is very real, and cannot be forgiven

TEACHING ON FORGIVENESS

without real agony of soul, the best and noblest strains in religious literature have always affirmed the conquest of good over evil to be the obliteration of all sense of offence and injury by a generous outflow of kindness to the offending person before that person has experienced repentance. There is, of course, another more popular phase of religious and moral thought which condemns any relenting towards an offender before he has repented; and this phase of thought belongs to the still sterner phase which counts all forgiveness immoral and would always mete out punishment according to the measure of the offence. It may be set aside, for unless the offended person has already the disposition to put himself in the other's place, to feel with the other's regret, the repentance of the offender will work no change; in other words, forgiveness must be latent in the heart of the offended person if the repentance of the offender will make it explicit. It is most important not to confuse for a moment forgiveness of an injury with indifference to the moral quality of the offensive action; and, indeed, the best that is in man has always acknowledged that human holiness is more truly expressed by the free forgiveness of an injury which the forgiving person justly abhors, and by generous conduct towards the offender even while his attitude is repulsive, than by any attitude of loathing, any fierceness of wrath. Wrath against sinners, threats of punishment, are by the best men never held to be noble when the moralist who gives expression to them has been personally injured. If we think of God as being Himself the One against whom all sin is an offence —" against thee, thee only, have I sinned "—and if we admit, as Jesus certainly did, the argument from

Free forgiveness not to be confused with indifference to sin.

the nature of human goodness to that of the divine, it follows that it belongs to the very nature of God to forgive, that He cannot do otherwise. We must, then, admit that tears and entreaties for mercy, if they are aimed at the softening of His heart, are insults, that offerings of bulls and of goats must always have been irrelevant absurdities.

Man models himself on his conception of God.

There is nothing so evident in the whole of human history as man's godliness—god-like-ness. Whatever a man thinks his God is and does, that he seeks to be and do, and generally succeeds. If his gods are sexually immoral, such is he, and that even in his worship. If his God is a God of war, he is truculent. If God is one among many and jealous, unable to abide other gods, His followers are jealous of the prestige of any nation but their own, unable to abide other nations. If God is conceived as the One Absolute Reality, rational but impassible, man holds himself above human joys and sorrows in Stoic aloofness. If God is cruel, demanding to be appeased by the death of victims and human suffering, man cuts himself with stones, indulges in ascetic deprivation and self-torture, and, demanding the same of others, is profligate of human happiness and human life. If God's holiness consist in the vindictive punishment of wrong, and His glory consist in the power to coerce His creatures into obedience, human civilization will express itself in a penal code and will be founded on military force. If to men who worship a God of penal justice and coercing force a prophet should come who should proclaim another God, their whole religious instinct would be gathered up in the cry: " Let us alone ; what have we to do with thee, thou Jesus of Nazareth ? Art thou

TEACHING ON FORGIVENESS

come to destroy us ? " But they would not add, as the poor demoniacs are said to have added, " I know thee who thou art, the holy one of God."

Yet it must have been this new idea of God that Jesus, if he was consistent, proclaimed, for no man has the true inward disposition to forgive his enemies, to do good to them who do ill to him, to bless them that are a curse to him, unless he is quite sure that God forgives freely and blesses without thought of desert or hope of reward. To forgive because God is trusted to avenge is a psychological impossibility. But, on the other hand, to recognize that the offender is doing what incapacitates and injures himself, promotes compassion and forgiveness. Calling ill-consequence punishment, men believed they must, and hence could, worship an avenging God and also practise forgiveness towards the unrepentant. This fallacy has made so-called " Christian forgiveness " a byword with the world.

Rejecting a legal and penalizing God in favour of a God that saves only by forgiveness and saves to the uttermost, we get the answer both to the problem of God's cruelty and the problem of God's power as they are so graphically presented in Jewish apocalyptic. Ill-consequence, cruel as it seems, is the product of a vast creative method not acting with personal adaptation. Persons to live well must adapt themselves to it; but it is not a penal code. A penal code cannot command obedience, as the Jews discovered; but a Living Love, give it time and free scope, does adapt men to the good life. Love is thus kinglier and more majestic than law, for it rules free spirits. It is the only power that can leave men free while yet it controls their action.

THE LORD OF THOUGHT

Ambiguity of the word "forgiveness." Jesus taught that the attitude of God to sinners was embodied in that full and free forgiveness that love always accords to its own. This teaching is obscured by the fact that the word "forgiveness," and its synonyms in other languages, often confuse two distinct things in one—the attitude that cannot do other than forgive a beloved culprit, and the attitude that can only exist when the culprit responds to kindness. This last is not properly forgiveness at all, but only its natural result under certain conditions

Heartfelt forgiveness without remission of penalty may be illustrated by the case of a parent or guardian forgiving a boy or girl and, while complete reconciliation is effected, still inflicting a penalty if such penalty is judged to be the best educational method. On the other hand, if a penalty has been threatened it may, on the culprit's repentance, be remitted without forgiveness while the offended person still harbours a heartfelt grudge. In this latter case the mere remission of penalty is often loosely called forgiveness of the offence; though what we have is remission of penalty without forgiveness. Again, the offended parent may entirely forgive an erring son, and be eager only to embrace the offender and do him good; but if the son does not desire reconciliation, or admit that he is in the wrong, the parent cannot act towards him as he would if repentance were felt and expressed. The same is true between friend and friend; while affection is repulsed there can be no reconciliation. We can thus have forgiveness without reconciliation. The reconciliation, when it comes, is not only called forgiveness but, for lack of clear thinking, is thought of as forgiveness, while in reality it is only the expression of a forgive-

TEACHING ON FORGIVENESS

ness that already existed. Thus in the Epistles passages may be found where the reconciliation of the soul or the world to God is spoken of as God's forgiveness.

Many of these various uses of the word forgiveness seem to arise from identifying the goodness which God desires in man with mere innocence in relation to a written law, whence follows the identification of forgiveness with remission of penalty following on repentance.

Jesus analyzed the confusion, and the distinction between innocence and goodness is clearly indicated in that saying of his, "To whom little is forgiven the same loveth little." Stones are innocent; babes are innocent; idiots are innocent; but if God has created and fostered this world with a purpose, the product that can fulfil that purpose is the development of human lives with all their instincts and impulses sublimated to ends wise and benevolent. A soul who had thus developed would ultimately certainly have the quality of innocence in the sense that from the time it became wholly wise and kindly it would not even desire to do or be what was out of harmony with its highest perception of goodness. Innocence is therefore a necessary attribute of mature goodness. But unless in the case of a heart wholly good from the beginning, as a good tree is good or a pure spring of water is pure, human goodness must grow in the conflict of impulses, and the cold, sluggish soul who has fewest impulses to excess in anger or acquisitiveness or sexual passion is by no means the noblest or capable of the highest development. It is clear that a human being in the making could only be innocent in relation to some law. In so far as such a law was good, legal innocence would be

Distinction between innocence and goodness.

good as far as it went. But innocence in relation to such a law would be a low type of goodness, for no law could demand the depth and height of possible attainment. Further, unless the law were a perfect law —which no codified conception of obligation has ever been—demanding nothing that was foolish, demanding only what was good, legal innocence would not be entirely good even as far as it went. If, for example, a ritual law demanded from a man money which he ought to spend on the maintenance of his aged parents, innocence would not be good.[1] On the other hand, innocence might be compatible with a bad heart of which the law could take no cognizance.[2]

In lifting the conception of goodness above that of innocence, Jesus lifted the idea of forgiveness above that of remission of sin

In lifting the conception of goodness above the notion of innocence, in exalting a divine ideal for humanity, Jesus lifted the conception of forgiveness entirely above the notion that it must consist in the reversal of some former condemnation.

The teaching of Jesus on forgiveness chiefly lies in his almost exclusive use of the word "Father" for God,[3] together with the sayings and parables that make clear his conception of Fatherhood. There was nothing legal and magisterial about the Semitic idea of fatherhood as there was in Roman law and afterwards in the Latinized Church. The Jews have always been fond and compassionate parents, as they have always been fierce enemies to alien offenders. Their own moralists often warn against indulgence to children, showing to what virtue their failings leaned. The typical father referred to by Jesus knows what his children need, gives them what they ask as a matter of

---

[1] "Corban," Mark vii 11-13 [2] Matt v 21-22, 27-28
[3] Cf C W Emmet, Chap xviii

TEACHING ON FORGIVENESS

course. ("What man is there of you whom if his son ask bread, will he give him a stone?"[1]) It is impossible to read all that is said and implied by Jesus about the heavenly Father and believe that, because man is constantly offending, God is in a constant mood of offence. The forgiving soul is always forgiven, and no mention is made in this connection of repentance.[2] In Matthew's characteristic way it is added that the unforgiving soul will not be forgiven, and this was apparently copied later into Mark from Matthew. Its authenticity, on various accounts, is more than doubtful.[3] It remains true that the recognition of God's forgivingness—which recognition is constantly called forgiveness—is only really possible to the soul that forgives, for only by itself forgiving can it understand the divine nature. Conversely this most beautiful quality would be impossible in man if it were not derived from the divine nature.

[1] Matt vii 9.   [2] Matt vi. 14-15.
[3] Cf C W. Emmet, Chap xx.

CHAPTER XVI

TEACHING ON SIN AND SALVATION

Jesus affirms that no man is good.

THE teaching of Jesus upon sin was very simple. "There is none good but God." "Ye are all unprofitable servants." If your light is hidden; if you are insipid; you are fit for nothing. Whoever is angry with his brother, or despises his brother, or thinks improperly of a woman, or refuses generous service to an oppressor and fails wholesomely to forgive all wrong, is a sinner. To attempt to please God by only trying not to do wrong is hopeless, for it is only the effort of the soul to save itself, the consequence of which is loss. God, the Father of men, spends Himself in positive benefaction for men—both good and evil men. To come short of this perfection of God is to need His constant forgiveness, in the sense in which a child is always needing the parent's forgiveness, or in which the faults and failings of an ignorant and wayward companion are always needing the forgiveness of his friend and superior.

The best Jews were already disheartened by the universality of sin.

Some of the best Jews had already reached almost the same conclusion about sin, realizing that the spiritual requirements of God were without limit. Paul's sense of past sin is acute, although he could point to his record as a Jew and defy criticism. And we have seen [1] the pathos of the apocalyptic seers; thus again:

[1] Chapter vi.

TEACHING ON SIN AND SALVATION

" Who is there of those born who hath not transgressed thy commandment ? . . .
    For there is in us the evil heart which . . .
    hath led us into corruption,
    and hath shown us the ways of death,
    and made known to us the paths of perdition . . .
and this not of a few, but perchance of all who have been."—*Apocalypse of Ezra,* vii. 46-48.

Like Stoicism, Judaism held no doctrine of the grace —*i.e.* love—of God growing up gradually in a wayward man. Man on his own initiative must voluntarily repent, voluntarily reform, in order to be saved. God would aid, but, though His aid in the majority of cases seemed insufficient, He would do no more, and the time of probation was short, and the good qualities of the erring were of no value.

This, of course, was a higher conception of salvation than that of a salvation by magical rites—an idea common to various mystery cults of other nations. It fostered a true notion of individual responsibility, encouraged the highest aspiration ; but, as their literature attests, it failed to reform the nation or to give peace to the souls of those who hungered for righteousness and were not filled.

Because such good souls held the ideal of innocence ; because they thought that sins invalidated the virtues that grew side by side with them, because they could not understand the principle of the wheat and tares, they lost hope for the world. Yet the fact remained that, however universal sin was, good was also universal. There have always been good parents, good children, good brothers and good friends and loyal citizens the world over. And if God, immanent in all the good, had been thought of as overcoming the evil with inexhaustible patience, it would have been possible for them to rejoice in human virtue rather than despair over human sin. But the gloom of these more sensitive Jews was caused, not by the universality of sin, but by the other beliefs which they associated with that. The first was the mistaken notion of goodness; the second, that they had to rely on the human will, with at best but a little aid from an external God, to overcome unruly impulses; and, not recognizing any robust natural virtue, they thought that sin was always victorious in their souls and in the world. Weeping over a perishing world, Salathiel, wistful for a command that comes not, cries that if God would only command him he would pray:

The cause of Judaic moral despair.

" Do thou give us the seed and culture of a new heart whence may come fruits, so that everyone that is corruptible may be able to live " (*i.e.* live righteously so as not to be destroyed at the judgment).—*Apocalypse of Ezra*, viii. 6.

The salvation Jesus offered.

It was just this " seed and culture of a new heart," growing in the imperfect, impulsive life of man, that Jesus offered in his doctrine of the constant, inalienable friendship and forgiveness of God, and of the life of prayer by which man can enter into this friendship.

The goodness that Jesus taught was to come by the inspiration of God, whose character was such that sin awakes in Him only compassion and provokes Him only to impart His own energy of goodness to all who ask.

" Ask and it shall be given you;
Seek and ye shall find;
Knock and it shall be opened to you;
For everyone that asketh receiveth."

Matt. vii. 7-8.

TEACHING ON SIN AND SALVATION

The emphasis is upon the "everyone." That was one point in which Judaism failed. It taught that some works, some correct emotion, were necessary to constitute a claim upon God before there could be any assurance that the prayer would be heard. Christian teachers also have taught that conditions were laid down by God, and only on the fulfilment of these would the Holy Spirit be given. Jesus said, "Men ought always to pray and not to faint." The "always" is futile if it means only "sometimes when certain conditions are fulfilled." Jesus went about among all sorts of his countrymen saying, in practice, Whether is it easier for God to inspire goodness in you or to heal your diseases? If I by the power of God heal your diseases and insanities, then you have access to the kingdom—that condition of inspired goodness in which the *hopeless* struggle with sin is for ever over. In the *Book of Enoch* the reign of God is thus described:

<blockquote>
"All shall walk in his ways since righteousness never forsakes him:
With him shall be their dwelling-places, and with him their heritage."—lxxi. 16.
</blockquote>

The gift of the Spirit.

It is part of every apocalyptic description of the reign of God that those who attain to a share in it should be without sin.

Jesus not only taught that the Holy Spirit is to be had by all men for the asking,[1] but that the Spirit is essential to the good life. This present necessity of constant divine co-operation—*i.e.* inspiration or inward help—was new. A life of goodness and power, upheld

---

[1] Before Christ the gift of the Spirit was conceived as a rare and supernatural experience; Jesus, as it were, naturalized the Spirit in the town of Mansoul. The initial and principal factor in human holiness before Christ was man's will; after Christ, the Spirit of God

THE LORD OF THOUGHT

by the influence or inspiration of God, was, as we have seen,[1] a common idea in connection with the life of the righteous in a future reign of God :

> " They shall be made like unto the angels,
> And be made equal to the stars,
> And they shall be changed into every form they desire,
> From beauty into loveliness."
> *Apocalypse of Baruch*, xlix. 10.

> " The souls of the righteous are in the hands of God . . .
> They that trust in him shall understand truth,
> And the faithful shall abide in him in love."
> *Wisdom of Solomon*, iii. 1, 9.

In teaching that this kingdom, thought of as future, was already existing in the unseen, within the reach and grasp of men who could draw it into the visible and temporal order, Jesus taught that the goodness and power of such men—*i.e.* the children of the kingdom—were to be of God. Everyone could see that the lily is clothed by the unfolding of the life within, as the stature of a man is attained by inward vitality ; that the food of the birds also is of natural growth, and their faculty for finding it is within them.[2] To assert that God is acting in such ways was to assert divine immanence in the simple and the common things of life.

Pre-Christian doctrine of the Spirit. Before Jesus came men did not recognize this power of the Spirit to make and keep them good, because they looked for evidence of his operation in wrong ways, in negative ways, hoping merely to overcome bad habits and resist temptation, or in positive ways expecting supernatural excitement to give knowledge or delight. The parable of the house swept and garnished shows that the negative way is not God's

[1] See Chap vi pp 79-81   [2] Matt vi 26-30

TEACHING ON SIN AND SALVATION

way.[1] In our Lord's teaching a good heart brings forth good fruit as naturally as a good tree. The gift of God to men that ask is the good heart that always shows loving-kindness to friend and foe, that out of its good treasure of traffic with God brings good things for the world. "Come with me and I will make you fishers of men." "Man shall not live by bread alone." "Have salt in yourselves and be at peace with one another." "If thine eye be single thy whole body shall be full of light." "Blessed are your eyes for they see." "Many prophets and kings have desired to see the things that ye see." These are all sayings that suggest that the salvation which God would give freely to those who ask Him was energy for a new benevolent activity which would be like a lusty overgrowth of good from under which an old, evil crop would dwindle. The kingdom in the heart would be like a grain of mustard seed, and, moreover, it would grow while he who had received it slept and waked and knew not how it grew; but the grain, the crop, the outcome of good, would be obvious. It was not a doctrine that interfered with the doctrine of causation: the seeds of evil brought forth evil, but just as evil habits would choke off the seed of good intentions which were not rooted in the good heart inspired by God, so faith that appropriated the generous energy of God would produce a crop that choked off the weaker plants of evil.

The teaching as to receiving the kingdom, or God

---

[1] Matt xii 44 The saying about the kingdom, or house, divided against itself (Luke xi 18)—understood by the evangelists to refer to Beelzebub casting out demons—is extraordinarily suggestive of a soul trying to negate some unruly impulse or bad habit and failing in that, and, because attention is centred on the sin, in all else

THE LORD OF THOUGHT

Himself, or the divine energy of Jesus, into the heart expresses an idea of a personal salvation that operated from within the heart outwards, filling the whole life with a world-saving energy, " Whoso shall not *receive* the Kingdom of Heaven ... he shall not enter therein" (Mark x. 15). "Whosoever shall *receive* me *receiveth* him that sent me" (Mark ix. 37). "Whoso *receiveth* you *receiveth* me, and he that *receiveth* me *receiveth* him that sent me" (Matt. x. 40). It is evidently "spiritual hospitality" that is intended in these texts, as God the Father could not otherwise be entertained. What is included in "receiving" the kingdom, the Father, Jesus himself, or the apostle, or even " a little child," is the notion of a life not only wholesome and dynamic, but expansive with regenerative outward force. Such a force had been evident in the greatest of the long line of prophets, and was most obvious to them all in the Baptist; "nevertheless he that is least in the Kingdom of Heaven is greater than he" (Matt. xi. 11). The greatness of " the least" could only be by the in-dwelling of God.

<small>The true nature of the gift of the Spirit.</small>

Again, the inspiration given freely by God to man was not supernatural power or knowledge.

First, it was not supernatural power. The healing of sick people or "demoniacs" by an authoritative word may be a natural power which works by suggestion received by the inward faith which is a necessary condition. It is of God, as is all beneficent action. It is the healing of the bad habits of the body-governing part of the human mind, just as reformation produced by conversion is the healing of the bad habits of the conscious mind. The power of healing and converting by imparting faith and suggestion was certainly to

TEACHING ON SIN AND SALVATION

be a natural outcome of the Spirit which God would give. As we now know, but Jesus alone then divined, it was not in itself supernatural power, nor did it imply the possession of magical powers.

Supernatural knowledge was certainly not offered. The disciples certainly "received Jesus," and, according to the teaching, "received the Kingdom" and received the Spirit in their hearts; but they misunderstood Jesus frequently, and misunderstood at times the whole spirit of his gospel. "Ye know not what spirit ye are of." "Ye know not what ye ask." Further it is said, "No man knoweth the times and the seasons but the Father." Neither to the individual nor to the community was offered supernatural theoretic knowledge or infallibility about the things of God; yet part of the salvation of Jesus—one fruit of this imparted divine energy to be received by faith—was the clear insight of the individual mind as to the right word or right action for the hour—a practical, not a theoretic, wisdom.

The teaching of modern psychology about the manner of human development is in entire harmony with this teaching. Psychology shows us that no man is good; for, while man's primitive habits of mind, latent in the most highly civilized, are constantly producing unruly impulses and conduct of a lower type than the reason approves, it is also true that man's perception of what is fitting or desirable or good is constantly advancing. He who almost succeeds in living up to his own ideal to-day will to-morrow have a higher ideal to which he finds himself unable to conform. Thus the man or the community that does not seek to live up to what is seen to be good, sins—*i.e.* *Modern psychology gives an account of man in harmony with the teaching of Jesus.*

Sin is universal

transgresses or comes short—and the man or community that almost attains, at once acquires a higher notion of goodness to which the half-trained, impulsive life fails to conform. Sin, therefore, is universal. The spiritual requirements of the good are without limit, just because life is a development. The nature of man is such a combination of intelligence and will and instinctive life that to all the practice of civilized virtues will always be both possible and so difficult that effort will flag; the sow of the animal soul will always return at times to the wallowing that for untold ages in the past was its legitimate delight but is now its vice. It is impossible to get rid of the inconvenient fact which religion calls " sin " by being irreligious.

and is not to be overcome by efforts to attain sinlessness.

If again we turn to the psychologist who has thus explained the nature of sin and ask, How, then, can man come at peace and harmony within? how can he unify his older and newer natures, which St Paul called " the old Adam " and " the new man " ? we shall be told that bracing the will, with self-chiding and self-abasement, is futile; and so also is an easy pace along the line of least resistance. By either of these methods man only reaches greater discontent or drugged despair. The right way of reaching unity is to fill the imagination, not only with the ideal to be attained, but with the thought of the self as attaining. The mind must be nerved and nourished by the suggestion that attain-

Vision and inspiration required.

ment is possible. This vision of the ideal, this belief in his own power to attain, is enough; the suggestion will work without conscious effort, and, slowly or quickly, a unification of the nature will take place, and man will be a new creature, harmonious with his progressive environment. This is the salvation which the

TEACHING ON SIN AND SALVATION

psychologist points out. What he says is true. The trouble is that the ideal right seldom intrigues the human imagination, and self-inspiration is so dull a process that few persist in its practice.

Let us now turn back to the insight of religious genius which Jesus of Nazareth flashed upon this human condition. He also saw that the sinner's imagination must be filled with the idea and with the conviction that it could be attained; but the ideal was not abstract and passive, as mere ideals of right are; it was the living, loving, personal God, invisible but not unknowable, outwardly an alluring attraction, inwardly the dynamic of a new life. *Jesus declared God to be the object of vision and the bestower of inspiration.*

" Be perfect as your Father in heaven is perfect "— your Father whose activity is manifested in the beauty and growth and care-free life of plant and bird, and in the natural parental and brotherly goodness of your hearts. Be inwardly inspired by this Father, who will give His Spirit to all who ask. Compare with this St Paul's personal experience, repeated down all the ages of Christendom, " I can do all things through Christ that strengtheneth me." [1]

---

[1] "If the spirit of God's love is as a breath over the world, suggesting, strengthening the love which it desires, seeking man that man may seek God, itself the impulse which it humbles itself to accept at man's hands; how much more is this love of God, in its inconceivable acceptance and exchange, the most divine, the only unending intoxication in the world."—Arthur Symonds.

CHAPTER XVII

SUMMARY

<small>The call of Jesus.</small>

WE have realized that the Jewish thirst for retributive punishment for the unrighteous, and the Greek longing for a refuge in which individual souls could save themselves out of a lost world, are the contemporary currents of thought which would be the most likely to have filtered into the oral tradition of Jesus' teaching before it was written in final form. We have seen that these two ideas appear to be inconsistent with the hope of the world as preached by Jesus, and that by eliminating them from the story of the ministry and teaching, we have in that story the call to a salvation that is the more intensely personal because it is a group salvation and international. What is that call?

<small>Self-denial not in the forefront of the call.</small>

Many would lay the first emphasis upon the demand which Jesus made for renunciation. "He that loveth father or mother or house or lands more than me cannot be my disciple." "Take up the cross." "Leave all in which you delight." All that is in the "good news" of Jesus, but it does not come first. It comes in a place where it is as natural as are any other of the renunciations of love.

We have seen with what black shadow and lurid light the Jewish thought of the coming of the Reign of God was invested; and yet, while John, living in this shadow, offered reformation of life and baptism as a

SUMMARY

merciful means of escape from world-wide destruction, he made no demand for entire self-sacrifice. His appeal was to the motive of self-interested fear; and Jesus spoke of John's preaching as a call to mourn. If the more drastic demand of self-denial that Jesus made upon his followers could be contrasted with John's call as wedding music contrasts with the dismal wail of mourning, it is evident that the demand for entire self-sacrifice must have been associated with a joyful purpose and inspired by natural longing for its achievement. A mother whose child's life can be saved in sickness by toil of hers; a father who sees that his son can be saved from disaster by some effort of his; a lover who must renounce much to win what he supremely desires; a patriot who knows that the land he loves can be successfully defended—these do not heed hunger or thirst or cold or contumely or loss or pain. Their vocation is not to the incidental loss but to the assured gain. The love of self and of possessions is overbalanced by the longing for something else: the vision of the accomplishment of their purpose makes them almost oblivious of what they lose or set aside. It was Jesus who finally drove home the lesson that, except as incidental to altruistic purpose, self-immolation was irrelevant to salvation.

Jesus called his followers to the joy of unbroken and confident friendship with a God wholly kind, the joy of co-operation with that God in saving the whole world. The Jews, as a race, had developed a beautiful conception of God as the friend of the righteous. They had learned and taught that personality is a divine attribute, and that man can find in God, not only his own ethical values, but a living, personal friendship whose influence *Call to friendship with God and co-operation with Him in bringing new life to the world.*

THE LORD OF THOUGHT

raises his values and helps to their realization. As the idea of God is the most formative of all ideas, this—which was so far the highest idea of God—was the priceless contribution of the Jewish race. We all recognize the intense friendship that Judaism realized between God and the righteous man or righteous community. "Underneath are the everlasting arms." "I have trusted in thy loving-kindness." "The Lord is my shepherd ... he restoreth my soul." But, as contemporary literature shows, such privilege was thought of as only for the righteous. The description of their perfect enjoyment of such friendship, after all sinners had been destroyed, was frequent in the Jewish writings:

> "And the righteous shall be in the light of the sun,
> And the elect in the light of eternal life : ...
> And they shall seek the light and find righteousness with the Lord of Spirits :
> There shall be peace to the righteous in the name of the Eternal Lord.
> And after this it shall be said to the holy in heaven
> That they should seek out the secrets of righteousness, the heritage of faith :
> For it has become bright as the sun upon earth,
> And the darkness is past."—*Book of Enoch*, lviii. 3-5.

But a God who could thus be in communion with some human beings and yet destroy the great majority of their fellows has always been a cause of stumbling and offence to the humane. The more zealously and clear-sightedly an avenging God is worshipped, the more religion dehumanizes.[1] The more man by the

[1] The dehumanizing process may be seen in the persecuting activities of powerful sects and the anti-social exclusiveness of weak sects. In Christendom all instances of persecution and exclusiveness would seem to be due to the acceptance of, and emphasis on, Jewish eschatology.

SUMMARY

love of God becomes humane, the more he has always slurred over or explained away this doctrine of divine destructiveness. Again, the difficulty of deciding by what means or character the good could justly be raised so far above their fellows has produced in religious thought unending subterfuge and division. I believe that Jesus cut this Gordian knot by the sword of the Spirit when he said that none were righteous, but God was the friend and Saviour of all.

I have tried to show that, starting with the prophetic conception of a coming Golden Age or reign of God into which all nations should gather, Jesus, *first*, set before his followers exactly what every reformer to-day acknowledges to be the great need of humanity—the rational and good-natured co-operation of all men with their neighbours, all classes with each other, all nations with one another. This could only be attained by sublimating the combative instinct into an effort to overcome the evils, moral and physical, which hinder the development of our common humanity. It could only be had by the development of common sense—that is to say, by a reasonable way of looking at what is the common good of all and being guided by that. Individual propaganda of good nature and common sense.

Secondly, Jesus taught that the method of this salvation was the teaching of every man by his neighbour. This suggests why such sayings as that about the mote and the beam were expressed with such extraordinary strength of figure; and why the warnings, "Do not judge; do not condemn; do not be annoyed or call your brother a fool," were coupled with forecasts of the dire results of disobedience to the warning. Alas for the world! alas for the Church! how little has he been heeded! The house has been built upon the sand again and again, and again and again we have seen it fall.

This method of man to man, woman to woman, propaganda was the means whereby the universal salvation became intensely personal, because it was the intensive cultivation of group excellence. It was a responsibility laid on every man, woman and child to sweeten the home, the village, the town—to convert the world by attraction. Clearly this could not be done by any neglect of the proper business of each, but only by excellence and sweetness of spirit. Jesus set the example by beginning to teach and to heal in his own community and, as Luke would have it, in his own village. Can anyone read the passage, Luke vi. 27-42, concerning love to enemies, consideration for neighbours, and the necessity for unassuming and undidactic behaviour, without realizing that Jesus taught that it was only by making his neighbour forgiving as well as himself that each man could be saved? To tempt the neighbour to be thus forgiving, the convert of Jesus had to be "very nice" to that neighbour. This was easy enough while he was a person who was nice to the Jews; but when he was the collector of Roman taxes, the Roman policeman, the Roman civil servant—ask the members of any conquered and oppressed nation if that was easy! Or again, if the neighbour was a brother who had done a bitter wrong, then again it was not easy. But even all this might have been easy in the sense of being easygoing had it not been necessary at the same time to uphold all the principles of truth and equity. Justice is coupled with the love of God: the new righteousness must exceed that of the law. Any breach of righteous behaviour would bring, sooner or

SUMMARY

later, terrible consequences which could not by any means be cancelled or annulled but only overcome of good. Thus we see that the mutual, unconditioned forgiveness of all men, the mutual recognition of the law of moral consequence, was the distinctive method of Jesus.

Thirdly, permeating both the demand for fine fellowship and for the personal dissemination of kindliness, is the practice of God's presence. The prayer of childlike petition, of confiding expectation, is only half of the duty implied by the new doctrine of divine inspiration taught by Jesus. As common as the feeding of children by earthly fathers, so common is God's good gift of the Spirit. The Spirit was given for the asking; and the inspired souls, the children of the kingdom, were to be known by their fruit. Beneficence of life was the test. He that humbly serves mankind receives God within his soul. But, likewise, no man can adequately serve mankind, working for the ideal welfare of the world, without that change of mind, or repentance, that makes him conscious of his dependence upon God for constant revelation and inspiration. "Can the blind lead the blind?" God reveals, even to babes, the wisdom essential to goodness. God gives, for faithful asking, spiritual riches that those who do not ask do not get. "This kind cometh not out but by prayer."

Finally, some motive was needed to make men eager to live with God for God-like ends. The passion of personal love to God, the vision of God that attracts personal love, could alone suffice. The motive which causes men to perform wonders in disregard of all other nterests is always love—love of kindred or country.

<small>The almightiness of God reveals itself in attracting free spirits to the divine life.</small>

THE LORD OF THOUGHT

God had to be seen as the nearest and dearest of kin, and as the whole in which all that was near and dear could safely abide, in order that all the instincts that make for the persistence, the well-being and the protection of the race should be gathered up in such love to Him as would make service natural, the intention of disloyalty impossible, and the renunciation by the will of all that might hinder, a matter of course.

It was such love that Jesus called the " faith " to which God's power is given. He said that God would give this faith, revealing Himself to those who prayed as men pray when they are in need. And some men, looking at Jesus, loved him, and therefore believed his message and coveted the life unto God which he lived. Through him they realized God. He not only taught them what God is, he became at once their symbol for God, the greatest of all symbols because living intensely, loving greatly, dynamic with passionate desire for the welfare of the world.

Jesus died because he would not compromise with a lower thought of God or with the low idea of man implied in an exclusive religion. In his death God revealed Himself as the power which attracts the perfect and glad allegiance of the free. Compared with such power, any force that rules by being able to punish and destroy rebels is as nothing.

It is, of course, not within the scope of this small book to discuss the theology of the Cross. I would only ask the reader to pause here to realize that the power to benefit wicked men and at the same time suffer generously and uncomplainingly at their hands, thus attracting their allegiance, is greater than, and wholly opposed to, the power to crush, torture and destroy.

SUMMARY

To all who know that personal relations are of more account than all the universe besides, belief that God is and is good carries with it belief in the survival of personality after death. This life is not a good gift unless the values of personality survive death. The words of the Epistle of James apply here: "Every good gift and every perfect boon is from above, coming down from the Father of lights, with whom can be no variation, neither shadow that is cast by turning."[1] We need not, then, turn first to any transcendental doctrine to explain the belief that death could not hold or change the soul of Jesus. That the friendship of Jesus for his friends was stronger than death, that so ardent and vivid a personality as his must survive, and be no faint reflection, no pale ghost, but more strong and vivid when set free from material conditions, would be a natural belief to men who lived in theocratic habits of thought. "God is not the God of the dead but of the living."

> "But the souls of the righteous are in the hands of God, . . .
> In the eyes of the foolish they seemed to have died ; . . .
> But they are in peace. . . .
> They shall judge nations, and have dominion over peoples."
> *Wisdom of Solomon*, iii. 1-3, 8.

This is a fragment of Judaic, not Christian writing.

Turning now to history, we find that something certainly happened after the death of Jesus which gave to the depressed and frightened disciples a tremendous impulse of exalted joy and courage. One day we see them a small despised Galilean sect, all their crude hopes shattered, bereaved alike of their dearest friend and

---

[1] James 1 17 Some sound critical opinion still attributes this epistle to the brother of Jesus.

THE LORD OF THOUGHT

of the leader whose prestige gave them what little importance they had, disloyal, terrified, broken. Another day, soon after, we see them an indomitable band, strong with sheer joy in the face of persecuting authority, setting out with unwavering faith to bring joy and comfort and new power to mankind.[1] This much is historic fact, as is also the large result of it upon the world.

What concerns us further here is the undoubted fact that Jesus of Nazareth was believed by the members of the conquering school of his disciples to be living in the unseen a life of great power and glory, in touch with all who trusted him, supplying their spiritual needs; and that through this belief he became, in fact, the most powerful leader whom the Western world has seen. This constituted a triumph for Jesus only in so far as the character and methods believed to be those of the unseen Christ were the same as the character and methods of Jesus when on earth. We can see this by a glance at lesser instances. The Antinomian movements that from time to time founded themselves upon the teaching of St Paul did not vindicate St Paul's doctrine. The excesses and formalism of the followers of St Francis of Assisi, contradicting the very spirit of his evangel, testify only to the power of tendencies which he gave his life to oppose.[2] These cases were no sign of the triumph of the cause they nominally represented, but the reverse. In so far as the Church has taken over the vindictive, exclusive spirit of Judaism, and enthroned these with Jesus in the heavenlies, the victory has been to his opponents, not to Jesus.

---

[1] Cf *The Mind of the Disciples*, by Neville Talbot
[2] See *Life of St Francis*, by Paul Sabatier, latter half of Chapter xv.

SUMMARY

We have seen that the simplicity and the richness of the truth which Jesus brought into the world was concerned with the two ideas of God and of man. These ideas in the mind of Jesus were not blurred in any pantheistic conception, but were distinct, in the sense that, for Jesus, there could be friendship between God and man. Self cannot have friendship with itself: for friendship there is need of one and another or others. God and man were not different in kind, *i.e.* there was kinship between the divine Spirit and each human spirit. We see his conviction of this kinship expressed by Jesus in dispensing with all the common terms in use to suggest divine power in favour of the one term, " Father "; and the great truth was confirmed by the impression Jesus in some way undoubtedly gave his followers, that " Son of Man " and " Son of God " were equivalent terms. Thus the distinction between God and man was so enclosed in the larger unity of kin that the Father could not be conceived as hostile to or abhorring man. The Father's love was the all-inclusive power within which man must live throughout existence, an enclosing sphere beyond which man's soul could no more wander than could a denizen of earth rise above our atmosphere. There is in this conception a sense of proportion strangely at variance with those theocratic schemes of thought which present God as injuring man on account of ill-conduct. The infinite, omnipresent, omnipotent, creative Love, having chosen to give birth to what is little, local and frail, cannot, without contradiction, be thought of as deviating from

THE LORD OF THOUGHT

the course of creative love on account of any use the creature may make of such limited freedom, although the created and finite clearly can only be thought of as acquiring power and transcending its limitations by becoming receptive to the infinite power of the Creator, and only acquiring happiness by becoming obedient to the method of the eternal creation.

The notion that a moral power, which can be thought of as an energy of all good, could vent anger on what is only beginning to be, because of insubordination, is a notion that can only exist when God and man are thought of as, in some sense, on equal terms.

In the days of the prophets even the greatest minds of the Jewish race could do this because their highest conceptions of God were even more limited than ours. God was but super-man. God was thought of as appearing under some imaginable guise, and as acting among things and people with human infirmities of thought and will and feeling, needing, as human rulers need, to support righteousness by penal exactions; needing, as human chieftains need, a following of tribe or army exclusively His own.

But after the time of the prophets new habits of thought had permeated the countries of the Mediterranean basin. In the first place, knowledge was increasing. The world, as man knew it, was becoming wider and more complex; it was becoming more difficult to think of its Creator and ruler as super-man. Secondly, philosophical speculation about the Mind at the back of the universe, the supreme Power, the supreme Reality, had tended to put the pictures of God which abounded in Jewish literature in the same

SUMMARY

class as the images of other mythologies. These could now be conceived as symbols or aspects of what was behind, what was beyond and above the power of human imagination. No nation, however separatist in doctrine, can live in a watertight compartment of thought; a passing word, a scrap of parchment, a rude drawing, is enough to convey to the active mind a new idea to which existing notions must be adjusted. Certainly, in the flux of armies, of trade, of travel, in the period between the Macedonian conquests and the time of Christ, even the home-staying Jew of Palestine —and these were few compared with the Jews of the Dispersion—could not, and did not, lock out the philosophic thought of the Greek world. The genius of the Jew was for poetry rather than philosophy; but we see, during this epoch, the God of his thought retiring into a more distant heaven, because more unapproachable, more unthinkable. As a necessary consequence, Jewish literature of this period abounds in divine agents, mediating between God and man, as over the Empire the imagination of the Gentile was centring devotion and hope upon such divine agents as the Saviour-Gods of the Mystery Religions. Among the Jews devotion turned to such divine emanations or agents as the Angel of the Covenant, the Wisdom, the Word of God, etc.

We need to realize clearly that imagination—the power of representing intuitions or inferences of reason under some concrete mental image—is essential to the human mind. The moment that man realizes that God is beyond man's power to know fully and as He is, he must either give up trying to deal with Him —*i.e.* give up religion—or he must seek to know such aspects of God as may be possible to human thought, and these aspects will be grasped by him through mental images which are symbols. He may think of supreme Power as an energy, like electricity; he may think of supreme Wisdom as a pervasive atmosphere, healing and refreshing; but these images, although without definite shape or colour, are none the less images and symbols.

The advanced religious thought of the Mediterranean world at the time of Christ was coming to believe that God must be thought of as supreme Power and Goodness, and that to His Goodness must belong Love and Truth and Beauty. To this Greek philosophy and the Roman genius for order and proportion in things social had contributed; but the most notable contribution had come from the ethical insight of the Jewish prophets. The Greek translation of the Old Testament was very widely read by serious Pagans. Everywhere there were desire and questioning. The world of the first century was crying out for some adequate common symbol or manifestation of a transcendent God. Agreement in common language and common ideas had become possible, and as long as there was disagreement in religious thought, religious energy was dissipated in intensifying national or class distinctions rather than conserved for the search for goodness and truth. Everywhere men were trying, according to the measure of their insight, to find the right idea of God.

We know that whenever a great genius has appeared in history, lesser minds have been at work on the problems that he solves. It was the hour best fitted to produce a genius in religious thought. In this little

SUMMARY

book, while attempting to show that Jesus Christ gave a wholly new conception of power and of goodness, it has been desirable to keep entirely within the bounds of history for my facts. It is not within my scope to discuss whether, in transcending the separation caused by death as other men do not transcend it and making himself known to men as still living and teaching though invisible, he offered himself to the world as an immortal manifestation and agent of God. I would only suggest that the world was then in desperate need, not only of an ideal interpretation of goodness and truth, but of just such a living symbol or mediator or agent as the early Church believed Jesus to be.

We have seen that, while there is reason to believe that Jesus gave his own unique interpretation of power and goodness, the Church has sought to glorify both God and Christ by ascribing to Deity a character to which Jesus laid no claim, and which he did not attribute to God, a character fashioned out of cruder and more primitive human notions. Yet the Church has passed on to each generation of Christians the belief that in the unseen world the same Jesus who lived on earth is still adequate helper, guide and friend to those who seek him, captain of souls, urging on his votaries to do and die for the salvation of the whole world and the bringing about of an earthly paradise. But this belief in him is the treasure of the humble. It is not vouched for by the theology which sets him upon the throne of the apocalyptic God, or identifies him with the Messiah as agent of the world's final doom who at best can attract to his offered salvation only such fortunate souls as have received the proper initiation.

THE LORD OF THOUGHT

If we think of the majesty of God as opposed to, or different from, the humility Jesus exemplified; if we think of the power of God as in no way subject to limitations of life as Jesus was subject; if we think of the glory of God as a blinding magnificence which did not shine forth in the gentleness of Christ; if we think of God's holiness as something opposed to friendly association with sinners—then to call Jesus God is rather to vindicate the Judaism that opposed him than to be loyal to the spiritual illumination he offered.

But if by divine transcendence we mean an eternal creative Love which, entering by lowly doors, is able to develop beauty and truth and goodness in all that is—such a belief may bring us near to the heart of " the truth as it is in Jesus."

We can only be depressed by current controversies concerning the Godhead, but if Jesus, in his participation in human joys, in his fellowship with the faulty and the fallen, in his humorous criticism of the righteous, in his stern denunciation of the self-righteous, in his love of fine character, in his passion for truth and the welfare of men, in his power to cure the ills of mind and body, in his dependence on human friendship, in his majestic victory over defeat—if in all this the historic Jesus is the true and living revealer of the transcendent God, how great is our hope!

PART III
CRITICAL VERIFICATION

CHAPTER XVIII

WHAT DO WE KNOW OF THE TEACHING OF CHRIST?

How far is the view taken in the preceding chapters consistent with the record of the teaching of Christ as preserved to us in the Gospels? In answering this question we are bound to distinguish between the record and the actual teaching. For by general consent the Gospels cannot be regarded as giving us the *ipsissima verba* of Christ himself. We have indeed to allow for several stages in the growth of the record: *The teaching and the record.*

1. The original teaching as given on various occasions.

2. The impression made on diverse groups of hearers (not necessarily altogether identical with the meaning intended by the speaker), the modification of this impression as time went on, and the attempt to convey it to others by word of mouth. This is the stage known as "oral tradition."

3. The earliest written records, whether in Aramaic or Greek. The most important of these is the document known as "Q." The symbol comes from the German *Quelle* or Source; it is simply a piece of shorthand, used for convenience, and we might equally well use S (from the English "Source"). It stands for the supposed document from which is derived the

THE LORD OF THOUGHT

matter common to Matthew and Luke but not found in Mark.[1]

4. Finally we come to our existing Gospels.

It is obvious that in all these stages, however carefully and reverently the words of the Master were preserved, there is danger of misunderstanding, modification and the intrusion of alien elements. The differences found in our present Gospels, even in recording such things as the Lord's Prayer, the Beatitudes, or the words used at the Last Supper, prove that changes in the tradition did occur, and the fact that they are found in sayings belonging to a particular occasion, *e.g.* the reply to the High Priest at the Trial,[2] shows that we cannot always account for them by supposing that Jesus was in the habit of repeating his teaching in slightly different forms. No doubt this did sometimes actually happen, and it may explain

---

[1] When we analyze the three first Gospels we find in all three a good deal of material which is in substance common to all this is derived from Mark But Matthew and Luke have also a further series of passages in common, mainly, though not entirely, concerned with the teaching of Christ It is generally held that they drew this from a document (Q), possibly written by the Apostle Matthew. On this view it contained all the non-Marcan matter which is found in both Matthew and Luke, though we cannot tell how much more it contained, since parts of it may have been reproduced by either Matthew or Luke alone.

Canon Streeter has lately suggested (*Hibbert Journal*, xx No 1) that we can discover in the Third Gospel an earlier document, probably written by Luke himself, which consisted of (*a*) the sections of Q which he incorporates, (*b*) the large amount of matter peculiar to this Gospel These two elements really make a complete Gospel; subsequently Luke added to this the Marcan sections This view seems very probable and has been received with great favour. If it is true, it is of great significance for our purpose, since the peculiar matter of Luke is then very early in date, and the apocalyptic elements in it are very slight It is therefore an important confirmation of the hypothesis that these elements did not form part of the authentic teaching of Jesus. See p 293 ff. A fuller statement of Canon Streeter's view will be found in his book, *The Four Gospels*.

[2] See below, p 290

THE TEACHING OF CHRIST

some of the variations, but it is clear from a comparison of the Gospels that in most cases these are to be accounted for as modifications which have taken place in the course of tradition. One important cause of such modifications would be the unconscious influence of contemporary ideas and beliefs, whether the ideas of Judaism inherited by the first disciples, or the desire for immediate escape from a lost world, or the later ecclesiastical conceptions which developed with the growth of the Christian Church and of Christian doctrine. Criticism has recognized fully the influence of this last class of ideas on the Gospels; our hypothesis is that we have also to allow for the influence of the two first, and especially of the ideas inherited from apocalyptic.

Having said so much, we must beware lest we exaggerate the extent to which the teaching has been altered and jump to the desperate conclusion that we can know nothing of what Jesus really taught. The teaching as preserved in the Synoptists has in its main outlines a consistency and originality which is the guarantee of its authenticity. Even if—which is far from being the case—we could not feel any absolute certainty about the genuineness of any single saying, taking them one by one, this would not mean that the teaching as a whole could be regarded as a later invention attributed to Jesus by the pious imagination of his followers. There must have been a model to suggest imitations, a nucleus round which accretions could gather. And the most certain parts of this nucleus are the original, the unexpected, the half-understood and the little practised elements, about which there was no particular controversy in the early

[margin: There is a nucleus on which we can depend.]

days of the Church and which it was not to the interest of any particular party to emphasize. This is not to say that everything which might conceivably be ascribed to any such controversial influence is necessarily a later addition; but it is a sound principle of criticism that features which cannot be so accounted for are most likely to be genuine, and that features which can be explained in this way, and are also inconsistent with what is clearly original, may well be unauthentic.

<small>Is our method subjective?</small> It is, of course, often argued that we have no right to reject as interpolations anything with which we may not agree, when our MSS. give us no ground for doing so, and that such criticism is purely subjective. It should, however, be understood that, except in a few cases, it is not argued that a passage the authenticity of which is disputed was not part of the Gospel as originally published. The modifications or additions had been already made, or were made by the writer of the Gospel himself. Further, it is misleading to speak of "interpolations," unless in a few special cases. The term suggests a fixed record of Christ's teaching, such as might come from a modern reporter, to which additions were made more or less deliberately. But, as we have seen, we have to do with a long-drawn-out process during which alterations crept in almost insensibly as the teaching passed from one to another. Nearly all scholars recognize this as a fact, and if so, it must be our duty to recover so far as we can the original form of the teaching. One means of doing this is the careful comparison of the Gospels by which we attempt to reconstruct the original sources which lie behind them. Another is the general

THE TEACHING OF CHRIST

criterion of consistency with the nucleus and general spirit of Christ's teaching. This last may be to some extent "subjective," in that each reader must form his own judgment on historical and religious grounds as to what Christ really stood for and how far his view of life and of God was really of a piece.

But wherever we find a general consensus of opinion as to what was characteristic of Christ, the standard ceases to be "subjective" in any depreciatory sense. When we read in the apocryphal *Gospel of Thomas* (chapters iii., iv.) stories of the child Jesus turning a companion who annoys him into a withered tree, or causing the death of another by a word, we do not need elaborate discussions of the date and authenticity of the document from which they come. We reject them at once because we are sure that Jesus did not do such things.

Among the original elements in the sayings of Jesus none is more important or more certain than the teaching about the Fatherhood of God. It meant putting God in a new light, and consistency with this may well serve as a touchstone for other elements of the narrative and teaching. *The originality of the teaching of the Fatherhood of God.*

We are indeed sometimes told, and we have been told lately, that there is nothing original in this central doctrine, that "the Fatherhood of God is a characteristically Jewish doctrine, found in equal abundance in the Old Testament and in Rabbinic literature. . . . Until controversy with Polytheism began, there is no sign that Christianity ever claimed to be a new message as to the nature of God. The God of Jesus and of his disciples is identical with the God of the Jews."[1]

[1] Lake and Foakes-Jackson, *The Beginnings of Christianity*, Part I p. 401 ff.

THE LORD OF THOUGHT

But what are the facts? It is true that we do occasionally find in the Old Testament and in the Apocrypha general references to God as Father: "I will be to him a father," "Like as a father pitieth his own children"; or we read in the *Book of Wisdom* (xiv. 3), "Thy providence, O Father, guideth it along." *Ecclesiasticus* (xxiii. 1, 4) twice has a prayer beginning "O Lord, Father and Master of my life." And in Rabbinic literature, though *always* of a date *later* than the first century A.D., God is spoken of as "Heavenly Father" or "Our Father in Heaven." But in all such cases this is only one among many names for God, one among many conceptions of His nature and relationship to man, nor is it ever a common name We find strings of titles, and what most of them emphasize is the power or the aloofness of God. Look at these from 3 *Maccabees*: "Lord, Lord, King of the Heavens and sovereign of all creation, Holy among the Holy ones, only ruler, almighty"; "King of great power, most high, almighty God, who governest all creation with loving-kindness." No doubt among such titles the term "Father" is found, as it is once found in this very book, but how much else besides!

It may then be true that Jesus did not invent the title. In a limited sense he "adopted this term for God from the popular usage of his time."[1] But when we look at the Gospels, what do we find? Jesus simply puts aside all these other titles of previous and contemporary religious thought and concentrates entirely on the single phrase "Father." He appears never to have used the terms "Almighty," "Lord of Hosts." "Master" and "King" occur once (Matt.

<small>The avoidance of other titles by Jesus.</small>

---

[1] Dalman, *Words of Jesus*, p. 188.

THE TEACHING OF CHRIST

v. 35; xxiii. 8); even "Holy," apart from its special application to the Holy Spirit, is not used of God in the Synoptists.[1] The prayer in the Garden of Gethsemane and the Lord's Prayer begin with the simple "Father"; in the Lord's Prayer there is even some doubt about the additional words "which art in Heaven." To the Jew it seems to have been little more than an accident which term he happened to use of God; to Jesus there was just one name and no other.

Again, as is well known, there had grown up among the Jews a habit of avoiding any direct reference, not merely to the name "Jehovah" but even to God Himself, outside prayer or worship. They referred to Him by phrases such as "The Holy One," "The Blessed," "The Highest," or else substituted evasive terms such as "Heaven," "The Glory" or "The Word." This habit, due to a mistaken reverence and a sense of the aloofness of God, is rarely, if ever, followed by Jesus[2]; the term "Kingdom of Heaven," found only in Matthew, is a very doubtful exception. He is not afraid to speak of God directly. Dalman remarks that "all three Synoptists record the use by Jesus of 'God,'" and finds this "surprising."[3] He questions whether "they reproduce the original form of what was said by Jesus."[4] The doubt is quite

Jesus is not afraid of speaking of God directly.

---

[1] It is found in John xvii 11, "Holy Father."
[2] For a possible exception in the reply to the High Priest (Mark xiv. 62) see below, p. 291, cf also Luke vi. 35. It is not necessary to consider whether the exceptions noted here and on the preceding page represent the actual words of Jesus. Even if they are all original, they do not upset the principle of his normal use of the term "Father." This is found 4 times in Mark, 45 times in Matthew, and 17 times in Luke
[3] *Words of Jesus*, p. 194.
[4] P. 196.

needless. It is entirely in accordance with the spirit of Jesus that he finds no difficulty in speaking quite directly and simply of God and encourages his followers to do the same. To him God is not a dangerous, distant, unaccountable Being, to whom it is only safe or reverent to refer with great reserve and by way of allusion. He is just our God, our Father, and Paul rightly feels that in the fearless intimacy of the prayer " Abba, Father " he is expressing the spirit of Jesus.

Here, we may justly claim, is real originality. Christ does not merely shift the emphasis, making the idea of fatherhood more prominent than it was before. By his concentration on this one term he showed that he had a new conception of God. And just because there can be nothing which is more far-reaching in its influence on the life and thought of mankind than a true idea of what God is like, we are abundantly justified in finding in this new conception the heart of his revelation. Much else there is, but it all follows in the end from this postulate.

The ideas suggested by the term father may and do differ. In some stages of society this term brings to the mind the *patria potestas*, an absolute and undisputed authority which controls the action and the very life of the child in small things as well as in great, which may mean the giving of a daughter in marriage to one she has never seen, or an arbitrary right of corporal punishment, even of death, which no one may challenge. But it is obvious that this legalistic conception of fatherhood was not in our Lord's mind. His use of the idea carries with it reverent love and joyful obedience on the side of man, and on the side of

THE TEACHING OF CHRIST

God His unwearied affection for the erring son, His watchful protection and His unstinted giving of the best. It means not the degradation or the parody of fatherhood but its ideal. God's is the perfect Fatherhood from which all earthly fatherhood is derived.[1]

Christ, then, brought to the world for the first time in its clearness the good news of the Fatherhood of God. The question before us is whether with this he combined other conceptions of God. Did he sometimes present Him as the omnipotent King who punishes and avenges, who in the last resort falls back from the attractive compulsion of love to the threatening force of a destructive judgment? Those who see no inconsistency between the two sides will answer without hesitation; the Gospels, they urge, no less than the Apocalypse, point to the wrath of the Lamb. But those who feel that the attempt to combine the two is " to walk with unequal legs," must, as already pointed out, choose between two alternatives. Either Jesus was not clear-sighted enough to see the contradiction, but retained the inherited and contemporary ideas side by side with his own new vision; or the apparent contradiction does not belong to the original teaching, but is an accretion which has crept in during some of those various stages through which Christ's words passed before they reached their present form. In the chapters which follow we shall consider which of these alternatives is the more probable from the point of view of a critical study of the Gospels.

_{Had Christ a consistent idea of God?}

---

[1] See Eph iii 15, "The Father from whom every family in earth and heaven is named." The word for family is πατριά, derived from πατήρ (father)

CHAPTER XIX

ANGER AND PUNISHMENT

A DISTINCTION has been drawn in earlier chapters between consequence and punishment, the former denoting the working out of a law of retribution which, as part of the scheme of a moral universe, represents the general purpose of God, while the latter suggests a definite penalty inflicted on the individual *ad hoc* by a personal agent who wills this particular thing. In considering the teaching of the Gospels it will be important to bear this distinction in mind.

Is God angry? We may first note a very significant feature which affects the New Testament as a whole. God loves, but we are never told in the New Testament that He is angry. We read indeed of the wrath of God (or of the Lamb, Rev. vi. 16), but this phrase, or more often the wrath alone, is used in a curious impersonal way which suggests "a process directed or controlled by a person" rather than an emotion in the mind of that person.[1] It is the law of consequence, not the personal anger of God. We may instance the passage in Rom. i. 18 ff., where "the wrath of God" is revealed in the consequences of sin to which God leaves the sinner. It is this principle of deterioration and moral

---

[1] See on this whole question the admirable treatment by C. H Dodd in *The Meaning of Paul for To-day*, p. 62.

ANGER AND PUNISHMENT

blindness which constitutes the real horror of sin.[1] While, then, the Old Testament has no hesitation in speaking quite simply of God as being angry or wroth, the follower of Christ feels instinctively that he must avoid the expression.

To turn to the Synoptic Gospels, the impression that Jesus taught the wrath of God and His personal action in punishment is chiefly derived from the parables. It has already been suggested [2] that the " King " or " Master " in many of them is not to be understood as referring to God personally and directly, but is, as we should say now, a kind of personification of consequence. The parable is an illustrative story, not an allegory where the figures and incidents correspond exactly to something else. As these things happen in the earthly story, so do things happen in the realm of the spirit; but it does not follow that what is done as a direct personal action by the potentate in the parable is to be thought of as done in exactly the same way by God Himself. In view of the fact that anger and punishment are not attributed to God in the ordinary teaching of Christ, we are justified in refusing such an interpretation of the parables unless it is forced upon us. On the other hand, Christ did wish to emphasize beyond the possibility of mistake the unrelenting law of consequence and retribution; it was necessary that it should be presented vividly and dramatically, and it may well be that one of the reasons for his choice of the parabolic method was

Parables are not allegories.

---

[1] Cf 2 Thess ii 11, 12   In the same way in the Septuagint God is never the object of the verb "to appease," as He is in Pagan writers; there is an instinctive feeling that in the last resort He does not need to be appeased.

[2] See p. 172.

that it enabled him to teach the working of consequence in this vivid way without attributing it to the personal action of the Father.

<small>The danger of pointing the moral.</small> In examining the parables it is also important to distinguish between the core of the parable and the explanations or comments which seem often to have been added in tradition or by the evangelists themselves. Such comments are particularly common in the First Gospel,[1] and they nearly always have the object of emphasizing the aspect of punishment. The preacher or catechist in repeating the parable would always want to bring out the moral, and the moral might not always be precisely that intended by Christ. And this additional comment, when often repeated, would easily come to be attached to the parable itself as though it were part of the original.

<small>Matthew's additions.</small> The double phrase about "outer darkness" and "weeping and gnashing of teeth" occurs as such a comment in Matthew's versions of the Wedding Feast and the Talents (Matt. xxii. 13; xxv. 30); it is absent from the corresponding Lucan parables of the Great Supper and the Pounds. The second half of the phrase also occurs at the close of Matthew's parables of the Tares (xiii. 42, in the explanation), the Net (xiii. 50) and the Faithful and Unfaithful Servants (xxiv. 51).

The whole phrase is found in the prediction of the exclusion of the sons of the Kingdom (*i.e.* the Jews), which follows the healing of the Centurion's Servant (Matt. viii. 12). Luke has the latter part—the only

---

[1] This Gospel was written for Jewish Christians, and we are not surprised to find the influence of Jewish apocalyptic far stronger here than in the other Gospels. The following pages will supply many examples.

ANGER AND PUNISHMENT

occurrence of the phrase in his Gospel—in a different context (xiii. 28): "There shall be the weeping and gnashing of teeth when ye shall see Abraham and Isaac and Jacob and all the prophets in the kingdom of God, and yourselves cast forth without." Here the application is different; it denotes regret for lost opportunity, with no reference to future or eternal punishment.

Particularly instructive is the comparison of the two pairs of parables: (*a*) the Wedding Feast and the Great Supper; (*b*) the Talents and the Pounds. Both of these occur in different versions in Matthew and Luke.[1]

(*a*) The Lucan parable (xiv. 15) is a straightforward story of the refusal of an invitation by those originally invited and its acceptance by others, ending with the comment, "None of those men which were bidden shall taste of my supper." *The parable of the Great Feast*

Matthew's version (xxii. 1) adds the ill-treatment and killing of the servants, with the result that the king sends his armies and burns their city (the reference is clearly to the national disaster of the fall of Jerusalem); it also includes the episode of the man without the wedding garment. Archdeacon Allen[2] holds that this is the conclusion of another parable, in which a rejected guest is dismissed the palace. We have already noted the other addition of the comment about outer darkness and gnashing of teeth. In Matt. xxii. 14 there is the final moral, quite unsuitable to the latter part dealing with the wedding

---

[1] It will make no difference to our argument whether it be held that both versions are derived from Q, or that Matthew and Luke have drawn them from different sources.

[2] *International Critical Commentary*, ad loc.

THE LORD OF THOUGHT

garment: "Many are called, but few chosen." It does not appear that this suits the original parable either, since those finally admitted would seem to be as many as those who rejected the invitation. In any case there would seem to be at least three features in Matthew's version which do not belong to the original.[1]

The Talents

(*b*) We have also already noted the addition of the conventional comment in Matt. xxv. 30 at the close of the parable of the Talents. But in this case it is Luke who makes the chief modifications (xix. 11 ff.). He adds the features of the nobleman going into a far country to receive a kingdom, the counter-embassy of his subjects, and the command on the part of the new-made king to slay his opponents before his face (xix. 27). This last verse comes in as a complete surprise after the apparent close of the parable [2]; if it and verse 14 be omitted we have a quite straightforward parable, running parallel to that found in Matthew. The additions seem intended to bring out the parallel between Archelaus who went to Rome to receive a kingdom and Christ who ascended to his Father in heaven, the continued refusal of the Jews to accept him as King, and their imminent destruction at the second coming. We can indeed almost hear the catechist making up the naive story implied in this subsidiary parable, drawing on his knowledge of what happened in the case of one of the Herods, and

---

[1] Dr Stanton, speaking of this parable, says: "I do not think it can be denied that it is easier to suppose that the special features in St Matthew were added to the original form, than that the original form contained them and was stripped of them, so as to give the form we find in St Luke" (*The Gospels as Historical Documents*, II. p. 340).

[2] Montefiore (*The Synoptic Gospels*, ad loc.) and others regard this verse as an addition.

ANGER AND PUNISHMENT

pointing the moral of what, in his view, Christ would do on his return.

At any rate, when we examine these two pairs of parables, we can see how a simple original has been modified and complicated, and we note the significance of the fact that the additions all have the object of emphasizing the idea of punishment. It is clear that the destruction of enemies was an obsession to that generation, and that additions suggesting this were made to parables which had originally no such reference.

In the parable of the Tares (Matt. xiii. 24-30, 36-43) The Tares. the whole explanation is probably a later addition. It is separated from the parable itself by several verses, and is represented as given in private to the disciples. This may be taken to imply that the explanation was not known in the earliest tradition and suggests why it had hitherto remained unknown. It is full of " the crude and fierce imagery of Jewish Apocalyptic thought," and " can hardly have emanated from Jesus."[1] It turns the parable into an allegory, attempting to find the exact equivalent to every feature, in a way which seems quite alien to the general method of Christ. The original warned the hearers that as some would not receive the message at all (see the preceding parable of the Sower), so even those who received it would include good and bad. The disciples must rest content with this situation till the end, which is briefly described in imagery proper to the setting of the story; the later explanation

---

[1] Winstanley, *Jesus and the Future*, p. 150 Note also that the explanatory section represents Jesus as speaking of himself as Son of man in a clearly Messianic sense, which he certainly did not do at this early stage of his ministry, if indeed at all See below, p. 279.

THE LORD OF THOUGHT

expands this into the terms of a definite apocalyptic scheme.

The Unjust Judge. In the parable of the Unjust Judge (Luke xviii. 1-8) we have a case where it is clearly impossible to say that the central figure (" an unjust judge who fears not God nor regards man ") is God Himself. The teaching is the need of perseverance in prayer, as in the parable of the Friend at midnight. The application that God will " avenge his elect who cry to him day and night " seems to reflect the questionings which arose in the Church owing to the delay in the Coming, and is probably not original. It encourages patience on the ground that God will soon punish the persecutors of the faithful. As has been shown, this is a frequent feature of the apocalyptic literature. In the New Testament it occurs in 2 Thess. i. 4 ff., and constantly in the book of Revelation. See especially Rev. vi. 9, where the souls of those who had been slain for the word of God and for the testimony which they held, cry from beneath the altar, " How long, O Master, the holy and true, dost thou not judge and avenge our blood on them that dwell on the earth ? " But it is not easy to read the Sermon on the Mount and believe that Jesus encouraged this temper of mind.

Passing from the parables, we may consider certain other outstanding Gospel passages often taken as confirming the doctrine of punishment.

1 Sayings common to Mark and Q.

The sin against the Holy Ghost. The passages about the unforgivable sin have always been a difficulty to preacher and reader alike, just on the ground that they cannot be understood in a way which is consistent with the general tenor of Christ's teaching. The versions of the whole saying (Mark iii. 28; Matt. xii. 31; Luke xii. 10) vary considerably

ANGER AND PUNISHMENT

and the question of their relation is complicated; it seems to have been recorded in different forms in Mark and Q. It is probable that Luke follows Q rather than Mark, and that Matthew, as usual, combines both. W. C. Allen, Harnack and Streeter, all arguing on purely literary grounds and with no desire to eliminate or tone down references to punishment, agree that the Lucan form of the saying is nearest the original, and this is simply "shall not be forgiven him," with no reference to eternal punishment such as is found in the other versions. Christ is speaking of the heart which refuses to recognize the good when presented to it, and so cannot open itself to the divine forgiveness. It is a solemn statement of inevitable consequence, which must follow on certain states of mind so long as they remain, not a statement that certain sins are excluded from the range of the divine forgiveness.

"If thy hand or foot offend thee, etc." (Mark ix. 43; Matt. xviii. 8; Matt. v. 29 [Q]). This is clearly consequence; what a man makes of himself persists, even when he enters "into life"; there is no question of God cutting off his hand or foot as a punishment.

"Offending" the little ones (Mark ix. 42; Matt. xviii. 6; Luke xvii. 1); cf. the saying to Judas (Mark xiv. 21). Offences must come, but the personal responsibility of those who bring them remains. The result is a deterioration of their character, so terrible that death were a better fate.

Throughout Q there is a constant stress on consequence with a marked absence of any idea that God Himself punishes. "With what judgment ye judge" (Matt. vii. 2), "the broad way leading to destruction"

2. Passages probably derived from Q.

243

THE LORD OF THOUGHT

(vii. 13), the good and bad tree (vii. 16; xii. 33; Luke vi. 43), the houses built on the rock and the sand (Matt. vii. 24), "the blind leading the blind" (xv. 14)—these all express in one way or another the warning given to a world where effect follows cause.

Matthew's treatment of the good and bad tree in vii. 16 is instructive. He adds, as so often, an editorial comment, derived in this case from the teaching of the Baptist (see Matt. iii. 10), "Every tree that bringeth not forth good fruit is hewn down and cast into the fire," thus bringing out the ideas of punishment and destruction rather than of simple consequence.

"More tolerable for Sodom and Gomorrha, etc." (Matt. x. 15; Luke x. 12). Here Christ seems to be speaking of the result of national folly on a nation, not of an external sentence which is to be passed by a judge on a city for something it has done long ago.

"Fear him." "Fear him who is able to destroy both soul and body in hell" (Matt. x. 28); or "Fear him who after he hath killed hath power to cast into hell" (Luke xii. 5). On the view taken by most commentators that the object of the fear is God, this is the one passage from Q which speaks of Him as destroying and punishing by His own personal action. But in view of the general trend of Christ's teaching it is far more probable that the reference is to the devil or the power of evil, which does ultimately destroy body and soul. In the following verses Jesus describes the Father as essentially the Saviour, the protector even of the sparrows.[1]

"The house swept and garnished" (Matt. xii. 43; Luke xi. 24). Here is a clear statement of the conse-

[1] See above, p. 173 Cf Heb 11 14, *the Devil* has the power of death

ANGER AND PUNISHMENT

quence not merely of sin, but of a state of mind which contents itself with a passive and negative attitude towards life; the heart of such a one is in the end invaded by "seven other spirits worse than the first," and this is its punishment. But obviously God is not thought of as sending the spirits as a direct judgment.

The Woes on the Pharisees (Matt. xxiii.; Luke xi. 42). This is a warning of inevitable consequence coming upon certain classes as the result of their attitude towards life; the "woe" is a statement, not a curse or a prayer for vengeance. This is especially clear in Luke; Matthew, as we should expect, is fuller; his most significant addition is verse 33, "Ye serpents, ye offspring of vipers, how shall ye escape the judgment of hell?" This is practically taken over from the teaching of the Baptist; see Matt. iii. 7; and, if we are right in contrasting the teaching of the Baptist and the teaching of Jesus, it is not in place here. The final issue is the national disaster when the blood of the martyrs from Abel to Zechariah " shall come upon this generation "—so Matthew. Luke twice has the more personal " shall be required of this generation "; Harnack prefers the Matthean phrase as more Semitic.[1]

Warnings of national destruction.

" As it was in the days of Noah, etc." (Matt. xxiv. 37-41; Luke xvii. 26-37). Though this occurs in "the Little Apocalypse" (see p. 288), it probably comes from Q. We should note the marked reticence of the passage in contrast with similar pictures from the apocalyptic books. God is not represented as the agent of punishment or as avenging. The doom is

[1] *Spruche und Reden Jesu*, p. 73 (Eng tr, *The Sayings of Jesus*, p 103)

THE LORD OF THOUGHT

the inevitable result of previous folly and unpreparedness. This also holds good of the lament over Jerusalem (Matt. xxiii. 37; Luke xiii. 34), and the prediction of its fall (Luke xix. 41); it is most significant that none of these passages say that *God* will destroy it. In view of the fact that this would be the natural way of putting it at the time, we have a right to argue with some confidence that Christ deliberately avoided it.

3. Marcan passages.

Most of these have already been discussed under previous heads; only two remain.

The purpose of parables (Mark iv. 12 and parallels). Christ says that he speaks in parables " *that* seeing they may see and not perceive, etc." The explanation is recognized as a real difficulty, and many critics hold that the words cannot, as they stand, have been spoken by Jesus. In any case, it will be agreed that he cannot have *desired* the increasing blindness of the Jews; his attitude is, " How often would I have gathered thy children." The meaning of the saying, whether authentic or not, must be that blindness is the necessary consequence of sin, not that Christ wished to bring it about. The distinction between purpose and result (" in order that " as opposed to " so that ") was not very clearly marked in Hebrew or Aramaic, and in the later Greek represented in the New Testament the particle ἵνα was used in a more general way to express result and not purpose.[1] Hence Matthew's version (" because [ὅτι] seeing they see not ") probably gives the right meaning.

The cursing of the fig tree (Mark xi. 13, 20 ff.; Matt. xxi. 19; not in Luke). This again has always pre-

[1] See Moulton, *Grammar of New Testament Greek*, p 206

ANGER AND PUNISHMENT

sented a difficulty, not only from the strangeness of the miracle but from its apparent inconsistency with Christ's character. There are two possible explanations: (*a*) that the story is a mistaken dramatization of the parable of Luke xiii. 6; (*b*) that when Christ failed to find the figs he expected, he saw the signs of death in the tree and made a statement that no one would eat of it again. This was changed into a "curse," as Peter calls it (Mark xi. 21), "No one eat of thee." In either case the lesson is the same as that of the Lucan parable—the inevitableness of national doom where there are no fruits of righteousness.

The fact that the incident as related in Mark connects very badly with the subsequent sayings about the power of faith and of prayer suggests that the tradition has somehow become confused.

The teaching of the New Testament on the subject of hell has already been dealt with by the present writer at some length in the article "The Bible and Hell," published in the volume of Essays, *Immortality*, edited by Canon Streeter. I have there tried to show that in the New Testament in general there is far less about future punishment than is usually supposed. The stress on it is practically confined to a single group of books, Matthew, 2 Thessalonians, 2 Peter, Jude and Revelation. At first sight these books may not seem to have much in common, but they are connected by the fact that in them the influence of apocalyptic ideas is specially marked; they may therefore be regarded from this point of view as "a group." All of them derive their language about punishment after death from a common source, extraneous to the teaching of Jesus. For it is from

Hell.

THE LORD OF THOUGHT

the earlier Jewish apocalyptic books that the idea of future punishment really comes. It is there connected quite unmistakably with the very human desire for vengeance on the enemies of the nation, regarded as identical with the enemies of God, or on classes within the nation, whether heretics or apostates, to which the writer is hostile. It also appears that even the passages in which future punishment is stressed, whether in the apocalyptic books or in the New Testament, do not really imply that it is everlasting; as a rule, the language used suggests annihilation or else punishment till the end of an "age."

We are here, however, concerned only with the teaching of Jesus himself as recorded in the Gospels. The belief that he taught an everlasting hell is almost entirely derived from the First Gospel, the Jewish Gospel; this, as we have seen, frequently introduces apocalyptic ideas which are absent from the parallel passages in the other Gospels, and also emphasizes the belief in punishment and an external judgment. The outstanding example is the Matthean parable of the Sheep and Goats (Matt. xxv. 31 ff.), which we shall have to consider further in another connection.[1] We are here concerned primarily with the words, "Depart from me, ye cursed, into the eternal[2] fire which is prepared for the devil and his angels" (verse 41; cf. verse 46). This idea is, of course, a commonplace of apocalyptic, and indeed throughout the whole section apocalyptic influence is at its height. Almost every phrase may be paralleled from the earlier

---

[1] See p 291

[2] The word is "æonian," which means "lasting till the end of an age" (or *æon*); it does not mean "everlasting" in the sense of unending

ANGER AND PUNISHMENT

literature.[1] The features which are peculiar and original are: (1) the stress on sins of omission; (2) Christ's identification of himself with his "little ones," which is also found in Mark ix. 37. If, then, we suppose an original parable of Jesus developing these features, the marked apocalyptic additions may well be due here, as elsewhere, to tradition or to the Evangelist.[2]

To sum up: Jesus emphasizes again and again the truth that man has his lot in a moral universe, the laws of which cannot be evaded; what a man soweth, that shall he also reap. But he markedly avoids the language of contemporary Judaism which represents God as taking a fierce vengeance on evil-doers, whether here or hereafter. A very few phrases are attributed to him which might suggest that he occasionally shared this attitude, but they can all be readily explained as later glosses, added in oral tradition or by the Evangelists. Here, as elsewhere, his conception of God is harmonious and self-consistent.

Summary of the chapter.

---

[1] See *Immortality*, p 196 ff

[2] It is worth noting that popular taste has not shrunk from using the idea of a division into sheep and goats in all kinds of humorous connections, but no reverent person would make a jest out of the words, "Inasmuch as ye have done it unto the least of these my brethren" This instinctive difference of treatment would seem to indicate real insight. Criticism and the religious intuitions of the ordinary man agree more often than is sometimes supposed

CHAPTER XX

TEACHING ABOUT FORGIVENESS

BOTH in the Sermon on the Mount and in the Lucan parables, such as the Pharisee and the Publican, the Lost Sheep, the Coin and the Prodigal Son, the divine forgiveness is represented as always ready; God loves the evil-doer all the time and is actively seeking for him. There is no question about His attitude, and this attitude, with its absence of resentment and anger and with its active purpose to resume the relations which have been broken by the offender, is what we have defined as forgiveness. The second stage is the resumption of these relations, or, in the case of God and man, the inauguration for the first time of that loving intimacy which has always been the purpose of God but has often never been actualized in the experience of the individual. This stage depends on man's response. But God's forgiveness in the deepest sense is there all the time. God takes the initiative, and this initiative does not denote a change of mind or attitude on His part, as though He passed from a prior stage of anger to one where He became ready to forgive.

<small>Forgiveness and reconciliation.</small>

There are one or two features in the Gospel teaching which require some discussion from this point of view.

1. We find prayers for forgiveness, *e.g.* in the

TEACHING ABOUT FORGIVENESS

Lord's Prayer. Does this imply that God does not forgive till He is asked? Once, in the parable of the Publican (Luke xviii. 9), we find the cry "be merciful." Does this mean that there is a stage where God is not merciful, or needs propitiation? The answer will certainly be "No"; and yet, quite apart from any question of the frequency of such language in our Lord's teaching, the cry for forgiveness in whatever phraseology is clearly a deep-seated religious instinct. But if Christ's conception of God be true, must not this mean in the last resort "make me forgivable"; "teach me to open my heart that Thy forgiveness may find its way in"? This would seem to be suggested by the prayer, "Father, forgive them, for they know not what they do." It is really a prayer that their eyes may be opened that they may know, that they may come to their true selves and return to their Father. One of the conditions for the entry of forgiveness is that we should recognize "what we do," confess that we have sinned. But such confession and prayers for forgiveness do not imply that God has to be turned from a previous state of anger in which He is not ready to forgive. Even in human relationships the friend or the father can say, "I forgave you from the first," and yet it is natural, for the sake of the offender, that he should look for an acknowledgment of wrong and a request to be forgiven. It may help us if we realize that after all this particular problem is the same as the problem which arises with regard to all prayer. God knows our necessities before we ask; He is "more ready to give than we to receive"; "His nature and property is always to have mercy and to forgive." It is generally agreed that we ask, not as persuading God

Why pray for forgiveness?

Prayer is not persuading God to relent.

but because the asking represents the spiritual condition on which alone the blessing which He is eager to give can be appropriated by us. We can apply the same principle to prayers for forgiveness. And this will mean that we shall choose our language accordingly. We shall prefer phrases implying confession of sin, or simple prayers for forgiveness and for the deepening of our own repentance, rather than petitions such as " spare us," " be not angry with us for ever," or those reiterated cries for mercy which in their origin undoubtedly implied, and which suggest even now, an offended God who has to be persuaded to change His mind, or has intimated that He is ready to abandon His anger if He is asked in the proper way. We shall never forget that we are addressing, not an arbitrary potentate, but the Father who hastens to greet us when we are yet a long way off.

God's forgiveness and our forgiveness of others.

2. Forgiveness is sometimes represented as dependent on certain conditions, especially on our readiness to forgive others. This is central in the Lord's Prayer, and the same point is emphasized in Mark xi. 25 (" forgive . . . that your Father . . . may forgive you ") ; Matt. vi. 14. We must obviously understand this as referring to the second stage of forgiveness—its acceptance by the offender. The spirit of malice and hatred towards our fellows closes the heart as nothing else, so that we cannot be in that relationship to God in which His love is realized. The parable of the

The Unmerciful Servant.

Unmerciful Servant (Matt. xviii. 23—peculiar to this Gospel) teaches the same general lesson, dramatizing the inevitable working of consequence. But it is one of those cases where the comment of the Evangelist and the desire to produce a rounded allegorical parallel-

TEACHING ABOUT FORGIVENESS

ism seem to have given a wrong turn to the parable. The closing verse, 35, " So shall also my Heavenly Father do unto you, if ye forgive not everyone his brother from your hearts," reads like a later and mistaken comment. The context of the parable is the duty of free and unfettered forgiveness, " till seventy times seven." [1] The attitude of mind which makes this possible cannot be brought about by a threat, " God will deliver you to the tormentors until you have paid all that is due for your sins, unless you forgive your brother from the heart." You can no more get the true spirit of forgiveness out of fear than you can get true charity or loving-kindness out of the principle, " Whatever, Lord, we lend to Thee, repaid a thousand-fold shall be." There is no hint in the Sermon on the Mount that we are to forgive our enemies only if they forgive theirs or if they come to us saying, " We repent." Here, as elsewhere, we must choose between the admission that at certain times Christ fell below the level of his own teaching, and the belief that a single verse tacked on to the end of a parable in a single Gospel may be a well-meant but a misleading gloss. It is just the sort of addition which might be made in order to round off the instruction when the story was told orally.

Once more in Matt. vi. 15 we have the double statement, positive and negative, " For if ye forgive men their trespasses, your Heavenly Father will also forgive you. But if ye forgive not men their trespasses, neither will your Father forgive your trespasses." The

"If ye forgive not."

---

[1] Luke xvii. 3, 4 has the parallel, "If seven times a day he sin against thee and seven times turn again to thee saying, I repent, thou shalt forgive him " We note that the condition of repentance is absent from Matthew.

THE LORD OF THOUGHT

former half is a comment on the clause in the Lord's Prayer and may be understood as already explained. It shows us what we must be like in order to respond to God's forgiveness. But it is a different thing to say that He refuses to forgive us except on this condition, and the negative statement seems to have been added by the Evangelist, or in oral tradition, in order to point the moral as the average teacher would conceive it. In the parallel passage in Mark xi. 25, 26 we can actually trace the process at work. The true text has, "Whensoever ye stand praying, forgive, if ye have aught against anyone; that your Father also which is in heaven may forgive you your trespasses." But some scribes, not satisfied with this, have added in later MSS., "But if ye do not forgive, neither will your Father which is in heaven forgive your trespasses."

The latter verse stands in the A.V., but is omitted and placed in the margin in the R.V., following Westcott and Hort and other editors. It is not found in ℵ or B, the two oldest MSS., or in the Old Syriac. It should be noted that there are in it several verbal differences from Matt. vi. 16, indicating that it has not been added in Mark simply in order to bring the two Gospels into agreement with one another.

In Matt. xviii. 15 ff. ("If thy brother sin against thee go shew him his fault, etc.") forgiveness is not in question; if it were it would contradict the teaching which follows in verse 21 to forgive till seventy times seven. The point is the virtue of helping the brother to recognize his fault, which may best be done by one who has already forgiven him. This he may do privately, or before one or two witnesses, or before "the congregation." Whether our Lord can ever

TEACHING ABOUT FORGIVENESS

have said " let him be unto thee as the Gentile and the publican " is another question. In view of his teaching and attitude to publicans and Gentiles it is not likely that he should have used these terms contemptuously, or as a type of those with whom the Christian ought to have no intercourse.[1]

The sayings about " binding " and " loosing " (Matt. xvi. 19; xviii. 18) are again of doubtful authenticity. But in any case they do not refer to forgiveness of sins, but are technical terms in Rabbinic literature, referring to legislation; they denote the actions which are allowed or prohibited in the community.

[1] Dr Headlam (*The Doctrine of the Church and Reunion*, p 32) defends the authenticity of the words on the ground that when the Gospel was written there were no longer any publicans, and the Gentiles were admitted to the Church; they must therefore be spoken from the standpoint of a Jewish community. But in this case it is more likely that they represent one of those Judaic touches which we find in the First Gospel than that Jesus himself should have suggested that Gentiles or publicans were to be avoided A Jewish Christian might use Gentile in the sense of "unbeliever," and publican might retain its sting even after the class had disappeared

CHAPTER XXI

THE KINGDOM OF HEAVEN

The sovereignty of God. As has already been shown, Jesus came with a new message about God and His relation to man which, if accepted and acted on by the nation to which he first appealed, would establish a new age for the world as a whole. It would sweep away selfishness, strife and war, and would bring in a fundamentally new condition of things, in which man would do the will of the Father completely, as in heaven so on earth. This he called the Kingdom of God, or of Heaven, a term which in Jewish thought meant the sovereignty or rule of God.[1] From one point of view indeed God had reigned from the first, but His reign could only be effective on the one condition that individuals and nations alike should joyfully accept the yoke of the Kingdom and perform the divine will.

Dalman[2] quotes many Jewish sayings to illustrate both these points. "'Before our father Abraham came into the world, God was, as it were, only the king of heaven; but when Abraham came, he made Him to

---

[1] See on this point Dalman, *The Words of Jesus*, p 94 ff The fundamental meaning is "the full realization of the sovereignty of God" Cf also Lake and Foakes-Jackson, *The Beginnings of Christianity*, Part I , p 270 ff

[2] *Ibid.*, p 96 ff.

THE KINGDOM OF HEAVEN

be king over heaven and earth.' Thereafter, at the Red Sea and Sinai, Israel gave allegiance to this sovereignty of God." The proselyte to Judaism "takes upon himself the sovereignty of heaven." A Rabbi of 100 A.D., speaking of the time when all service of other gods shall be abolished, says, "Then shall God alone be absolute in all the world, and His sovereignty will endure for ever and ever." Another ancient prayer runs, "Our King, our God, make Thy name one in Thy world, make Thy sovereignty absolute in Thy world, and make absolute the remembrance of Thee in Thy world."

It must, of course, be recognized that these sayings are of different dates, and probably no one of them goes back quite to the time of Jesus. But this does not mean that he cannot have held a similar conception of the Kingdom, for our documents do not give us evidence of any alternative conception which he might have entertained. In the Old Testament we do not find the phrase "Kingdom of God," but we constantly meet with the ideas of God as King and of His rule.[1] In such cases the reference is to the "sovereignty of God" in much the same sense as in the Rabbinic quotations just given. There is, however, a good deal of uncertainty as to the method by which this sovereignty is to be made a realized fact. It may come either by some kind of missionary enterprise, or by the sudden act of God at a moment of time, in which case its establishment must be regarded as practically coincident with "the Day of the Lord." In many cases the thought of the writer seems to hover between the two.

The sovereignty of God in the Old Testament.

It is indeed strangely suggested by Lake and Foakes-

---
[1] See especially Psa. xciii., xcvi.-c, cxlv.; Dan. vii.

THE LORD OF THOUGHT

The Kingdom of God and missionary enterprise. Jackson [1] that "the realization of the sovereignty of God over all the world was not expected to be the result of missionary enterprise, but of the self-determined act of God." This statement may be generally true of apocalyptic, but it is not true of the Old Testament. The preceding sentence to that just quoted gives a reference to Isa. xlv. 23, which runs, "I have sworn by myself . . . that unto me every knee shall bow, every tongue shall swear." This follows the words, "Look unto me and be ye saved, all the ends of the earth: for I am God and there is none else." The page before, collecting passages relating to the Kingdom, refers to Psa. cxlv.: "One generation shall laud thy works to another and shall declare thy mighty acts" (verse 4); "they shall speak of the glory of thy kingdom, and talk of thy power; to make known to the sons of men his mighty acts, and the glory of the majesty of his kingdom" (verses 11, 12); "my mouth shall speak the praise of the Lord; and let all flesh bless his holy name for ever and ever" (verse 21). These are not bad descriptions of "missionary enterprise"; they envisage the "Kingdom" as coming by the proclamation of those who have known God's goodness, and by the conversion of the Gentiles who hear. Passing beyond references actually given by Dr Lake, we may instance Psa. xcvi, "Tell it out among the heathen that the Lord is king," or the whole of Psa. lxvii.[2]

---

[1] *The Beginnings of Christianity*, p 271.

[2] The list of missionary passages from the Old Testament might be extended, especially by the inclusion of references from the second part of Isaiah, but we have confined ourselves to those which connect the idea of the realization of God's sovereignty with the proclamation of it by His people.

THE KINGDOM OF HEAVEN

The outstanding example in the Old Testament of the realization of the divine sovereignty by an eschatological intervention is Daniel vii., but we have no reason to assume that this conception is decisive for the interpretation of the Gospels. In the first place, we have the alternative conception to which we have just referred, according to which God's rule comes by the co-operation of His people. In the second place, it is important to note that the actual phrase " Kingdom of God " or " Heaven " nowhere occurs in literature earlier than the Gospels; there is one doubtful example in apocalyptic literature. We cannot therefore assume, as is so often assumed, that when Jesus announced that the Kingdom of God was at hand he was using a current apocalyptic idea which could only have meant that the world was coming to an end.[1] All it necessarily implied was that the long-expected sovereignty of God was at last to be realized.

The Kingdom of God not a current apocalyptic phrase.

How was it to come ? That is the real question.

It may be granted in the first place that there was a sense in which Jesus expected the Kingdom to come soon. Surely the new things he had to say about God and the nature of the obedience He asked for had only to be put before men for them to welcome them eagerly ; to those who knew the meaning of love his yoke was easy and his burden light and readily to be accepted, in contrast to those who laid upon men's shoulders things hard to be borne. To himself the truth and the attraction of his conceptions were so

The Kingdom was at hand.

---

[1] It is true that Matt iii 2 represents the Baptist as using the term, but it is not found in this connection either in Mark or Luke, and the view is probably right which regards its attribution to the Baptist as an addition made by Matthew in order to assimilate his teaching to that of Jesus.

THE LORD OF THOUGHT

obvious and clear that, like many teachers, he pictured them as winning their way very quickly; the Kingdom of God was indeed at hand, if men would listen to him. Whether, in fact, it came or not it was in any case there for the taking. No doubt there was to be a period of opposition to the sons of the Kingdom in which, just as he was to suffer himself, so his followers must expect persecution in their turn. But the Kingdom was there in their midst for those who could receive it; it was also near for the world as a whole if the nation would yield to his teaching.

But while in this sense Jesus looked on the Kingdom as near, there were in his teaching two fundamental differences from the popular eschatological view of the future.

It is not destructive. 1. The great *dénouement* which was expected was, as the preceding pages have shown, for many a catastrophe of destruction. But, even taking the Gospels as they stand, the main stress in our Lord's teaching is on the coming of the Kingdom as something positive and beneficent. It is essentially a good news, a gospel. There was indeed the inexorable working of causation by which some would find themselves outside the Kingdom, but it is not a great assize in which God as Judge will give free play to the wrath which His mercy has heretofore restrained. As has been pointed out,[1] when at Nazareth Christ quotes Isa. lxi., the good news of the release of the captives, he closes with the words, "To proclaim the acceptable year of the Lord"; it is not his mission, as it was the mission of the Baptist, to proclaim also "the day of vengeance of our God."

And this is no isolated example. Apocalyptic

---
[1] See p. 95.

THE KINGDOM OF HEAVEN

passages, referring to the Messiah, constantly harp on the destructive side of his work as described in Psa. ii. or Isa. xi. : "He shall bruise them with a rod of iron"; "he shall smite the wicked with the rod of his mouth." These are constantly quoted in the earlier books, but Jesus never applies them to himself, or suggests that this type of vengeance is, or is to be, part of his work, except in some of the more doubtful "Son of Man" passages which we shall examine later. Publicly, indeed, he does not declare himself as Messiah at all until the answer to the High Priest at the trial. The Entry into Jerusalem comes nearest to such a declaration, and it is remarkable that it deliberately looks back to Zech. ix. 9, a passage which explicitly pictures the Messiah as a king of peace, not as conqueror or judge ; he is righteous, having salvation, and lowly.

2. Again, in apocalyptic, the coming of the end was conceived of as solely an act of God, to come when He willed. No doubt His time was not purely arbitrary ; it had some relation to the state of the world. But it was not conditioned by man's readiness to receive it, but rather by his unreadiness. It is to come when wickedness and ungodliness are most near their triumph, when the oppressed righteous remnant sees no hope of good. It is the *deus ex machina*, interposing at the very last and most desperate moment.¹ Now for us it is beyond question a foundation truth that the Kingdom, like all else which is good, is a gift of God. Man cannot create or bring it of himself. But we have also come to realize more clearly the counter-truth that its

An act of God or conditioned by man's response ?

¹ This is true of the apocalyptic literature though, as we have seen, some of the Old Testament writers realized the part the nation might play as missionary agent And later Rabbinic thought rose to the higher conception that if Israel could repent, the Messiah would come.

261

THE LORD OF THOUGHT

coming must depend on man's response. If the consummation which Christ called the Kingdom were indeed simply a great assize in which the good were to be rewarded and the wicked punished, it might come just when God willed. But if it meant the state in which God's will is to be done by men co-operating with Him as free spirits, it could not be imposed from without at a predetermined point of time. It would not be in this sense the Kingdom at all if it came thus. This is now to us a commonplace which is accepted by almost every religious thinker. Why should we take it for granted that it was impossible for Jesus to realize this truth ?

If, then, the coming of the Kingdom is ultimately determined by man's response to God's offer, we must interpret the words " Repent, for the Kingdom is at hand" as including the meaning " Repent and the Kingdom will come." Repentance implied not merely sorrow for past wrong-doing but a complete change of attitude which could only come from the Spirit of God. And though God was always ready to bring the Kingdom, yet it was then near and possible in a special sense just because the presence of Christ implied a unique opportunity for this change of attitude. The cry also meant for the individual " Repent and the Kingdom will have come." It will have come already to you, though not to those who have not repented. As Jesus himself insists, it is like the treasure hid in the field, or the pearl of great price, which each one finds for himself, each in his turn and as it comes to him. It is the process by which we work out our own salvation as God works in us. But it is also corporate in that those who lend themselves whole-heartedly to

THE KINGDOM OF HEAVEN

doing the will of God are bound together in a fellowship which becomes the light of the world, the leaven in the mass. When the light shines as it should, when the leaven does its work, the Kingdom does so far come with power. In oriental imagery it might be said that the Son of Man—the ideal humanity—was manifested, seen at the right hand of God.

The great question, then, which emerges with regard to the philosophy of Jesus is not so much whether he foreshortened the process, seeing the triumphant climax as near in his own piercing vision of the truth and his conviction of the appeal of that truth to men, but whether he saw it as a process at all or merely as a single catastrophic act of God thrust on the world from without. Discussions on the significance of the Kingdom of God in the Gospels turn largely on the question whether it is present or future.[1] It is quite obvious that, if it means the actualization of the rule of God on earth, it must be spoken of, as it is spoken of in the Gospels, as both; the gift is offered to all and accepted by some; its universal acceptance is still in the future. But the real point is the method and condition of its coming. When it is shown that the Kingdom was regarded as future, it is frequently taken for granted that this is equivalent to saying that its coming was so pictured as to imply the acceptance of Jewish apocalyptic. It is hard to see the justification for this.

Present or future: process or catastrophe?

We have already noted that the actual phrase "Kingdom of God" or "of Heaven" does not occur at all in the apocalyptic literature, and there is no reason for supposing that the message of its nearness would neces-

[1] *E g.* in Lake and Foakes-Jackson, *op. cit*, p 278 ff.

sarily imply the end of the world in a catastrophic sense. Christ very seldom gave a direct answer to a question, but on being asked (Luke xvii. 20) when the Kingdom of God should come, he broke his rule and replied quite definitely that it did not come with observation; they should not say, "Lo, here or Lo, there"; for the Kingdom was within them.[1] It is quite true that the following section in Luke xvii. speaks of the coming of the Son of Man as the lightning visible to all and as happening at a point of time. But the Kingdom is not mentioned at all in that section. And it is, in fact, in connection with the Son of Man that we find the passages which really do have an apocalyptic colouring. We shall consider in due course the problems they raise. Meanwhile we note that, even taking the Gospels as they stand, with all their intrusive elements of Jewish apocalyptic, there are very few cases in which the Kingdom occurs in what is necessarily an eschatological setting.[2] No doubt there are other passages which admit such an interpretation—*e.g.* the central message that the Kingdom is at hand—but they do not require it.[3] They are understood in the eschatological sense only under the pressure of the general hypothesis, based on other

[1] The alternative translation "in your midst" comes to much the same thing from this point of view

[2] The most important are the explanation of the parable of the Tares (Matt xiii 37 ff), on which see p 241, and the saying in Matt. xvi 28, see p 283 In Luke xxi 31 ("Know that the Kingdom of God is nigh") the Kingdom occurs in a definitely eschatological setting. But Luke is here following Mark, and the phrase is simply a paraphrase of Mark's "Know ye that he (*or* it) is nigh at the doors" (Mark xiii 29), where there is no mention of the Kingdom On the whole section, see below, p 288

[3] This applies especially to the enigmatic saying at the Last Supper about drinking the new wine in the Kingdom of God (Mark xiv 25 and parallels, cf also Luke xxii 29).

THE KINGDOM OF HEAVEN

passages, that this feature is, in fact, authentic and central in the teaching of Jesus. But if the hypothesis is rejected, they at once become susceptible of another and an easier explanation. The Kingdom was to come as men learnt to do God's will on earth. Jesus was there to teach them that will and to help them to perform it.

CHAPTER XXII

SALVATION NATIONAL AND INTERNATIONAL

<small>Improving the world or ending it?</small> How far is the general trend of the teaching of Jesus consistent with the view we have taken of the significance of the Kingdom? Does it contemplate the improvement of the world or its speedy dissolution? Some at least of those who hold that the approaching end was the chief message of Christ have seen what this implies with respect to his moral teaching and its purpose. The ordinary reader takes it for granted that the practice of love and forgiveness is intended to make the world a better place to live in. Not so, say the supporters of " the eschatological theory." The commands to give and to forgive are simply the rules by which the individual may secure his own place in the Kingdom and escape the doom which is to engulf the rest.

<small>" Interims-ethik."</small> It is urged that only on this supposition can we explain Christ's attitude towards wealth, family and social life, his commands to give to all, to resist not evil, to forgive enemies, together with the ignoring of political and æsthetic interests. The ulterior effects of the conduct he requires may be put aside; the teaching is not meant for men living under normal conditions. It is for a temporary crisis, where, as in war, the considerations which hold good in ordinary

SALVATION NATIONAL & INTERNATIONAL

life are suspended.[1] The supreme need is that the disciple, by obedience to these otherwise extravagant and impossible demands, shall secure his place in the coming Kingdom. Compared with this, nothing else now counts, and here is the sole motive for obedience. According to Weiss, just, as in the case of Jesus himself, his readiness to love his enemies was mainly a proof of his detachment from the world, so the commands to the disciples to do the same are addressed to men who have here no abiding city, but seek the Kingdom of God.[2] " We are to do good to those who hate us, not so much in order to help them, but much more in order to prove that we ourselves are free from enmity and selfishness. Certainly prayer for enemies may benefit them, but in the foreground stands simply care for our own soul, which shows by such prayers that it bears a charm against hatred and bitterness."[3] So with regard to the command to resist not evil, " there is no suggestion that the enemy is to be shamed and reformed by patient long-suffering; that idea is quite alien. The whole stress lies on the readiness to suffer wrong." Weiss indeed admits[4] that at other times Jesus does speak more as a preacher and reformer than as the herald of the Kingdom, and that he sometimes attempts to improve and help the world, as though it might be expected to continue. But with regard to this admission, as with regard to all others which he is forced to make of the existence of other moods in the thought of Jesus, he urges that it does not represent his real mind. This is to be found rather in despair of the world and in an insistent constraining of

[1] J. Weiss, *Die Predigt Jesu vom Reiche Gottes* (2nd ed), p 139.
[2] P 149   [3] P 150.   [4] Pp 137, 145

THE LORD OF THOUGHT

the individual to secure his own salvation while he may.

In considering this somewhat remarkable position we may at least note that forgiveness of enemies had not been a prominent feature in previous apocalyptic thought, and, if Jesus was simply adopting the same general outlook, it is not quite clear why he should have laid such stress on this particular point as the thing which really counted in the preparation of the individual. But with all due respect for the learned and sincere thinkers who have taken this view it is difficult to treat it very seriously. It obviously robs love of others of all its meaning by making it simply an enlightened form of selfishness; and the remarkable thing is that, *e.g.* in the Sermon on the Mount, what may seem the extreme commands to love and to forgive are never associated in any way with the idea that the time is short.[1] We are not told to give away our coat because there is not going to be another winter and we shall not want it for long. It is not surprising, therefore, that more recent supporters of the eschatological view have quietly dropped this side of the theory. But we are entitled to insist that it shall not thus be dropped. The issue is fundamental. If Jesus really thought that the world was quickly coming to an end there could be no point in trying to improve it.

Does the Sermon simply state the conditions on which a few may escape the common doom?

---

[1] For a fuller discussion of this theory, which is known as "Interimsethik" (*i e* an ethical teaching intended only for a short interval), I would refer to my article, "Is the Teaching of Jesus an Interimsethik?" (*Expositor*, viii. 4), I have ventured to reproduce one or two paragraphs from it I have also examined the views of J. Weiss and Schweitzer at greater length in *The Eschatological Question in the Gospels*. I should now modify the position there adopted by being less ready to allow the possibility that the expectation of a catastrophic end may have held even a subordinate place in the thought of Jesus.

SALVATION NATIONAL & INTERNATIONAL

If, on the other hand, he looked out on life as he knew it with a clear and piercing vision of what it might become if man would only let God in and try His methods of love and persuasion, there was no room for the expectation of the immediate external catastrophe. We must choose between the two points of view unless we are to believe that the outlook of Jesus on the world and its future was entirely vacillating on this question of principle.

We take it, then, that Jesus did mean his followers to improve the world and not merely to save their own souls from the coming doom. It would seem that he also meant them to save the world as Jews. In the forefront of the Sermon we have a series of sayings which set before his hearers the ideal of proving themselves the salt of the earth and the light of the world, the city set on the hill, the lamp illuminating all in the house. Their light is to shine before men that they too may be drawn to the Father; the meek are to inherit the earth. There is nó real reason for supposing that these words are addressed only to a little group with the idea that they in their turn should influence other little groups. They are quite general in their application, spoken to all who have ears to hear. As has been suggested above,[1] they become doubly significant if understood as an appeal to the Jewish nation to rise to its opportunity and become the salvation of the earth. No doubt the work will be begun by the nucleus among them who accept his teaching. These are the grain of mustard seed, the little leaven, of which the parables speak. But the seed is to grow till it becomes a tree in which the birds take shelter;

Christ's hope for the Jew.

[1] See Chap. XII.

the leaven is to expand till it leavens the lump. First, this is to happen within the nation; then within the world. One of Christ's somewhat rare quotations from the Old Testament is the great saying of Isa. lvii. 7 which sees in the Temple the house of prayer for all nations. His indictment of the religion of the day is precisely that it makes this impossible.[1]

<small>The instinct of patriotism.</small> The Jews have always been essentially patriotic, with a keen sense of their race, its greatness and its possibilities, and the contemporaries of Jesus were no exception. The history of the first century A.D., with its conflicts with Rome culminating in the great revolt and the fall of Jerusalem, proves this completely. Now a deep-seated, emotional instinct of this type cannot be ignored. Adopting the principles of modern psychology, one of three things may happen: (1) The instinct may attempt to find its immediate and direct expression in the kind of action to which it obviously points; *i.e.* it may vent itself in political and imperialistic attempts at conquest. With many Jews of the first century this actually happened in the futile resistance to Rome, a policy with which Jesus had nothing in common.

<small>Apocalyptic its psychic equivalent.</small> (2) Where the natural outlet was impossible, as it was to those who realized the absurdity of attempting to overcome Rome by force of arms, the instinct might by suppression become a "complex," finding for itself another outlet. Apocalyptic, with its glorious visions of a supernatural future, was just such an outlet. For a later period it has been pointed out that "chiliasm" was most popular in Phrygia, Egypt and Roman Africa, where patriotism was both

[1] Mark xi. 17.

SALVATION NATIONAL & INTERNATIONAL

naturally strong and also repressed. " Chiliasm was a psychic equivalent for patriotism." [1]

" So far as his conscious mind was concerned, the Phrygian might be perfectly reconciled to Roman political supremacy. . . . Yet the emotional energy of his patriotism remained, and it naturally associated itself with any idea that lay at hand. Chiliasm happened to be at hand. The glorified divine Kingdom of the Saints of God on earth was the psychic equivalent of that Phrygian Kingdom whose national existence had been for ever extinguished by Rome." The heretical chiliasm of Phrygia placed the reign of Christ not in Jerusalem but in Pepuza, a small town of Phrygia. " Similarly the national patriotism which under other historical circumstances might have found expression in the glory of an independent Egypt now found expression in the borrowed phraseology of Jewish and Christian apocalyptical literature." [2]

This seems to have happened no less with the Jews of the Christian era. What we find in apocalyptic is not a purified or spiritualized nationalism, but a nationalism which projects itself upon the future and looks for its satisfaction in the completely miraculous act of the national God, who will somehow meet the wishes of His people. It is really parallel to the day-dreams which we all experience in some form or another.[3] The powerful ambition which sees no prospect of its satisfaction in the natural course of

---

[1] See L P. Edwards, *The Transformation of Early Christianity from an Eschatological to a Socialized Movement*, p 80 By "chiliasm," or millenarianism, is meant the expectation of the Messianic Kingdom on earth for "a thousand years"
[2] Edwards, *op cit*, p 82
[3] Cf Chap. ii

THE LORD OF THOUGHT

events pictures itself as receiving some fairy gift or magic secret which will lead to a triumphant success. Another, with an enthusiasm for music, but with no corresponding power of execution, dreams of himself suddenly dowered with a talisman by which he plays as never man played before. The struggling golfer sees himself with the infallible secret of straight and long driving; the halting speaker with a sudden gift of golden oratory. Apocalyptic on a larger scale offered the same imaginary compensation to the baffled patriotism of the Jew. Again, if our contention is right, Jesus refused to lead him along this road.

Missionary enterprise the sublimation of patriotism.

(3) But an instinct may be deliberately sublimated, *i.e.* consciously directed into a worthy channel, so that it makes for itself an expression which is of service both to the individual and to the community. The sublimation of patriotism is to be found in the missionary spirit which, with no thought of the glorification of its own Church, *qua* Church, is filled with the enthusiasm of a message and a vision which it desires to see the property of the world at large.

It has been pointed out in the last chapter that such a sense of missionary vocation, the conviction that God had chosen Israel not for its own glorification but that it might be the light and saviour of the Gentiles, is found in the best of the prophetic teaching, notably in the latter part of Isaiah and in some of the Psalms. In a remarkable recent book, *Early Judaism*,[1] it has been suggested that the history of the Jews after the exile is largely a conflict between this principle and the opposing principle of national pride and exclusiveness. The latter triumphed, and the self-contained satisfac-

[1] By L E Browne.

SALVATION NATIONAL & INTERNATIONAL

tion which this triumph brought in its train was the main cause of the rejection of the Messiah when he came. It is clear, then, that Jesus in setting before his nation a missionary ideal was both going back to the best of the prophetic teaching and also offering to the aspirations of his nation the one channel in which they might find satisfaction. He likens his teaching in the breadth of its appeal to the teaching of Jonah at Nineveh [1]; the Queen of the South came to hear the wisdom of Solomon. The fame and the teaching of one who is greater than Jonah or Solomon will in the end spread no less widely. The acceptance of this teaching will be the vindication of Jesus, pictured as the Son of Man seated on the clouds of heaven.

The fact that his own mission was confined to Jews may be best explained by this conviction that they were the people of God, through whom his message would in the end find its way to all nations. Whatever view be taken of the authenticity of particular injunctions to evangelize the Gentiles, it cannot seriously be held on any theory of his teaching that he was indifferent to their fate. He concentrated on the Jewish nation, as by common consent he concentrated with even greater intensity upon the band of his disciples, in order that in each case he might perfect the instrument. To convert the disciples was the best way to convert the nation; and to convert the nation in such a sense that its practical attitude towards the world should become a visible expression of its

---

[1] Matt xii 40 makes the point of the reference the comparison between Jonah in the whale and the burial of Christ; a comparison with xvi 4 and Luke xi 29 shows that this is one of the frequent additions made by the editor of the First Gospel

THE LORD OF THOUGHT

new conception of God—this was in the end to convert the Gentile. And this task was the one outlet for the intense national spirit which Jesus could neither ignore nor yet endorse in the forms in which it had heretofore clothed itself.

CHAPTER XXIII

THE SON OF MAN

BEFORE discussing the meaning of this title in the Gospels, something must be said of its previous history.

(*a*) It is used in the Old Testament, especially in poetic parallelism, as equivalent to "humanity" or "man in general"; the plural "sons of men" is still more common. According to Hebrew usage, "son of" means the member of a class. Further, the word for "man" is Adam; when it has the article ("the") it means man; without the article it may mean Adam. In this particular expression the article is generally omitted; it might therefore mean, or at least suggest, "son of Adam." The outstanding example of its use as equivalent to man is Psa. viii.: [margin: "Son of man" in the Old Testament.]

> " What is man that thou art mindful of him ?
>   And the son of man that thou visitest him ?
> For thou hast made him but a little lower than God
>   And crownest him with glory and honour.
> Thou madest him to have dominion over the works of thy
>   hands ;
>   Thou hast put all things under his feet."

(*b*) Closely connected is the use in Ezekiel. It is applied to the prophet ("thou son of man") over ninety times, and is first used after he has seen "one

THE LORD OF THOUGHT

with the appearance of a man." " It is as though the Voice had said, I manifest myself to thee as Man, and thou art in my likeness ' son of man.' "[1]

(c) The use in Dan. vii. 9 ff. is in line with the Old Testament meaning, though it marks a definite development. The figure " like unto a son of man," who comes on the clouds of heaven and is brought to the Ancient of Days to receive the Kingdom, is definitely explained as symbolizing Israel, the saints of the Most High (verses 18, 22, 27). It is not the Messiah but a personification of the nation. In the seer's vision Israel stands for the true ideal of humanity, opposed to the " beasts," the hostile world-empires which embody brute force and all the elements which run counter to the purpose of God for man.

The Son of man in Enoch

(d) A further development is found in the *Similitudes of Enoch*.[2] On its first occurrence the phrase is " one whose face was as the appearance of a man,"[3] and afterwards we find " the " or " that " Son of man, referring back to the original description. It is not quite a definite title of the Messiah, but it is a description of him; and when the phrase had been thus prominently applied to the personal Messiah, it would at least tend to suggest him in circles where this type

---

[1] E A Abbott, *The Message of the Son of Man* The view adopted in this chapter is substantially that taken by Dr Abbott, though I cannot follow him in all his applications. For the more technical linguistic problems connected with the subject, reference may be made to Dalman, *The Words of Jesus*, p 234 ff , or to Dr Driver's article in Hastings' *Dictionary of the Bible*, iv p 579 ff.

[2] A parallel conception of the Messiah as "the man" is found in the *Apocalypse of Ezra*, xiii This is later than the time of Christ and the writing of the Gospels. But its use here is good evidence that the term was current in apocalyptic circles

[3] *Enoch*, xlvi. The general character of the references to "the Son of man" may be seen from the full quotations given above in chap ix.

THE SON OF MAN

of literature was familiar; it might then be used as a definite title. But Dalman is fully justified in his view that "a regular Jewish name for the Messiah never was formed from the passage in question" (*i.e.* Dan. vii.). He holds that the "two apocalyptic fragments" in *Enoch* and the *Apocalypse of Ezra* do not justify us in regarding "Son of man" as a current Messianic title.[1]

The question, then, is whether the phrase "Son of man" in the Gospels goes back primarily to this Messianic and eschatological use, so that the main idea would be of a heavenly Being who was to come on the clouds to exercise judgment on God's enemies and the enemies of the chosen people, and to reign in the Messianic Kingdom. Since the discovery and intensive study of the apocalyptic literature it has generally been assumed that this is the case. And with regard to certain passages of the Gospels as they stand, the truth of this view is undeniable; they are almost exact quotations from *Enoch*; *e.g.* Matt. xxv. 31.

What did Jesus mean by the phrase?

But here, as elsewhere, we have to consider whether this represents the thought of Christ himself. It is at least a possible hypothesis that he used the term in the sense in which it occurs in Psa. viii. and in Ezekiel, referring to himself as the representative man, the one who by his nearness to God realized completely His purpose for mankind in general. If so, it would almost inevitably happen that in the process of emphasizing the eschatological side, which we hold to have gone on in the growth of the Gospel tradition, his use of the phrase would have been unconsciously

[1] Dalman, *Words of Jesus*, p. 248.

THE LORD OF THOUGHT

modified so as to bring it into closer relation to the apocalyptic usage.

There are several indications in favour of this view:

Christ's use derived from Psa. viii.

1. The majority of the cases in which the term occurs in the Gospels, including the earliest cases (*e.g.* Mark ii. 10, 28; viii. 31), do not in any way suggest apocalyptic ideas, but seem rather to stand for man at his best.[1] Many critics, in fact, hold that in the first two of these passages " Son of man " has been wrongly substituted for an original " man." But this is only because they do not fit in with the supposed Messianic and eschatological meaning.

2. We can on these same lines go some way towards explaining the very curious way in which the expression is used as a kind of substitute for the first person. Though it includes the speaker, and in fact refers primarily to him, it is not just a periphrasis for " I "; it seems to mean himself as the representative of mankind; with the suggestion that what he does and suffers, mankind as a whole must do and suffer too.

3. It is noteworthy that the use of the term " Son of man " does not occasion any surprise either to the disciples or to the people. They ask what right Jesus has to forgive sins, not what right he has to speak of himself as " Son of man." But, if the expression had been understood to imply an identification of the speaker with the pre-existent " Son of man " of *Enoch*, it would have been received with a storm of protest. Clearly it was susceptible of a reasonable and natural interpretation, and this can only be found on the lines of the Old Testament usage. This would

---

[1] Cf Matt ix 8, "which had given such power unto men," with ix 6, "the Son of man hath power on earth to forgive sins."

THE SON OF MAN

be at least as familiar as the rather special use in *Enoch*. In our anxiety to bring out the newly-discovered influence of apocalyptic,[1] we must not forget that our Old Testament was the Jewish Bible.

4. That the term cannot have been understood in the *Enoch* sense is shown by the matter-of-fact way in which it was received; the same conclusion follows from a consideration of Christ's own attitude towards his Messiahship. It is clear from the questions asked at Cæsarea Philippi and by the High Priest at the Trial that he did not speak of his Messiahship in public at any time, or even to the disciples before Cæsarea Philippi. But if Son of man was really equivalent to Messiah, as it is in the apocalyptic use, his adoption of the term must have at once identified him as Messiah. Hence those who insist on the identification are compelled in one way or another to eliminate both the early and the public uses of the term. If however, as we suggest, the term was associated rather with the Old Testament the difficulty disappears. Christ in speaking of himself as Son of man would be understood as summing up in his own person the true ideal not only of Israel but of humanity, not as identifying himself with the Heavenly Being who was to appear as Judge on the clouds.

In Psa. viii. we have three ideas associated with "man" or "the Son of man"—humiliation, authority over the lower creation, and subsequent exaltation. These are precisely the three main ideas associated with "Son of man" in the Gospels. The first ex-

---

[1] The work done by Dr Charles in this connection will remain one of the great achievements of English scholarship, but he cannot be held responsible for the use made of the materials which he has placed at the disposal of students.

THE LORD OF THOUGHT

amples of its use emphasize authority to forgive sins and lordship over the Sabbath; the thought of humiliation and suffering is frequent ("hath not where to lay his head" and the predictions of the Passion); and so, in one form or another, is that of exaltation. It is in this last connection that the passages as they stand suggest *Enoch*, but it is also just at this point that the turn which emphasized the suggestion would naturally be given by Jewish reporters. If Christ had spoken of the exaltation which was to follow his humiliation, when the Son of man was to be "crowned with glory and worship," when true humanity was to triumph by the power of the divine love, the Beast to be crushed and the Kingdom established, and had done this in general terms, partly derived from Daniel,[1] a very slight change would assimilate these sayings to *Enoch* and introduce the idea of an actual coming on the clouds. What was figurative, poetical and inward would become literal and external. The change in wording might be very slight, but it was a change which made all the difference.

The intrusion of the apocalyptic idea.

And it is clear that this change would take effect very quickly after the Resurrection, indeed as soon as Jesus was recognized as the Lord of the world, the conqueror over death, and we find it, in fact, in the early speeches of Peter in Acts. His speedy return in triumph is expected, and the expectation is clothed in the language of eschatology (ii. 17 ff.; iii. 19 ff.),

[1] Dalman sums up his discussion of the term in these words: "Jesus called himself [Son of man] not indeed as the 'lowly one,' but *as that member of the human race (Menschenkind) in his own nature impotent, whom God will make Lord of the world*, and it is very probable that Jesus found another reference to the Son of man of Dan vii. in the verses of Psa viii 5" (*Words of Jesus*, p. 265; the italics are in the original).

THE SON OF MAN

though the term "Son of man" is not used except by Stephen in Acts vii. 56. Any sayings of Jesus which seemed to endorse this would quickly undergo the necessary modification. The marvel is not that they have been altered in this way, but that they have been altered so little.

It is important in this connection to consider the predictions of the Passion and the Resurrection.[1] No doubt there is some uncertainty as to the exact words used, and it is probable that they have been to some extent modified in the light of after events. But the point is that, if the thought of an immediate coming to judgment was central in the mind of Jesus, we should expect that the climax of the predictions would be the return on the clouds; instead of this it is always the Resurrection.[2] If the return had been mentioned by Jesus in these sayings, it would certainly not have dropped out in the tradition. And if it was not mentioned in these emphatic and repeated utterances, in which above all he set himself to open the eyes of the disciples to his future destiny, it is hard to believe that it had any place in his thought. *Predictions of the Passion and Resurrection.*

We pass on to consider the chief Gospel passages in which the Son of man figures in what appears to be the *Enoch* sense. We shall find good evidence, in comparing one Gospel with another, that the apocalyptic element has been heightened. And we must bear in mind the possibility that the process may have *Passages in which Son of man is used in the apocalyptic sense.*

---

[1] Mark viii. 31, ix 12, ix 31, x 32, and parallels
[2] It is noteworthy that Schweitzer regards these predictions as altogether unhistorical, they cannot, in fact, be harmonized with the eschatological theory. Jesus always speaks of himself in this connection as Son of man, and yet never introduces the idea of his coming on the clouds at the very point where we should expect it. On Luke xvii 25 see below, p. 286.

THE LORD OF THOUGHT

begun still earlier, in the oral tradition before Mark or even Q were written, and that the presence of the apocalyptic elements—the visible coming on the clouds and the judgment on enemies—is due to an early misunderstanding of sayings cast in a different mould. For if the tendency to introduce eschatology was strong enough to affect the written record of the teaching, it would operate still more readily while that teaching was still being handed on by word of mouth.

MARK viii. 38 ff	MATT. xvi. 27 ff.	LUKE ix. 26 ff.
(a) For whosoever shall be ashamed of me and of my words in this adulterous and sinful generation, the Son of man shall be ashamed of him when he cometh in the glory of his Father with the holy angels.	For the Son of man shall come in the glory of his Father with his angels; and then shall he render to every man according to his deeds.	For whosoever sh be ashamed of me and my words, of him sh the Son of man ashamed when he co eth in his own glc and the glory of t Father and of the hc angels
(b) And he said unto them, Verily I say unto you, There be some here of them that stand by which shall in no wise taste of death till they see the kingdom of God come with power.	Verily I say unto you, There be some of them that stand here which shall in no wise taste of death till they see the Son of man coming in his kingdom.	But I tell you of truth, There be some them that stand he which shall in no w taste of death till th see the kingdom of Ge

This passage in each of the three Gospels comprises two sayings. We shall deal with the two separately.

With the first saying, which has just been quoted in its Marcan form, we must compare another which is not in Mark and seems to have come from Q:

MATT. x. 32, 33.	LUKE xii. 8, 9.
Everyone therefore who shall confess me before men, him will I also confess before my Father which is in heaven. But whosoever shall deny me before men, him will I also deny before my Father which is in heaven.	Everyone who shall confess m before men, him shall the Son o man also confess before the angel of God: but he that denieth me ii the presence of men shall be denie(in the presence of the angels of God

THE SON OF MAN

We have, then, five variants of a single saying about confessing, or not being ashamed of, Christ—three being of the Marcan version and two from Q. Of these it is generally held that the Q form is the original.[1] We note at once that this does not refer to the end of the world. But in Mark viii. and Luke ix. the saying is brought into relation with the coming of the Son of man, who, however, appears as witness rather than as judge. Matthew gives the Q saying about denial in x. 32, and in xvi. 28 he makes the Marcan saying entirely eschatological. He omits in this context the whole idea of confessing Christ before men, and substitutes the explicit statement of a retributive judgment exercised by the Son of man, who appears as *judge*, not as witness: " Then shall he render to every man according to his works." The addition is an almost exact quotation from Psa. lxii. 12, and the idea of a judgment according to works is common in apocalyptic. We find, then, three stages in the tradition—a simple and non-eschatological Q saying, a Marcan and Lucan version where it is connected with the coming of the Son of man, and a developed eschatological version in Matt. xvi.

(1) Sayings about confessing Christ.

To pass to the second half of the Marcan saying quoted above (" there be some of them which stand here, etc."), Mark ix. 1 has " see the Kingdom of God come with power." Here, though the wording is vaguely apocalyptic, the reference might be to the visible triumph of Christ and the cause for which he stood, however brought about. This applies still more strongly to Luke's " see the Kingdom of God."

(2) " Till they see the Kingdom of God."

---

[1] For a discussion of these passages see Streeter in *Oxford Studies in the Synoptic Problem*, p 428.

THE LORD OF THOUGHT

But Matthew makes it refer definitely to a visible coming, " till they see the Son of man coming in his Kingdom." Once more we can trace the process by which an eschatological element was introduced.

(3) "Till the Son of man be come."

Matt. x. 23 : " But when they persecute you in this city, flee into the next : for verily I say unto you, Ye shall not have gone through the cities of Israel till the Son of man be come."

This is from any point of view a peculiarly difficult passage. It is sometimes assigned to Q, but it is very doubtful whether this ascription is justified. The sequence of ideas—warnings of persecution, being "hated of all men," and the promise, "he that endureth to the end shall be saved "—occurs with close verbal agreement four times in the Gospels : (1) Matt. x. 17-22 ; (2) Matt. xxiv. 9-13 ; (3) Mark xiii. 11-13 ; (4) Luke xxi. 12-19 (here, however, Luke substitutes for the injunction to endure to the end a corresponding climax, " in your patience possess ye your souls "). Now, in none of the other three passages do we find the words of Matt. x. 23, " Ye shall not have gone through the cities of Israel, etc." The charge to endure to the end in Matt. x. 22 forms a complete close to the section, as it does in the parallel passages, and verse 23, with which we are concerned, reads like an afterthought added by the editor, or derived by him from some other source.

What, then, do these words mean, and were they spoken by Jesus ? They now form part of the charge to the Twelve on their first mission, and, if original, we have two possibilities : (1) If they are correctly reported and taken in their obvious sense, we are forced to the view of Schweitzer, that Jesus at this period of his

THE SON OF MAN

ministry expected his manifestation on the clouds within a few weeks.[1] But, as we have seen throughout these chapters, the converging arguments against any such view are decisive, and we cannot attribute to Jesus so incongruous a belief on the strength of a single passage occurring in only one Gospel.

(2) It is possible, though not very likely, that Jesus may have spoken of something which was to happen very quickly, presumably his death, and that an eschatological colouring has been given to his words.

(3) More probable is the view, which is in fact adopted by the majority of critics, that the saying was not spoken by Jesus at all, but that it reflects the policy of a section of the Church at a later period. It justifies flight from persecution, and argues that as the time is so short it is better to confine evangelistic effort to the Jews rather than to go far afield to the Gentiles, as did Paul and his followers.[2] In this case the saying is really eschatological, but it is not Christ's, and, as we have seen, a comparison with similar passages in the other Gospels confirms this view.

---

[1] Schweitzer, in fact, rightly regards the verse as the pivot of his whole theory

[2] Cf the words earlier in the chapter, "Go not into the way of the Gentiles, and enter not into any city of the Samaritans" (x 5). These are also peculiar to Matthew It is true that we find the Gentile mission insisted on in this Gospel (e g Matt xxviii. 19); the editor seems to have been content to leave the two views side by side Perhaps he regarded the earlier limitation as revoked by the command given after the Resurrection But that the inconsistency must not be attributed to Jesus himself is recognized by so moderate a critic as Dr Stanton, who writes, with reference to Matt. x. 5, 6, 23, "In spite, however, of their emanating from the original home of Christianity, it is difficult in view of other sayings of Jesus and the general tenor of his teaching to believe that they accurately represent the mind of the Master" (*The Gospels as Historical Documents*, ii p. 330).

THE LORD OF THOUGHT

(4) The day of the Son of man will be as the lightning.

Luke xvii. 22-37: " Ye shall desire to see one of the days of the Son of man and ye shall not see it. . . . For as the lightning, when it lighteneth out of the one part under the heaven, shineth unto the other part under heaven; so shall the Son of man be in his day. But first must he suffer many things, and be rejected of this generation. And as it came to pass in the days of Noah, even so shall it be also in the days of the Son of man, etc."

This passage occurs in a shorter form in the eschatological discourse of Matt. xxiv., and probably came in substance from Q. The words in Luke xvii 25 (" first must he suffer, etc.") suggest a personal eschatological coming; the Son of man must die and then return. But though, as we have seen, we do not question the predictions of death as a whole, this particular prediction reads very much like a note added to the passage. The section is otherwise studiously vague in its wording: " so shall the Son of man be in his day "; " the days of the Son of man." The most definite expression is verse 30: " After the same manner shall it be in the day that the Son of man is revealed."

But, even allowing for this vagueness and omitting verse 25, the passage is not free from difficulty. It begins with the statement that many shall desire to see one of the days of the Son of man, which reminds us of the saying in Mark ii. about the Bridegroom being taken away. But it goes on to refer to the Flood and the destruction of Sodom, describing a crisis where one is taken and another left. This may naturally be understood of the time of horror which was associated with the fall of Jerusalem—hardly an event

THE SON OF MAN

which anyone would desire to see.[1] As already remarked, the section seems to have come from Q, and it would appear to be one of the few passages in that source in which the tendency to introduce an eschatological colouring already shows itself. The fall of Jerusalem, which probably was anticipated by Christ, is identified with one of the days of the Son of man, precisely as the prophets see in the national disasters of their time a "day of the Lord." Whether the identification was made by Jesus must remain doubtful. In the preceding section he has stated quite definitely that the Kingdom does not come with observation [2]; it is not probable that he went on at once to speak of his own coming, or of "a day of the Son of man," as a visible event. Matthew, as has been pointed out, combines part of this section with Mark's eschatological discourse, which we shall consider next. The same process seems to have been at work in both cases; sayings of Jesus about the fall of Jerusalem and commands to watch have been given an eschatological setting, though in this passage that setting is comparatively vague and indefinite.

Mark xiii.; Matt. xxiv.; Luke xxi. and xvii. 20 ff.

In this section,[3] known as "the Little Apocalypse,"

---

[1] The passage is not really parallel to the well-known section, Amos v. 18. "Woe unto you that desire the day of the Lord! wherefore would ye have the day of the Lord? it is darkness and not light." For Jesus does not say, "Ye shall desire to see one of the days of the Son of man, and when it comes ye shall wish it had not done so," but, "ye shall desire, and shall not see it." He then goes on to speak of something else which will come and is not desirable. The identification of this disaster with "a day of the Son of man" contradicts verse 22, he is more likely to have spoken of it in the terms of Luke xxii. 53, "this is your hour and the power of darkness."

[2] See p. 264.

[3] The chapters are too long to quote in full; the reader is advised to refer to them in a synopsis of the Gospels where they are printed in

THE LORD OF THOUGHT

(5) The great eschatological discourse.

we have a clear case of the heightening in Matthew of the apocalyptic element. The introductory question in Mark and Luke refers solely to the fall of Jerusalem: "Tell us when shall these things be and what is the sign when all these things shall be accomplished?" Matthew has "Tell us when shall these things be and what is the sign *of thy coming and of the end of the age*?"[1] In verse 29 he inserts the significant "immediately" before Mark's "after these things" in order to bring out the idea of the nearness of the Coming. Generally, though the closeness of the verbal agreement shows that Matthew is dependent on Mark, he is fuller, and his additional matter all has the same tendency to heighten the eschatological colouring; *e.g.* verse 30, "the sign of the Son of man" in heaven, and verse 31, the great trumpet. Luke generally follows Mark closely, except that he makes the references to the fall of Jerusalem more intelligible to Gentiles.[2] That part of his material which is not from Mark but from Q he places in chapter xvii.; Matthew has welded both sources together in the one chapter, xxiv.[3]

The greater part of the discourse admittedly refers to the fall of Jerusalem, with warnings of persecution (Mark xiii. 9-13) and of falling away (verses 21-23). But at verse 24 Mark passes on to speak quite clearly,

parallel columns, and to mark for himself Matthew's expansions of Mark

[1] The word here used for coming—*Parousia*—became the technical term for the Second Coming of Christ, it, however, occurs in the Gospels only in Matt. xxiv. Similarly the eschatological phrase "end of the age" is found five times in Matthew, and not elsewhere.

[2] See further, p. 294

[3] In the same way Matthew's treatment of the Q section is more eschatological than Luke's; *e g.* he introduces the technical *Parousia* in verses 27, 37, 39. Contrast Luke xvii. 21-35, on which see above, p. 286

THE SON OF MAN

though comparatively briefly, of the Coming in close connection with this. He closes with the parable of the Fig Tree, and with the warning that the day and the hour, though in that generation, are unknown. This section, *as it stands* in Mark, must refer, not to the fall of Jerusalem, but to the End of the world, which has just been clearly mentioned.

A full discussion of this chapter and its parallels would be long and complicated,[1] but it is widely recognized that it does not in its present form, even in Mark, represent an actual discourse of Christ. It is introduced as spoken in private; *i.e.* there was a time when it was unknown to the Church, a possible inference being that it was not part of the original teaching of Christ[2]; the extended use of apocalyptic imagery in a relatively crude form has no parallel in the rest of the Gospels; and nowhere else in Mark do we find a discourse of thirty-seven verses, a fact which suggests that he obtained it from some special source. Probably a little Apocalypse, written somewhere about 70 A.D., referring to the fall of Jerusalem and the Second Coming, has been combined with brief authentic sayings, vaguely understood, about the former event and with general commands to watch. Mark xiii. 30-32 ("This generation shall not pass away, etc.") may well be genuine; in its original context it would apply to the fall of Jerusalem, though, as we have seen, it must in its present setting refer to the Parousia. At any rate it is rash to use this chapter, even in its Marcan form, as evidence that Christ adopted apocalyptic

---
[1] See *e g* the discussion by Streeter in *Oxford Studies of the Synoptic Problem*, p 179 ff
[2] Cf the explanation of the parable of the Tares; see above, p. 241.

THE LORD OF THOUGHT

ideas; and if it is set aside, many other passages, which, if interpreted in its light, become eschatological, are susceptible of quite a different colouring.

(6) The reply to the High Priest at the Trial.	MARK XIV 62 Ye shall see the Son of man sitting at the right hand of power and coming with the clouds of heaven.	MATT XXVI 64. Henceforth ye shall see the Son of man sitting at the right hand of power and coming on the clouds of heaven.	LUKE XXII 69. But from henceforth shall the Son of man be seated at the right hand of the power of God

The exact wording varies, and Luke says nothing of the coming on the clouds.[1] It is never easy for bystanders to recall the precise words spoken at a time of great tension. They must have been reported by those who at the time were our Lord's enemies, and, since they formed the ground of his condemnation, they would naturally make them as extreme and startling as possible. It is clear that our Lord used language which recalled Dan. vii., and publicly identified himself for the first time with the Messiah, bringing the Son of man phrase into relation with it. But whether he spoke of a permanent sitting at the right hand of God, or used vague apocalyptic language in a deeper spiritualized sense, it is not easy to determine.

The record of the trials as a whole has the stamp of authenticity; probably some of the servants or soldiers present, if not some of the judges (we think of Joseph of Arimathea and of the company of priests who became obedient to the faith), became Christians and recorded their recollections. This may be said against those who, like Loisy, hold that we know nothing of what really happened on this occasion. But this does not justify us in building too much on the exact

[1] On the point that Luke's version of the saying is not a modification of Mark, but comes from an independent source, see below, p 294

THE SON OF MAN

wording of a saying, spoken in another language, and recorded in three different forms by our only authorities. We cannot assume that any one of them is absolutely accurate.[1]

From passages already considered it will be seen that the conception of Christ as a judge who will reward and punish at the last day is exclusively Matthean; it is found in Matt. xiii. 41 (see p. 241); xvi. 27 (see p. 283); and xxv. 31 (see p. 248). None of these passages can be regarded as authentic in their present form. It occurs also in Matt. xix. 28, " In the regeneration when the Son of man shall sit on the throne of his glory, ye also shall sit," etc. This is parallel to Luke xxii. 28-30, where the words " when the Son of man shall sit . . . glory " are not found. To quote Dr Stanton[2] once more, " The idea of the Judgeship of Christ, which is plainly expressed in the former [Matt. xvi. 27, 28], and implied in the latter [xix. 28], of these passages in St Matthew, is not elsewhere set forth in St Mark or St Luke."

Christ as judge.

In Matt. vii. 22 (" Many shall say to me in that day . . . then shall I confess to them, I never knew you ") we find the ideas of acceptance and rejection stated in comparatively vague language, which may be compared with the saying about confessing Christ before men. In the Lucan version (xiii. 25 ff.) " in that day " is not found, and its place is taken by a parabolic saying about the shutting of the door. With reference to this and other passages of the same type, Dr Stanton[3] argues that, in view of the way Matthew has modified

---

[1] The use of the term "power" as a periphrasis for "God" is contrary to the general habit of Jesus, see above, p 233.
[2] *The Gospels as Historical Documents*, ii p 351
[3] *Op cit*, p 352 ff

Mark, it seems probable that the peculiar features of the First Evangelist, such as "shall enter into the Kingdom of Heaven" in the eschatological sense (Matt. vii. 21; contrast Luke vi. 46), or the "in that day" of vii. 22, were introduced by him "in consequence of his own sense of what was fitting." The Evangelist would agree with the Rabbi [1] who taught that, if Israel were worthy, the Messiah would come with the clouds of heaven, but, if unworthy, he would come riding upon the ass. Jesus himself had a different standard of greatness and of power, which even his followers have been very slow to learn.

Summary. To sum up our discussion: it is clear that the passages which lend colour to the belief that Jesus spoke of the approaching end of the world and of his own return as judge on the clouds are passages connected with the Son of man rather than with the Kingdom. But, even so, the sayings which demand this interpretation are few in number, and may be explained on critical grounds as additions to, or modifications of, what he actually taught. And what was said in discussing the Kingdom passages holds good here also: there are a larger number of neutral passages which are capable of being understood in an eschatological sense, if the eschatological outlook has already been attributed to Jesus on the strength of the few sayings, of doubtful authenticity, which imply it. But if these are eliminated, the neutral sayings are at once susceptible of a non-eschatological interpretation.

Jesus, as we have urged, speaks of himself as Son of man in the Old Testament sense and refers in general

---

[1] See Dalman, *The Words of Jesus*, p 245

THE SON OF MAN

and figurative language to the coming vindication of himself, of his teaching, and of the purpose of God. In particular, he sees in the national disaster of the fall of Jerusalem an unmistakable manifestation of the moral law which rules the world of men, the inevitable doom upon national blindness and folly.

We have constantly contrasted the eschatological tone of Matthew with the more sober and spiritual version of the sayings found in Luke. If it were consistent with the religious genius of Christ, it might appear open to us to argue that Matthew is original and that Luke has modified the teaching. In reply to this position we would urge the following considerations: Luke or Matthew?

(1) In the early speeches of Acts, Luke has retained the eschatological elements.[1] He was certainly using here a source of some kind, and the conclusion is that, when he found eschatology in his source, he did not set himself to eliminate it, but preserved it faithfully. We have, in fact, in Acts i. 11 a most emphatic statement of the visible Second Coming: "This Jesus, which was received up from you into heaven, shall so come as ye beheld him going into heaven." He also introduces into the speeches of Paul clear references to the judgment to be conducted by Christ (Acts xvii. 31; xxiv. 25).

It is indeed commonly assumed that he has modified Mark's eschatology, but this does not appear to be the case. It is true that in ix. 27 he does slightly tone down Mark's "see the Kingdom of God come with power" by the omission of the last two words.[2] But otherwise he does not materially alter the small amount of eschatology he found in Mark; cf. Mark viii. 38 and Luke ix. 26; Mark xiii. 24-27 and Luke xxi. Does Luke tone down Mark's eschatology?

[1] See above, p 280   [2] See p 283

25-28; Mark xiii. 30, 31 and Luke xxi. 32, 33. The latter passages come from the eschatological discourse; if Luke's treatment of its Marcan sections be examined, it will be seen that he makes clearer the reference of the first part to the fall of Jerusalem, and in xxi. 25 omits the statement that the Second Coming will be " in those days " (Mark xiii. 24), or " immediately " (Matt. xxiv. 29). He also omits the warning that the exact hour is unknown even to the Son (Mark xiii. 32). But he retains the statement that this generation shall not pass away till all be fulfilled (xxi. 32), and in all essentials preserves Mark's eschatology.[1]

It is, however, often supposed that in his version of the reply to the High Priest he alters Mark, substituting the idea of sitting at the right hand of God for that of coming with the clouds.[2] But, here as elsewhere in the Passion narrative, Luke is clearly following a source of his own, with possibly a few modifications introduced from Mark. According to Luke xxii. 66 the trial before the Sanhedrin takes place in the morning, not by night as in Mark and Matthew; Luke omits the impressive section about the failure of the false witnesses. The verses immediately before and after the reply differ considerably from Mark, the common features being the question whether Jesus is the Christ (in Luke this is not asked

[1] Since this was written, a study by Prof Burkitt of *Luke's use of Mark* has appeared (*The Beginnings of Christianity*, vol ii) It happens that he takes this Eschatological Discourse as a test case, his conclusion confirms that taken above Though the vocabulary and style are largely Luke's, and though he emphasizes the "psychological" rather than the "material" element in "the terrors to come," "he has not altered the general tenor of what was in his source" (p. 114). " What concerns us is not that Luke has changed so much, but that he has invented so little " (p 115)

[2] The passages are quoted above, p. 290.

by the High Priest), the general tenor of the reply, and the retort, "What further need have we of witnesses?" But if the reports of the Trial go back to fact at all, these features would be common to all accounts, and are quite insufficient to prove that Luke is following Mark.[1] We conclude that he derives his version of the reply from another source, and that it is not a deliberate modification of Mark, made in order to tone down the eschatology.

It appears, then, that Luke has no particular bias against eschatology as such, but simply follows his sources. This conclusion is of the greatest importance for our whole investigation. Both with regard to Christ's teaching on punishment and with regard to eschatology we have found a constant divergence between Matthew and Luke in the passages common to them. These passages are naturally ascribed to Q and, without attributing verbal inspiration to that document, it makes all the difference in the view we shall take of Christ's own attitude which version we are to regard as the more original. Seeing, then, that Luke retains the eschatology of Mark and of his sources in Acts, there is no reason to suppose that he deliberately cut it out from Q. We follow him rather than Matthew as giving us the truer report of Christ's teaching where the two overlap. *Luke does not eliminate the eschatology of his sources*

It may be added that our conclusion is confirmed by a

---

[1] It may be noted that the rejection of Luke's dependence on Mark at this point eliminates one of the "agreements of Matthew and Luke against Mark," which have been used to suggest that they did not have Mark before them in quite its present form In this case Matthew begins the saying with "henceforth" (ἀπ' ἄρτι), and Luke with "from now" (ἀπὸ τοῦ νῦν), while Mark has neither On the view we take, the partial agreement here of Matthew and Luke is a coincidence

THE LORD OF THOUGHT

comparison of the general treatment of Mark by Matthew and Luke respectively. Luke sometimes omits altogether (*e.g.* the request of the sons of Zebedee, Mark x. 35 ff.), but, where he retains, his alterations are as a rule stylistic or explanatory.[1] On the other hand, Matthew does not shrink from substantial changes, even in the sayings of Jesus, when he has a theological purpose to serve; *e.g.* he alters the difficult " why callest thou me good ? " of Mark x. 18 into " why askest thou me about the good ? " (Matt. xix. 17); Luke here follows Mark. Or, again, in xxi. 2, 7 he substitutes the ass and the colt for Mark's single ass in order to bring out the fulfilment of the prophecy of Zech. ix. 9.

(2) According to the view of Canon Streeter referred to on page 228, the special matter in Luke, not derived from Mark or Q, represents, not a later tradition of Christ's teaching, but an early source. We have therefore ground for believing that it gives us that teaching in a relatively pure and uncontaminated form; and here there are practically no apocalyptic elements.

(3) The instinct of the Christian reader confirms the conclusion of the critic. The great parables of Luke, which are so free from eschatology, have been felt instinctively to bring us straight to the heart of Christ's thought and outlook on life. It is not unscientific to believe that, when instinct and criticism agree, we may trust their conclusions and use them as a touchstone by which to test what is less well authenticated.

---

[1] Harnack (*Sayings of Jesus*, p 115) comes to the same conclusion with regard to the general treatment of Q by Matthew and Luke It is to be noted that he approaches the question purely from the side of literary criticism, without any desire to eliminate any particular elements from the teaching of Jesus

CHAPTER XXIV

THE FUNDAMENTAL IDEAS OF APOCALYPTIC:
TRUTH AND ERROR

It may have occurred to the reader that, after all, the view we have taken of Christ's teaching about his Coming and the Judgment is in some respects a return to that generally held before the difficulties connected with the eschatological passages had been forced to the front. It was, for example, commonly taught that Christ spoke principally of "his Coming" in the destruction of Jerusalem, or in the sending of the Spirit at Pentecost, or in the victory of his teaching in the growth of the Church. But there are two outstanding differences from the older view, which must not be ignored.

1. We recognize explicitly that there are passages in the Gospels which cannot fairly be understood otherwise than as predicting an early and visible return to judgment, and as implying the acceptance of the apocalyptic scheme as a whole. Similar passages are found in various parts of the New Testament, especially in 1 and 2 Thessalonians, 1 Corinthians, the early chapters of Acts, and Revelation, and it is impossible to deny that the early Church believed in a literal and speedy Advent. But we argue that this belief is not derived from Christ, so escaping the grave

The New Testament teaches an immediate Coming

THE LORD OF THOUGHT

difficulty which is raised when we suppose him to have been mistaken both about the date of the End and its nature. On the other hand, we allow that large sections of the early Church, and some of the New Testament writers, did hold these erroneous views, deriving them from the current apocalyptic.

If the language about the date must be taken symbolically, why not the rest also?

2. The older view allowed that references to the date of the End—" this generation," " immediately," etc.—must be understood figuratively, but it maintained that the mass of the eschatology, though it had an immediate spiritual meaning referring to the death of the individual, yet had ultimately a literal meaning; all the language about nearness referred to the fall of Jerusalem, or else was symbolic, while the rest of the language referred to a literal, but indefinitely distant, Advent, a theory which is patently untrue to the text of the Gospels. This inconsistency of interpretation arises from a natural desire to preserve as much as possible of the literal accuracy of the New Testament, and it has maintained itself so long only because it is in a sense impossible to prove that it is wrong. It is always open to us to maintain that some particular event is going to happen to-morrow, and the prediction cannot be proved to be false till to-morrow comes. But when many " to-morrows " have come, and a series of predictions with regard to " to-morrow," such as we find in the expectation of the Second Coming, have not been realized, we have at least very strong grounds for arguing that the predictions themselves are mistaken, and not merely the date, the more so if they contradict our view of the way in which God works in His universe. The predictions of the Judgment have been proved to

FUNDAMENTAL IDEAS OF APOCALYPTIC

be wrong at the only point at which they can be tested—their nearness. It is now generally allowed that we can no longer uphold the accuracy of the language about immediacy in a literal sense, and must fall back on the spiritual truth which lies behind it. Why, then, should we not frankly do the like with the rest of the language about the fact itself and its accompaniments? We are the more encouraged to do so when we find that this language, as we have tried to show, does not go back to Jesus himself.

In this connection it is very relevant to remember that the nearness of the End, which has of necessity been abandoned, is not an excrescence which can easily be cut out of the scheme, but is an integral element in it, the dropping of which throws the whole out of gear. The Church has been slow to realize this. It took over a scheme which belongs to a pre-scientific view of the universe. In parts this scheme has obviously broken down, and these parts have been tacitly scrapped, but it has tried to retain the rest, and the result is an illogical compromise.

What, then, is the background which lies behind the pictures of the future found in apocalyptic and the New Testament? They presuppose a universe which is quite manageable both in its extent and duration. The earth is the centre of the visible world, with heaven, or a series of heavens, above it, peopled by spiritual beings who pass up and down in a quite literal sense. This universe had its origin in a definite act of creation at a point of time not very far distant. This act may have been split up into stages, as in Gen. i., but it was not thought of as a process of gradual evolution. The point is that the End was con-

The apocalyptic view of the universe.

ceived of on the same principles as the beginning. It was regarded as near, very near. History could be split up into a week of days, each of 1000 years, and the last of these days was drawing to its close, ushering in the final Sabbath. And the End would come, as the beginning came, by a single catastrophic act of God at a definite point of time. The whole attention was concentrated on the approaching Judgment, and the manifestation of what is known as the Messianic Kingdom. And it was thought of primarily in its effect on the nation as a unit, and on the generation alive at its coming. Generally speaking, past generations were strangely ignored. It follows that comparatively little interest was taken in the condition of the departed after death, in what we have come to call the intermediate state. There was indeed such a state, and it was depicted in various ways; but it had no real significance, being entirely subordinate to the privileges of the Kingdom which was so soon to be revealed. In the *Apocalypse of Ezra*, xiii. 24, it is held that, in spite of the horrors of the Messianic woes, which were to usher in the Kingdom, those who survive till its coming are more blessed than those who have died

The interval between death and the Judgment.

The same background is presupposed in much of the New Testament. In the Pauline Epistles we hear practically nothing of previous generations who have passed away. The problem which exercised men's minds related to the small number of Christians who might die before the Second Coming. We see this clearly in 1 Thess. iv. 13 ff. The survivors are not to sorrow as men without hope for those who die; they will not forfeit their share in the Kingdom on

FUNDAMENTAL IDEAS OF APOCALYPTIC

account of their premature death. They are now asleep, but soon the Lord will appear and bring them with him; their bodies shall rise (apparently to be united with the descending souls), and they and the survivors will be for ever with him in the new age. Nothing is said about sinners or unbelievers. It is surely obvious that this passage implies a Messianic Kingdom upon earth. For if the Thessalonians interpreted the future in terms of a bliss in heaven in our sense, into which men normally passed at death, why should they have been troubled about believers who died, in the fear that they should miss something that the survivors would enjoy? That is to say, the passage is not primarily a discussion about what we call "the future life" in the sense of the state into which we enter after death. The great thing is what will happen at the End.

We may notice that we have here the chief explanation of the origin of the belief in a bodily resurrection. As we have seen, curiously little interest was taken in past generations, but they could not be entirely ignored. And so the belief arose (first in Daniel) that the righteous should rise to receive their bodies, or new bodies, in order to enjoy the Messianic Kingdom, whether on earth or in heaven, and the wicked in order to receive the punishment they had escaped here. Meanwhile, it was held that they were waiting, asleep or disembodied, living a kind of half-life until they received their garments of light, their spiritual bodies. In Revelation the righteous are the souls beneath the altar, crying "How long?" But as a whole the state of the dead is not a pressing problem to the apocalyptic and New Testament writers,

The origin of the belief in the resurrection of the body.

THE LORD OF THOUGHT

simply because it is temporary and affects only a minority of believers. It was not an important part of the sequence of events.

It would, of course, be misleading to suggest that the scheme we have sketched was clear-cut and uniform. There are many modifications and variations, both in the apocalyptic books and in the New Testament. In particular, we find a modification which affects this very point of the interval between death and the End. For, as time went on, St Paul seems to have shrunk from the idea of a period of waiting after death, during which the soul should be "naked," and came to teach that the tabernacle or garment from heaven, the spiritual body, was to be received immediately after death. Whilst in 1 Thessalonians the dead may hope to be "with the Lord" after his coming, in 2 Corinthians and Philippians to die is to be with him at once. But in spite of modifications, the kind of programme which lies behind the detailed eschatological pictures of the New Testament remained unchanged.

Adjustment of the scheme in Christian theology. The Christian Church took over the scheme, but it found it very difficult to manipulate. For its pivot was, as we have seen, the near approach of the Judgment; when this did not come at once, it was of necessity thrust further and further away into the future. The belief in a kingdom on earth disappeared, and the Kingdom itself became identified with the heavenly state to be attained after death. Generation after generation of believers passed away; the period of waiting became longer and longer, and the actual fate and condition of the dead became of increasing importance. The intermediate state no longer affected

FUNDAMENTAL IDEAS OF APOCALYPTIC

only a few for a short time. But an indefinitely prolonged term of waiting for a judgment and a final entry into bliss or woe raised new problems and really dislocated the scheme with regard both to Judgment and the Resurrection.

(a) A belief grew up in an individual judgment at death, at which each one's destiny was decided, the sentence being, partially at least, carried into execution at once. But this made the final general Judgment otiose; though it was retained, it became only the statutory and public endorsement of a sentence pronounced and acted upon long ago. *Individual and general Judgment.*

(b) The postponement of the Resurrection also created a difficulty. Whatever our conception of the meaning of the " spiritual body " and its relation to the body which has decayed in the grave, we agree that it stands for the fulness of personality. It becomes difficult to conceive of those who have died in the Lord as living through ever-lengthening ages a " half-life," naked and still waiting for the tabernacle from heaven. Yet, in spite of 2 Cor. v., this has been the traditional, and probably the strictly orthodox, view. *Do we have to wait for our "spiritual body"?*

> " On the Resurrection morning
> Soul and body meet again. . . ."
>
> " Here awhile they must be parted
> And the flesh its Sabbath keep,
> Waiting in a holy stillness
> Wrapt in sleep."

In the Anglican Burial Service we are bidden to find our hope and comfort in a " general Resurrection at the last day," but it is not this which really comes home to the mourner so much as the truth that " the spirits

THE LORD OF THOUGHT

of them that depart hence in the Lord" live now with God, and that "the souls of the faithful" are already "in joy and felicity." This implies that they are already living a fuller and richer life than here, not a truncated half-life. The two views are inconsistently retained side by side, but if, apart from any dogmatic belief which we feel compelled to hold, we ask ourselves what has always been the most vital conviction of the Christian consciousness, is it not that those we have loved now live unto God, growing to perfection in the ampler day?

<small>Eternal Life</small>

This is, in fact, the fundamental teaching of the New Testament and especially of Christ himself, a teaching which goes far deeper than anything which stands in apocalyptic. We find it in St Paul's later view of death as a departing to be with Christ; we find it in the Johannine teaching of eternal life as knowing God, a present relation begun now and capable of indefinite perfection hereafter; we find it above all, as we should expect, in the outlook of Jesus. When asked about the Resurrection he does not base his argument upon some future assize and an ultimate coming together of soul and body, but on the profound truth that God is the God of Abraham, of Isaac and of Jacob. This is not a verbal quibble from Exodus; the meaning is that the relationship implied when we can say of the Eternal, "He is my God," is in its nature independent of death; "all live unto Him," now and always.

And so the phrases which haunt us, and which express our deepest longings, are such as these:

"The souls of the righteous are in the hand of God, and there shall no torment touch them."

FUNDAMENTAL IDEAS OF APOCALYPTIC

" In my Father's house are many mansions ; I go to prepare a place for you."

" Therefore are they before the throne of God, and serve Him day and night in His temple."

" They shall hunger no more, neither thirst any more, neither shall the sun light on them nor any heat ; for the Lamb which is in the midst of the throne shall feed them and lead them unto living fountains of water, and God shall wipe away all tears from their eyes."

These are independent of any apocalyptic scheme ; their keynote is not the hope of some distant Resurrection and Judgment day, receding ever further into an unknown future, but the conviction of a relationship begun here and growing to fuller completeness as we pass through the doors of death.

For this new life is not static ; it must be one of progress. Purgatory rightly interpreted is almost a necessity of thought. The mediæval purgatory was mainly a state of expiation of the punishment of sins already forgiven, and the teaching of Christ nowhere endorses the idea of a ledger account, with a fixed quantity of penal suffering to be shortened by various devices. But we shall hardly doubt that even the soul, which has made much progress here, must pass through an experience of further growth and purification, which may involve some pain, even though it be a " sweet pain." {Purgatory and Judgment}

Here it may be thought we shall find room after all for our apocalyptic " Last Day." For it may be argued that to us the " Last Day " marks the end of the process of discipline and development, when the soul passes from its purgatory or paradise to its heaven. But again there is an obvious difficulty. A universal " Last

Day" in this sense would imply that all reach their perfection at the same time. Is the prehistoric man, the ancient Egyptian, the Christian believer of the first or the nineteenth century—are those who die but a few hours before the End, all to attain their final climax of growth at the same moment? And if it be objected that this is to apply our ideas of time to a state often presumed to be timeless, we must reply that if we are talking about growth and change, followed by a Great Day at a particular moment which can be dated A.D. so and so, we are still thinking in terms of time and cannot escape from a real difficulty by suggesting that we are not. Heaven, as distinct from a paradise of growth, may be regarded as the final goal of perfection and nearness to God, beyond which further progress is impossible, the vanishing point of an infinite series, though such a conception has its difficulties. But it cannot reasonably be supposed that this heaven is reached by all at the same moment, its attainment being preceded by a simultaneous Resurrection and Judgment.

It is obvious that in speaking of the final goal of progress we pass to regions where thought must confess itself baffled. But it is not our purpose to produce an alternative scheme of the future, so much as to suggest that we need not allow ourselves to be hampered and confused by the particular apocalyptic scheme which Christianity inherited from Judaism (perhaps ultimately from Persia), and which later thought has vainly tried to adapt to a changed conception of the world. This scheme is a unity and must be taken or left in its completeness. We cannot tacitly ignore the idea of the nearness of the End, the

FUNDAMENTAL IDEAS OF APOCALYPTIC

trump of doom, the physical resurrection to a renovated earth, and attempt to combine the residue as literal and prosaic fact with a quite different view of the future and of life after death.

But, though we have passed beyond the scheme itself and many of the ethical ideas embodied in it, we must not forget that, in any great conception which has dominated religious thought, there is always some truth of which men have been dimly aware and which they have attempted to express according to their light. If our view is justified, Jesus clearly rejected the element in the Last Judgment which implies a great act of vengeance on a large proportion of God's children, but there are other ideas behind the apocalyptic conceptions which are of permanent value. It is indeed the subconscious sense of the underlying values which has been a main cause of the illogical compromise by which, as we have seen, they have been retained so long in their literal form. If we abandon the form, we must not lose hold on the truths they attempted to express. *The truths which underlie the apocalyptic drama*

1. The idea of "Judgment" embodies the idea of the inevitableness of consequence. It is often said that the war has vindicated the apocalyptic element in Christianity, but there is always a good deal of confused thinking in this statement. The war was not a catastrophic judgment in the sense of the first-century apocalyptists. It was not a special and direct divine intervention in history, still less its final consummation. It was something which happened within the evolutionary process, the result, in a sense the inevitable result, of what had gone before. No doubt it serves as a needed warning against the shallow idea that *Judgment and consequence.*

evolution is a smooth story of unbroken progress, but it is not what the apocalyptists meant by the Last Judgment. It was the sudden flaring up of the volcano, due to the bursting out of forces long at work beneath the surface. There are such crises in human history, as there are in the physical and moral history of the individual, when evil and materialism, selfishness and pride, come to a head. In that sense these crises are the sort of doom the prophets spoke of as "the day of the Lord," a day constantly recurring in different forms. In that sense we may say that the apocalyptic expectation was "fulfilled" in the fall of Jerusalem, or of the Roman Empire, so long as we recognize quite clearly that this is not the original meaning of the idea. On the other hand, such a transmutation of the idea of judgment from a single event to a long drawn-out series does preserve its fundamental value—the inevitable issue of sin and folly, working itself out by those social and psychological laws which are the expression of the divine will.

Process or single act? So regarded, judgment becomes a process, as the Fourth Gospel teaches us. In the same way, the coming of Christ is a process, the gradual appropriation of his vision of God, of the gift of his Spirit and of eternal life, both by the individual and by the society which is his Body. The coming of the Kingdom is equally a process, slow and difficult, as Christ himself taught, for all its joy and attractiveness. In that sense the Kingdom is embodied in the Church with all its failures, and more widely in all the varied operations of the Spirit upon the life and heart of man which make for the realization of the eternal values of truth,

FUNDAMENTAL IDEAS OF APOCALYPTIC

beauty and righteousness.[1] For this, as we have seen, is the Kingdom in the mind of Christ—the glad doing of the will of God in every sphere of life; His Kingdom comes as His will is done. It may help us to note the parallel in this respect between the changed conceptions of the last things and of the first. We now think of creation not as a series of isolated acts at a comparatively recent period but as an unceasing process, the origin of which goes back for uncounted millenniums and which is still going on under the operation of the Creative Spirit. So it is with the coming of the Kingdom. Just because this is so tremendous, so comprehensive, so spiritual, it cannot be the result of any single act or event external to the hearts of men.

2. The apocalyptic scheme expresses the conviction, ethical and religious, that right is right eternally and wrong is wrong, that the universe is such that they will be seen to be so, and that they have consequences for the individual, consequences which will be realized after death even if they are not clearly visible here. The Last Judgment and the belief in sharply contrasted rewards and punishments hereafter are simply the dramatic projection of these beliefs in terms of apocalyptic. But the projection has omitted the fundamental element, the love of God and the supremacy of the methods of love. Somehow we have to combine the two things, the eternal difference between right and wrong with their abiding consequences, and the belief that God will really behave as a Father to all *The final triumph of good*

---

[1] The establishment of the League of Nations as an effective force, changing the whole principle on which international affairs have been conducted, would be a true "coming of the Kingdom in power," a manifestation of "the Son of man seated at the right hand of God"

men always. The combination must come on the lines of the recognition that love is in the long run strong enough to conquer sin by changing the heart of the sinner in such a way that he ceases to be identified with his sin. In this sense we may give a deep meaning to the words "we believe that thou shalt come to be our Judge." The Judge is Jesus because loving-kindness, not what men have miscalled "justice," has the last word; because, as Son of man, he does not stand outside human life; because his teaching about the character of God, and his power, when lifted up, to draw all men unto him, will be seen to hold good to the end.

It is, indeed, sometimes said that the value of the belief in a literal judgment is its guarantee of this ultimate triumph of good; without it we could not be sure of the final victory. But this is surely to rest the pyramid on its apex. We do not in the last resort believe that good will conquer because we believe, on some other or stronger grounds, in the Last Judgment. If we do believe in the Judgment in this sense, we do so because our sense of values, our belief in God and in the purpose of the universe, make us confident of the triumph of right. The sense of values comes first. In the past an actual assize has seemed a natural corollary to this; to-day it appears superfluous, and even inconsistent with the hope that in the end God shall be all in all.

In conclusion, we would emphasize the fact that the difficulties which so many feel on this subject are at bottom ethical. The objection to the apocalyptic outlook does not spring from a materialistic belief in an automatic progress, or a dislike of supernaturalism

FUNDAMENTAL IDEAS OF APOCALYPTIC

or of miracle. It requires a greater faith to believe in the slow triumph of love than in the short cut of a supernatural intervention which will destroy the sinner. This faith must depend on the conception of God as Father, revealed in Christ, and the deeper insight into the relation of the world to God which is based on his teaching.

We owe to apocalyptic the growth of the belief in personal immortality; it also carried a stage further the distinctive belief of the prophets in God's vindication of Himself and of the principle of righteousness—the forward look which is the special characteristic of Judaism and Christianity among the religions of the world. But these beliefs were associated with the impatient desire of the unregenerate man for vengeance on his enemies, and with the superficial idea that sin could be overcome by the destruction of the sinner. In the last resort this makes nonsense of the world-process. It represents God as a chess-player, who can, when he sees fit, sweep his opponent's men off the board and order the opponent himself away to execution. As the Cross shows us, the age-long conflict with evil is not really like that; it is something far more serious both for man and for God. If, indeed, it is a question merely of the destruction of evil men and ugly things, no doubt "a flash of the will that can" may be conceived of as sweeping them away into nothingness in a moment. But if the divine purpose is the creation and development of independent spirits capable of a free fellowship with God and willingly co-operating with Him, this cannot be effected by any instantaneous display of omnipotent power or external catastrophe. The regeneration of the individual heart and the build-

[margin: Conversion of the sinner the only conquest of sin.]

ing up of such a society must be the slow and patient work of ages. The sinner is only defeated by being made into a saint. The regeneration of the world, the building of the New Jerusalem, whether on earth or in heaven, must be a process in which Creative Love reaches its goal by its own proper methods. In Christianity alone do we find a basis for the conviction that this is the meaning of the world-process. Many, indeed, among its adherents in all ages have lost their hold upon it; it has been maintained by some who, though they have drunk of the spirit of Christ, do not call themselves by his name. But it is distinctively Christian. It rests upon the revelation of the Fatherhood of God made by Jesus, and on the belief that in his life and teaching, and supremely in his death on Calvary, we read the secret of the divine character and of the manner in which the Father deals with His children. It is not a paradox to maintain that Jesus himself, the Lord of Thought no less than the King of Love, had also read this secret.

GENERAL INDEX

A

Abbott, E. A., *The Message of the Son of Man*, 276 n.
Allen, Archdeacon, *St Matthew (International Critical Commentary)*, 239, 243
Angels, 25, 27 ff , 48 f , 67, 87
Anger, analysis of, 176 f
—— and punishment, chap xix.
Antinomianism, 218
Antiochus Epiphanes, 14, 17, 20.
Apocalyptic, definition of, 1 f.
—— disappearance of, 23, 128 f
—— failure of, 52, 56 ff , 146, 188, 200, 202 f , 310 f
—— fundamental ideas of, chap. xxiv.
—— intrusion of, in Gospels, 113 ff , 186 f , 190, 228, 241, and Part III. *passim*
—— origin of, 14, 18, 20 ff.
Asceticism, 194
Atonement, 181, 237 n

B

Bacon, Dr B W., 89 n.
Baptism, 124
—— see also John the Baptist
Bevan, Edwyn, *Stoics and Sceptics*, 107 f , 143
Browne, L E , *Early Judaism*, 272
Bunyan, John, 14, 55
Burial service, Anglican, 303 f.
Burkitt, Professor, *Jewish and Christian Apocalypses*, 18, 20, 143
—— *Luke's use of Mark*, 294 n.
Butler, Bishop, *Sermons on Human Nature*, 64.

C

Cæsarea Philippi, 279
Causation, the system of See Creation, Evolution, Law, Will
Charles, Dr R. H., 279 n.
—— *The Book of Enoch*, 96 n.
Christianity, its foundation principle, 5.
Church and the Kingdom, 308
Consequence and punishment, 44, 55, 119 f , 132, 148 ff , chap. xiii , xiv , xv , 210, 215, chap. xix , 293, 307.
Conversion, 62, 79, 142, 146, 206, 311.
Creation, God's purpose in, 76, 79, 81, 100, 131 f , 151, chap xiii , 178, 205, 218, 220, 224, 236, 249, 293, 298 ff , 309 f , 311 f.
—— see also Evolution
Creeds, 182
Criticism, Higher, Introduction, 113 ff , 190 and *passim*.
—— see also Gospels, Jesus, Luke, Matthew.
Cross, theology of the, 216, 311.

D

Dalman, *Words of Jesus*, 232 n., 233 n , 256 n., 276 n., 277 n., 280 n., 292 n.
Dante, 14
Destructive agent of God, 85, 87 f , chap ix , 113, 124, 176, 187, 212, 223, 245, 283, 291.
—— see also Messiah, Son of Man.
Devil, the, 157, 166, 173, 244.
Dies Iræ, chap. viii. and *passim*.

Dispersion, the Jewish, 105, 138, 221.
Dodd, C H., *The Meaning of Paul for To-day*, 236 n
Dougall, L, article in *Concerning Prayer*, 139 n., 155 n
Driver, Dr, article in *Hastings' Dictionary*, 276 n.

E

Ecstasy, 39, 108.
Edwards, L. P, *The Transformation of Early Christianity from an Eschatological to a Socialized Movement*, 271 n.
Election, 43.
Emmet, C. W, *Fourth Book of Maccabees*, 70.
—— *Immortality* (essay on "The Bible and Hell"), 170, 247 ff
—— article on "Interimsethik" (*Expositor*, viii 4), 268 n.
—— *The Eschatological Question in the Gospels*, 268 n.
Escape from doom   *See* Salvation, World-abandonment
Eschatology, definition of, 2, 186
—— *see also* Apocalyptic
Eternal life, 304 f
Evil, the problem of, 28, 38 ff, 40, 46, 48, 51 f, chap. vi., 120, chap. xiii, 299, 309 f.
Evolution, 5 f, 9, 18, 38, 64, 131, chap. xiii., 178, 204, 218, 219, 224, 266, 299 ff., 306 f. *See also* Creation, Law.

F

Fall, the, 59, 67, 158.
Fantasy, compensations of, 14, 15, 17, 270 ff   *See also* Psychology.
—— Jewish, chap ii, 270 ff
Fatherhood of God, the, 231 ff., 312
Fear, 41, 86, 184 f., 210
Fireman, illustration of, 44 f.
Forgiveness, 29, 32 ff, 137, 140 f, 147 ff, chap. xv., 214, 242, chap. xx, 268, 278 ff
Francis of Assisi, 218
Free-will, 44 n, 79, chap xiii. 195, 215, 219.
—— *see also* Law.

G

Galileo, 55.
Genius, 3 f., 6, 16, 116, 124, 146, 222.
God, the idea of, 5 f, 23, 39, 45 f, 50, 89 ff, 100, 103 f, 107, 114, 117, chap xi, 140, 149 ff, 156 f, 170, 176 f, 180, 182, 184, 190, 194, 211 f, 219 ff, 231 ff., 274, 298 ff, 310
—— and inadequate salvation, chap vi.
—— as Judge, chap iii and *passim*.
—— destructive agent of. *See* Destructive agent, etc.
—— His love and cruelty, chap iv., 105, 156, 195.
—— practice of the presence of, 151, 215.
—— *see also* Immanence, Transcendence.
Goodness, the attraction of, 80, 93, 130, 150, 167, 176, 201, 235, 259.
—— *see also* Innocence.
Gospels, the, and other biographies, 7 ff.
—— devotional reading of, 1.
—— growth of, 227 f.
—— substantial truth of, 8, 9 f, 229
—— synoptic portrait of Jesus in, chap x, 229
—— teaching on consequence and punishment, chap xiii. and xiv
—— *see also* Jesus, Luke, Matthew.

H

Harnack, 243.
—— *Spruche und Reden Jesu* (*The Sayings of Jesus*), 245, 296 n.
Headlam, Dr A C, *The Doctrine of the Church and Reunion*, 255 n.
Heaven, 32, 305 f.
Hell, chap iii, iv, vi, vii, 247 ff.
—— *see also* Sheol.
Hellenism, 48, 64, 105, 116 f.
Heretics, 137, 248
Higher Criticism, Introduction, 20 ff, 113 ff, 190, and *passim*
Holy Spirit, the, 85 n., 87, 202 ff., 215
—— the sin against the, 243 f.
Hyde Park evangelism, 144.

I

Idea of God   *See* God
—— of Man.   *See* Man.

INDEX

Ideas, the dynamic of, 5, 55, 170
Immanence, the divine, 51, 162 ff, 170, 180, 201, 203 f, 206, 215, 219 ff
Immortality, 21, 22, 217, 311.
—— see also Survival, Resurrection.
Immortality (ed by Canon Streeter), 170, 247, 249.
Incarnation, the, 3, 182
—— see also Nature, Human and Divine.
Infallibility, 4, 9, 18 f, 38, 180, 207
Innocence and goodness, 15, 62 n, 64 f, 197 f
—— see also Goodness
" Interimsethik," 266 ff.
Intermediate state, the, 148 n, 301 ff
Intervention, divine. See Omnipotence
Intuition, 146, 296.
—— and criticism, 249 n.

J

Jerusalem, the fall of, 56, 119, 121, 162, 166, 168, 239, 270, 286 ff, 293 f, 308.
Jessica, 145.
Jesus and contemporary thought, 35 f, 55, 61, 140, 183, 190, 200, 210, 231 ff, 249
—— and the Son of Man   See Son of Man.
—— and the Suffering Servant, 101 f
—— and the Synoptic Gospels, 113, 186 f, 229 f   See also Gospels.
—— and nature, 131 f., 164, 183, 209
—— divinity, 5, 176
—— genius, 1 ff, 6 f, Part II especially, 24, 126, 146, 186, 204, 209, 222
—— inconsistency?, 2, 7 f, 9, 190, 235, 249, 253, 269
—— intellect, 3, 5, 114, 139, 190, 222.
—— originality, 1, 7, 9, 37, 91 f, 93, 113 ff, 126, 144, 175, 184, 198, 202, 223, 229 ff, 260, 268, 312.
—— philosophy, 2 ff, 9, 231, 263.
—— prayers, 94
—— temptation, 115 f, 153 n, 169
—— use of the Old Testament, 3 f, 85 f, 95.
—— works of healing, 94.

Jewish fantasy, chap II, 270 ff.
—— history, 13, 15, 20, 144
—— literature, its value, 18 n.
—— missionary ideals, 17, 46, 115, 135, 140, 146, 153, 257 f, 273 f.
—— philosophy, 39.
—— religion and Roman Catholicism, 13, 198
—— theology, its superiority, 15, 25, 40, 44, 47, 79, 91, 134, 211, 221
—— see also Apocalyptic.
John the Baptist, 63, chap VII, 93, 98, 115, 127, 137, 206, 210, 245, 259 f
Josephus, 89 f, 140

K

Kennedy, H A A, *St Paul and the Mystery Religions*, 108 f.
Kingdom, the, chap. VIII, 117 f, 140, 203 ff, 233, chap XXI, 276 f, 283 ff, 292 ff, 308 ff

L

Lake and Foakes-Jackson, *The Beginnings of Christianity*, 231 n, 256 n, 258 n, 263 n
Law, universal, 16, 21, 23, 24, 44 f, 54, 109, 118 f, 151, chaps. XIII. to XV, 205, 236 ff, 249, 293, 298 ff, 308
—— see also Creation, Evolution, Free-will
—— written, 15, 19 f and *passim*.
League of Nations, 309 n
Legalism in morality and religion, 15, 62, 91, 113, 133, 158, 182, 201.
Life, definition of philosophy of, 2 f
—— development of   See Evolution, Creation.
Loisy, 290
Loom, illustration of, 161 f.
Lord's Prayer, the, 148 f, 163, 166, 192, 228, 232 f, 251 f.   See also Prayer.
Luke, use of sources by, 293 ff.
—— see also Matthew, special characteristics of.

THE LORD OF THOUGHT

M

Man, Jewish idea of, chap. v
—— the idea of, 6, 23, 49 ff, 53, 57, 74, chap. xi, 149, 194, 200, 212, 219
Matthew, special characteristics of, 238 ff, 248, 252 ff, 264, 282 ff, 288, 290 ff
Mercy and retributive justice, 152, 210, chap iii
Messiah, 187, 223, 261
—— see also Destructive Agent of God, Son of Man.
Messianic birth-pangs, 96.
Milton, John, 14, 55
Miraculous, the, 16 f, 116, 118, 126, 160, 192, 271, 311
—— see also Omnipotence
Montefiore, C, Contemporary Jewish Religion, 19, 64 f
—— The Synoptic Gospels, 139 f, 240 n.
Moulton, Grammar of New Testament Greek, 246
Mystery Religions, 106 ff, 114, 144, 181, 201, 221, 223
Mystical intuition, 146, 296
Mythologies, 221   See also Symbolism

N

Nature, the relation between human and divine, 5, 6, 118 f, 123, 133, 191, 194, 216, 219
—— see also Incarnation

O

Oesterley, Dr, Wisdom of Ben-Sira, 53, 68
Omnipotence, 146, 163, 182, 195, 219, 235, 257 ff, 271, 300, 311

P

Pacificism, 148 n.
Pantheism, 219.
Parables, the need for, 155 f, 246.
—— their explanations, 168 n, 237 ff, 246 f, 253
—— their teaching on natural consequence, 171 f, 237 ff
Parousia, the, 242, chap. xxiii, 297 ff., 308.

Paul, St, 7, 47, 62, 129 ff, 179, 184, 189, 200, 208, 218, 234, 285, 302.
Peake's Commentary, 3 n., 19 n., 46 n., 64 f.
Penalties and rewards, 15 f, 23, chap. iii, 44, 53, 55, 73 ff, 79, 119, 130, 132, 147, chap. xiii, xiv, xv, 210, 216, 220, 309 and passim
—— see also Punishment.
Penn, William, 55.
Persecution, 137, 150, 167, 212, 285
Personality, 44, 157, 163, 208, 211, 217, 220, 303.
Philosophy, 2 f, 64, 79, 220, 222.
Phrygian chiliasm, 270 f.
Plato, 3, 7
Plutarch, Lives, 8
Prayer, 161, 155, 242, 247, 250 f
—— the Lord's   See Lord's Prayer.
Private judgment, 4.
Proselytes, 144
Providence, 161, 181
Psychology, 14 f, 20, 72, 106, 109, 142, 150, 156, 160, 172, 177, 179, 192, 195, 205 n, 207 ff, 213, 230, 251, 270 ff, 294, 307 f
—— and popular fiction, 15, 22
Punishment and consequence   See Consequence.
—— delight in, 26, 30, 48.
—— eternal, psychology of believers in, 156
—— teaching concerning, chap xiv.
—— see also chap xiii, xv., xix., 243 and passim
Purgatory. See Intermediate State
Puritanism, 14
Pythagoras, 109.

Q

Q, meaning of, 84 n, 227

R

Rabbinical sayings, 255, 257, 292
Rationalism, 4 f, 19 f, 38 ff., 178.
Reconciliation, 196.
Re-incarnation, 21
Remnant, the righteous, 103, 106
Renunciation. See World-abandonment
Repentance, 63, 74, 81, 86, 136, 199, 215, 261 f. See also Forgiveness

INDEX

Responsibility, 49 f, 57, 59, 73 f, 155, 157, 214.
Resurrection, 21 f, 35, 87, 102, 108, 113, 123, 217, 280 ff, 285 n.
—— of the body, 301 ff
—— see also Immortality
Revelation, 5, 16, 63, 73, 122, 126, 180, 211, 215
Revenge, 177 f.

S

Sabatier, Paul, *Life of St Francis*, 218 n
Sacraments. See Mystery Religions
Salvation, international and national, chap xii, 210, chap xxii.
—— the problem of inadequate, chap vi
—— and sin, chap xvi.
—— see also 39, 106 ff, 114, 121, 164, 201, 213, 223.
Schoolmaster, illustrations of, 45, 78.
Schweitzer, Dr A, 268 n., 281 n., 284, 285 n
Second Coming, the See Parousia
Servant, the Suffering. See Jesus.
Servants, Jewish idea of, 70 ff.
Sheol, 27, 102
—— see also Hell.
Sin and salvation, chap. xvi.
—— punishment and consequences of, chap. xiii, xiv.
—— remission of, chap. xv.
—— see also 119, 192, 242.
Socrates, 7
Son of Man, 26, 96 n, chap ix, 220, 261 ff, 273, chap. xxiii., 310.
—— see Destructive Agent of God.
Stanton, Dr, *The Gospels as Historical Documents*, 240 n, 285 n, 291 n.
Stoicism, 194, 201
Streeter, Canon B. H., article in *Hibbert Journal*, xx. No. 1, 228 n., 296 n.
—— *The Four Gospels*, 94 n, 228 n.
—— *Oxford Studies in the Synoptic Problem*, 283 n., 289 n.

Streeter, Canon B. H, *The Spirit* (article on "Christ the Constructive Revolutionary"), 146 n.
—— see also 243, 247.
Sublimation, 106, 109, 177, 213, 270 ff.
—— see also Psychology
Survival, 217
—— see also Immortality.
Symbolism, 21, 22, 87, 96, 105, 107, 122 f, 161, 165, 175, 190, 216, 220, 221, 222, 224, 298
Symonds, Arthur, 209.

T

Taboo, 91.
Tacitus, 8
Talbot, Neville, *The Mind of the Disciples*, 218 n.
Temptation, the, 115 f, 153 n, 169.
Tennyson, Lord, *In Memoriam*, 39.
Theology, moral, 161.
Thomas, Gospel of, 231.
Transcendence, the divine, 40, 59, 73, 88, 100, 163 ff, 202, 215, 217, 220 ff.
—— see also Omnipotence.

U

Universe, morality of the. See Creation, Law

V

Vicarious suffering, 17, 267, 278.
Victorian eschatological outlook, 98.
—— person, story of a, 14.
Von Hügel, Baron, *Essays in the Philosophy of Religion*, 2 n, 3 n

W

Weiss, J., *Die Predigt Jesu vom Reiche Gottes*, 267, 268 n.
Will, salvation and holiness, 202 f.
Winstanley, *Jesus and the Future*, 241.
Woman, Jewish idea of, 66 ff, 133 f.
Wood, H. G, 2.
World-abandonment, 17, 81, 98, chap. ix, 144, 210, 229.

INDEX OF
BIBLICAL, APOCRYPHAL AND APOCALYPTIC
PASSAGES

THE LORD OF THOUGHT

OLD TESTAMENT

Genesis, i.	299	Isaiah—continued.	
vi 2-4	67 n	xix. 23 ff.	136 n
Exodus, xxxiv 6 f.	92	xl 3	85
2 Samuel, vii. 13	232	23 f.	258
Ezra, Book of	67	xlix 6	136 n
Esther, Book of	34 f	lvii 7	270
Job, Book of	17, 40, 47, 52	lxi. 1 ff	95, 86, 260
Psalms, Book of	129, 272	lxiii. 9	176
—— imprecatory	34	Jeremiah, xxiv. 7 ⎫	
Psalm ii.	261	xxxi. 33 ⎬	79 n
viii	275, 277, 279	xxxii. 40 ⎭	
5	280 n	Ezekiel, vii 1-9	34
xviii 35	134 n	Daniel, Book of, 16, 23, 34, 103, 105,	
xxiii	212		185
3	164	iv 17	143
li 4	193	vii. 257 n, 259, 277, 280, 290, 301	
10	79 n	9 ff.	96, 141, 276
lxii. 12	283	viii.	34
lxvii	258	xii. 1	96
lxxxv	47	2	35 n
lxxxvi 5, 9	47	Joel, Book of	185
xciii	257 n.	ii. 30 f.	96
xcvi.	258	Amos, v. 18	287 n.
10	47	Jonah, Book of 17, 46 f., 146, 177	
xcvi —c.	257 n	Zechariah, Book of	185
cxiii 13	232	viii 20 ff.	136 n
cxix.	40	ix. 9	261, 296
32	79 n	Malachi, Book of, 83, 85, 87 ff., 128,	
cxxxvii 5	143		165, 185, 275, 277
cxlv.	257 n.	i 11	88
4, 11, 12, 21	258	iii. 1	85 n.
Isaiah, the Second 17, 47, 146, 272		1, 2, 18	84
Isaiah, ix. 1 f.	94	1-3	88
xi.	261	iv.	34
10	136 n	1-3	84, 88
xiii. 9	96		

APOCRYPHA

Wisdom of Solomon, 20 ff., 62, 68,		Wisdom of Ben-Sira (Ecclesiasticus),	
116 n., 129, 185		53, 62, 128, 185	
i. 11	182	i 11-13	42
iii. 1	304	ii. 7-11	42
1-3, 8	217	13-14	33
1, 9	204	v. 4-8	53
iii. 11 f	50	x. 2	80
iv. 19 f.	34	xvi. 11	33
vii 22b-27	41	xviii. 8-12	54
xi. 24–xii. 2	50	xxi. 9 f.	33, 181
xii. 2	52	xxii. 3	69
xii. 10-12	51	xxiii. 1, 4	232
xiv. 3	232	xxv 13, 5-20, 24-26	69
xv. 1-3	41	xxvi 6 f.	69
xxxviii.	103 n.	13 f.	68

320

INDEX

Wisdom of Ben-Sira—continued		Wisdom of Ben-Sira—continued	
xxxiii. 24-26, 28-31	71	xlii. 9, 11, 11-14	70
xxxvi 21-24	68	23-25	81
xxxix. 28-30	34	xliii 26-28	81
31-34	81	Maccabees, Book III.	62, 232
xl 1-6	54	Book IV.	62, 70
xli. 1 f	55		

APOCALYPTIC LITERATURE

Enoch, Book of, 20 ff., 26, 48 f., 62, 67, 105, 107, 170, 185, 276		Abraham, Apocalypse of, xxi. 67 n.	
		Baruch, Apocalypse of, 20 ff., 55 f., 62, 129, 182, 185	
i. 3-8	97		
9	26	iii 4-8	56 n.
v. 4, 5	27, 181	v 1.	56 n.
6	97	xii 1-4	56 n.
ix. 1-11	74	xiii 3-8	56 n
x 4-13	29	xiv 2-6	57 n.
xii 3-6	29	10-14	78
xiii. 1-6	29	xvi –xviii	77
xiii, xiv	49	xxv	98
xiv 4-7	30	xlviii. 14-17, 25 f., 39 f.	57
xxi 7-10	30	xlix 10	204
xxii 9	27	l	58 n
xxvii 2 f.	27	li 1.	58 n
xli 2	28	lii 2 f	58
xlii 2 f	74	liv 21 f	36 f.
xlvi	276 n	lv 3-8	58
xlix, 1 f.	80	lxxiii 1 f	43
liii 1, 3-5	28	lxxiv 1	43
lviii 3-5	212	lxxv 1-5	43
lxii 1-5, 9-12	101	Ezra, Apocalypse of, 20 ff., 58 f., 62, 129, 182, 185, 277	
lxiii 1, 5-8, 11	104		
lxvii 4-13	31	iii 4-5, 7-10, 12, 17, 19 f., 22, 27, 35 f	59 n.
lxviii 2-4	49		
lxxi. 5, 8, 9-11	42	iv 10 ff., 22 f	60 n
15-17	80	v. 1, 4, 5	97
16	203	vi 17-20	97
cii 5	102	vii 33, 36-38	35 f
ciii 5-8	92	46-48	201
cviii. 3	181	62-68	61
Testaments of the Twelve Patriarchs, 20 ff., 32, 67, 128, 170		119 f	131 n
		119-126	184
Reuben, v. 1-3	68	viii. 1-3	36 n.
vi 2-4	68	6	202
Levi, iii. 1-3	32	7-14	79
xv 1-4	32	20, 23, 28, 30, 37-39	183
Judah, xv. 5-6	68	27-34, 41, 44	75
Gad, vi. 3-7	141 n	35 ff.	141 n.
7	33	55-59	36
Asher, 1. 6-8	66	ix 9 f.	76
ii. 3-5	66	15 f.	36 n.
vi 4	66 n	19-22	75
Sibylline Oracles, Book III 46-56	141	29-37	77
		xiii	276 n.
Moses, Assumption of, x. 7-10	102	24	300

321

THE LORD OF THOUGHT

NEW TESTAMENT

St Matthew		St Matthew—continued	
.	247		
iii. 1-17	84 n	x. 40	206
2	259 n	xi. 11	206
7	245	13	91
7-12	84 n	17	99
10	244	18	93
1 ff.	115, 117, 123 n., 153, 169, 205	25	215
		27	121
10	294	xii. 31	242
v –vii	118, 131 ff, 189, 200, 205, 213, 250, 268 f.	33	244
		43	244
10	144	40	273 n.
21 f	198 n	44	205 n
25 f	147 n.	xiii. .	171
27 f	198 n	3 ff	241
29	243	16 f	205
35	233	24 ff.	134, 165, 170 n, 241
38-48	142 n	36-43	241, 289 n.
43-48	104	37 ff	264 n
44 f.	149 n	41	291
45	118 n, 141	42	238
48	209	50	238
vi. 9 f	148 f, 163, 166, 192, 232, 233, 251, 252, 254	xv 14	147 n, 244
		xvi 4	273 n.
14	252	19	255
14 f.	199	23	125
15	253	27	291
16	254	27 f	291
22 f.	152 n.	27 ff.	282 f.
25-29	164, 169 n	28	264 n
26-30	204 n.	xviii. 6	243
vii 1-5	147 n	7	168
2	243	8	243
7 f	202	15 ff.	254
7-11 and parallels	117 n.	18	255
9	199 n.	19	117 n.
13	244	21-35	142 n.
16	244	23 ff.	252 f
21	292	xix 17	296
22	291, 292	28	291
24	244	xx 1-6	169 n.
24-27	173 n	22	125, 207
27	120-133	xxi 2, 7	296
viii. 12	283	19	246
ix 6	278 n	xxii 1	239
13	175	11-14	172 n.
22	164	13	238
x 5	285 n	14	239
5 f	285 n.	xxiii.	245
15	244	8	233
17-22	284	33	245
23	284, 285 n.	37	246
28	244	xxiv.	287
28-31	173 n	9-13	284
29 f.	119, 120, 131 f, 165	27	153, 286
32	282 f	29	294

322

INDEX

St Matthew—continued.	
xxiv. 37-41	245
51	238
xxv 1-13	170 n.
14-30	172 n.
30	238, 240
31	277, 291
31 ff.	248
31-46	170 n
41-46	248
xxvi. 13	153
64	290
xxviii. 19	285 n
St Mark, 1. 2-6	85 n
14 and parallels	89
15 ,,	62
17 ,,	93, 205
24 ,,	195
11. 9	176
10	278
19 and parallels	94
20	286
28	278
iii 28 and parallels	164, 242
iv. 1 ,,	171
12 ,,	246
26 ff	205
30 ff and parallels	205
v. 7 f ,,	195
34	164
vii 11-13	198 n.
viii 31	278, 281 n
33	125
36 and parallels	153
38	293
38 ff.	282 f
ix 12	281
29	215
31	281 n
37	206, 249
42	242
43	242
x. 15	206
18	135, 200, 296
29 and parallels	210
32 ,,	281 n.
35 ff.	296
38	207
39	125
42-45	104
52	164
xi. 13	246
15 and parallels	122
17	270 n
20	246
21	247
25	252
25 f.	254
xii. 26 and parallels	304

St Mark—continued.	
xii. 27 and parallels	217
xiii	245, 287 ff.
11-13	284
24	294
24-27	293
29	264 n.
30 f.	294
32	294
xiv 9	153
21	243
25 and parallels	264 n.
62	233 n , 290
St Luke, iii 3-22	82, 84 n.
7 ff	84, 88
11, 14	115 n.
11-14	128 n.
16 f.	84
iv. 1 ff.	115, 117, 123 n , 153 n, 169, 205
18	260
18 f.	94
v 39	120, 168
vi 27-38	142 n.
27-42	214
35	118 n , 233 n.
35 f	149 n.
36 f.	179 n.
39	215
43	244
46	292
49	120-133
vii. 26-28	84
27	85 n
32 f	99
33	93
47-49	173 n.
50	164
viii 5-8	168 n.
11	171
48	164
ix 22-27	183
26	293
26 ff.	282 f.
27	293
47-48	183, 206
55 R.V m.	207
x. 1 f.	169 n.
12	244
21	215
23 f.	205
xi. 2 f , 148 f ,163,166,192, 232 f, 251 f , 254
5 ff.	242
13	118 n., 203, 209, 215
18	205 n.
20	164
24	244
29	273 n.

323

St Luke—continued.			St Luke—continued.	
xi. 29-32 and parallels	177 n.		xxi. 25-28	. 294
34	152 n		31	264 n.
42	. 245		31-33	. 294
50	. 168		xxii. 26 f	117 n.
xii .	119 f., 131, 165		28-30	. 291
4-9	173 n.		29	264 n.
5 .	. 244		53	287 n.
8 f.	282 f.		66	. 294
10	. 242		69	. 290
14	. 123		xxiii. 34	. 251
22 ff.	. 164		St John, iii. 16	. 183
32	. 165		xiv 2	. 305
37	117 n.		9 .	. 175
49	. 153		xvii 11	233 n.
54-56	168 n.		Acts, i.–xii.	. 297
58 f.	147 n.		i. 11	. 293
xiii. 1 ff.	. 167, 173 n		ii 17 ff.	. 280
3 .	139, 192		iii 19 ff.	. 280
6 .	. 247		vii 56	. 281
25 ff.	. 291		xvii 31	. 293
28	. 239		xxiv. 25	. 293
34	. 246		Romans, i. 18	. 236
xiv. 7-11	172 n.		ii. 14 f.	. 62 n.
15	. 239		vii	. 131
26 f	. 210		vii 10-24	. 184
xv. 4-7	. 105		vii 15–viii 1	. 180
8 ff.	. 250		viii. 1	. 189
11 ff	. 250		viii 38 f	. 156
xvi. 16	. 91		1 Corinthians	. 297
xvii.	. 264		2 Corinthians, v. .	. 303
1 .	168, 243		5-8	. 302
3 f.	. 253		Ephesians, iii. 15	235 n.
10	. 200		Philippians, i. 23	. 302
20	. 264		iv. 13	. 209
20 ff	287 ff.		1 Thessalonians	. 297
22-37	. 286		iv. 13 ff.	300, 302
25	281 n.		2 Thessalonians	247, 297
25 ff.	. 286		i. 4 ff	. 242
26-37	. 245		ii 11 f.	237 n.
xviii 1	. 203		Hebrews, ii. 14	244 n
1-8	. 242		James, i. 17	217 n.
9 .	. 251		ii 10	. 65 n
9 ff	. 250		2 Peter	. 247
xix. 10	. 104		1 John, i. 9 .	180 n.
11 ff.	. 240		Jude .	. 247
14	. 240		Revelation	247, 297
27	. 240		vi. 9	242, 301
41	. 246		16	. 236
xxi. .	287 ff.		vii 15 f	. 305
12-19	. 284		xviii 20	. 36 n.
25	. 294		xix. 1-3	. 36 n.

www.ingramcontent.com/pod-product-compliance
Lightning Source LLC
Chambersburg PA
CBHW050837230426
43667CB00012B/2041